TM Church
Univ. Delaware

D0072416

EARTH AND THE HUMAN FUTURE

Also of Interest

Natural Resource Economics: Selected Papers, S. V. Ciriacy-Wantrup, edited by Richard C. Bishop and Stephen O. Andersen

Renewable Energy for Industrialization and Development, David John Jhirad

†*Energy Futures, Human Values, and Lifestyles: A New Look at the Energy Crisis,* Richard C. Carlson, Willis W. Harman, Peter Schwartz, and Associates

Critical Energy Issues in Asia and the Pacific: The Next Twenty Years, Fereidun Fesharaki, Harrison Brown, Corazon M. Siddayao, Toufiq A. Siddiqi, Kirk R. Smith, and Kim Woodard

Science and Technology in a Changing International Order: The United Nations Conference on Science and Technology for Development, edited by Volker Rittberger

Cooperation in Science and Technology: An Evaluation of the U.S.-Soviet Agreement, Catherine P. Ailes and Arthur E. Pardee, Jr.

†*Global Order: Values and Power in International Politics,* Lynn H. Miller

Atoms for Peace: An Analysis After Thirty Years, edited by Joseph F. Pilat, Robert E. Pendley, and Charles K. Ebinger

Global Nuclear Energy Risks: The Search for Preventive Medicine, Bennett Ramberg

The Environmental Effects of Nuclear War, edited by Julius London and Gilbert F. White

China Among the Nations of the Pacific, edited by Harrison Brown

The Challenge of Man's Future, Harrison Brown

†Available in hardcover and paperback.

About the Book and Editors

During the second half of the twentieth century, great changes have occurred in the natural sciences, spawned by the leap forward in physics during the war years and the growth in understanding of earth's history and place in the cosmos. Also, with the new and terrible consequences of full-fledged war, the nuclear age has brought to the fore the need for humanity to work internationally to seek global resolutions for its age-old conflicts. And humanity in this period has begun to see its fate in broader terms, in the context of its interactions with resources and environment. The career of Harrison Brown has spanned this period and these subjects. His major contributions in the physical sciences, global resource problems, and international cooperation are related in essays by his colleagues, each of whom shares with Brown a prominent place in these disciplines.

Kirk R. Smith is research associate at the East-West Center's Resource Systems Institute. **Fereidun Fesharaki** is energy program leader at the Resource Systems Institute of the East-West Center. **John P. Holdren** is professor of energy and resources at the University of California, Berkeley.

EARTH AND THE HUMAN FUTURE

ESSAYS IN HONOR OF HARRISON BROWN

Edited by KIRK R. SMITH, FEREIDUN FESHARAKI, *and* JOHN P. HOLDREN

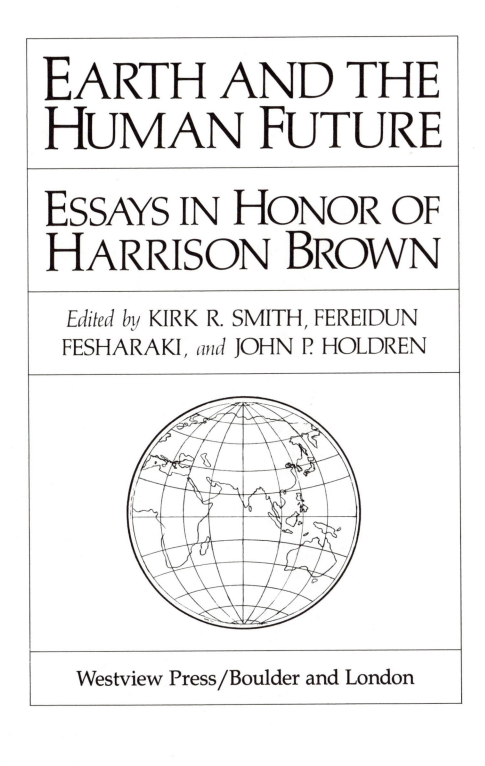

Westview Press/Boulder and London

All rights reserved. No part of this publication may be reproduced or transmitted in any form or by any means, electronic or mechanical, including photocopy, recording, or any information storage and retrieval system, without permission in writing from the publisher.

Copyright © 1986 by the East-West Center

Published in 1986 in the United States of America by Westview Press, Inc.; Frederick A. Praeger, Publisher; 5500 Central Avenue, Boulder, Colorado 80301

Library of Congress Cataloging-in-Publication Data
Main entry under title:
Earth and the human future.
    1. Natural resources—International cooperation—
Addresses, essays, lectures. 2. Brown, Harrison Scott,
1917–   —Addresses, essays, lectures. 3. Earth
sciences—Addresses, essays, lectures. 4. Environmental
policy—Addresses, essays, lectures. I. Brown,
Harrison Scott, 1917–   . II. Smith, Kirk R.
III. Fesharaki, Fereidun. IV. Holdren, John P.
HC59.E33 1986   333.7   85-17843
ISBN 0-86531-690-2

Printed and bound in the United States of America

10   9   8   7   6   5   4   3   2   1

CONTENTS

TABLES AND FIGURES

FOREWORD

The East-West Center is fortunate and proud to have had Harrison Brown as the director of its Resource Systems Institute for one-quarter of its twenty-five-year history. As one can see from the contributions in this festschrift, at one time or another Harrison has addressed essentially all the global concerns that either led to the creation of the center or are the subjects of its inquiries. Central to Harrison's career, as well as to the work of the center, is the belief that interdisciplinary study and international cooperation will lead to better understanding of the common problems facing humanity and to better solutions to them.

I first met Harrison in the early 1970s when he was engaged in beginning scientific exchanges with China. I remember thinking what an awesome intellect and engaging human being this man is. A decade later, I was privileged to work with him at the East-West Center for two years before he retired. In the course of our interactions, I was impressed with the breadth of vision and wisdom he brings to discussions of international resources and scientific questions. As any who knows him can attest, he is one of those rare people who can uplift the tone of a group by just joining it—a man with a presence. The East-West Center is indelibly marked by Harrison Brown's ideas and beliefs.

The reader will find in these essays the reflection of a remarkable career. It is remarkable not only for its span, from geochemistry through scientific diplomacy, but also for its prescience. Harrison very frequently has been among the first to identify and articulate issues that soon become major matters of general concern. We look forward with great anticipation to his future contributions.

Victor Hao Li
President
East-West Center

xi

PART ONE
Earth, Planets, and Cosmos

INTRODUCTION

KIRK R. SMITH

Harrison Brown graduated in 1938 from the University of California, Berkeley, where he had studied chemistry, and he left for graduate work at Johns Hopkins that same year. There he worked with Maria Mayer and Joe Mayer, among others, and at the time Pearl Harbor was bombed, he had nearly completed his doctoral dissertation under Robert Fowler on the separation of isotopes by thermal diffusion of gases. His particular focus was the separation of uranium isotopes. Just as he has often done during his career, he had become interested in a topic that soon would become of critical importance: Isotopic separation of uranium shortly became vital to the war effort through the Manhattan Project.

The only available gaseous compound of uranium was UF_6, the synthesis of which was not well understood. Harrison thus had to learn to develop new techniques in fluorine chemistry in order to obtain the material he needed for his thesis work. At this time, both Harrison and Phillip Abelson, then at the Carnegie Institution in Washington, D.C., developed techniques to convert UF_4 to UF_6, a dangerous task from which Harrison still bears scars from fluorine explosions.

In 1942 Glenn Seaborg, who had known Harrison as an undergraduate at Berkeley, asked him to come to the University of Chicago to work on the fluorine chemistry of plutonium. Soon after, Harrison left for Oak Ridge, where in 1943 he became assistant to Warren Johnson, director of the chemistry group charged with, among other tasks, the first separation and characterization of gram quantities of plutonium.

Harrison's roles in the Manhattan Project are related in Part 2 by Glenn Seaborg and are mentioned here only as background to his career in geo- and planetary chemistry, which developed immediately after the war. He began this concentration at the University of Chicago in the Institute for Nuclear Chemistry and the Department of Chemistry.

Stimulated originally as an undergraduate by reading the Baker Lecture given by George von Heavesy at Cornell in 1935, Harrison began investigations of the abundance and origin of elements. He applied methods of analysis such as neutron activation and thermal-ionization high-resolution mass spectrometry that were only just then becoming available.

In Chapter 1, Harrison Brown's first two graduate students, Ed Goldberg and Clair Patterson, describe in both personal and professional terms how their association with Harrison directed their careers at that time. They worked on the analysis of the distribution of elements in meteorites. In 1946, Harrison received the American Association for the Advancement of Science (AAAS) Award in Pure Science for this pioneering achievement. Early in this period, Harrison sent a meteorite sample for analysis to Al Neir, who, at the University of Minnesota, had one of the world's best labs for mass spectrometry. The same week, a similar sample arrived from Hans Suess at Hamburg, who was investigating the same question. What both were seeking was a determination of the isotopic ratio and thus the age of lead in the meteorites. The analysis revealed that the lead was modern, i.e., that it did not vary significantly in age from samples of Earth rocks.

Harrison, however, was not satisfied for he believed that both samples were probably contaminated by anthropogenic lead sources, such as combustion of leaded gasoline. This belief eventually caused him to encourage Clair Patterson to develop the first truly lead-free laboratory where accurate isotopic ratios could be determined. The association with Hans Suess led to persuading Suess to visit the faculty at Chicago in 1949. Eventually Suess, like Harrison and many other scientists in this period, was enticed to move west. In this case it was Roger Revelle who brought Suess to La Jolla to the University of California, San Diego, to join the Mayers, among others.

In 1951 Harrison left Chicago, along with his student Clair Patterson, for the California Institute of Technology. There the Atomic Energy Commission gave him funds to conduct a broad range of geochemistry research on uranium. This led him to speculations on "burning rocks," described by Alvin Weinberg in Part 2.

As he had done at Chicago, Harrison continued to work on the implications for the origin of the solar system of measured elemental abundances in Earth and meteorites. For this work he received the American Chemical Society Award in Pure Chemistry in 1952. In 1955, at the relatively young age of thirty-six, he was elected to the National Academy of Sciences.

Among others whom Harrison helped entice to join the growing planetary geochemistry group at Caltech was Bruce Murray from MIT.

Chapter 1 concludes with Bruce Murray's description of Harrison's farsightedness in helping to establish the Lunar and Planetary laboratories at Caltech.

Chapter 2 is by Jesse Greenstein, an astronomer who preceded Harrison in the move west from Chicago to Pasadena. He describes the importance to astronomy of Harrison's work on elemental abundances and illustrates some of the current areas of investigation that have origins in Harrison's work.

In Chapter 3, Sir Fred Hoyle describes Harrison's significant role as a geochemist in addressing some of the important astronomical questions of this century. He shows that Harrison's work on the abundances and origins of the elements has become part of the conventional wisdom and basic framework of extraterrestrial chemistry and astrophysics. More intriguing, however, is Hoyle's discussion of another line of Harrison's research: the implications of the present distribution of rare gases for the origin of Earth's atmosphere. This work, according to Hoyle, has still not been properly assimilated by the scientific community in spite of the thirty-five years that have elapsed since it was published.

Hoyle attempts to show how Harrison's conclusions about the origin of Earth's atmosphere, which were based on geochemical evidence, are compatible with arguments based on considerations of solar system dynamics. He differs, however, with Harrison's conclusions as to the origin of some of the principal gases in Earth's atmosphere, preferring cometary genesis rather than outgassing. He ends, appropriately, with the provocative hypothesis that conventional thinking about the origin of these materials may be as changed by consideration of extraterrestrial biological processes as thinking was changed in the past by Hoyle and others' addition of chemical processes.

Chapter 4, written by geologist Richard Sheldon, departs somewhat from the others in this section. Rather than being a description of the perspicacity and longevity of Harrison's approaches and speculations, it is itself an exercise in intelligent conjecture. Grounded in observation and documentation from the geological literature, Sheldon argues for the existence of ancient ring systems orbiting Earth, analogous to those around Saturn, but made of rock, rather than ice. Just as Harrison found chemistry a fertile ground in which to nourish astronomical hypotheses, Sheldon has identified a potentially exciting astronomical interpretation of anomalous geologic data. These speculations are admittedly unorthodox and lead to tentative conclusions that will not be readily accepted by most astronomers without considerable additional evidence. Nevertheless, they are appropriately found in this volume in honor of a man whose intuition and intelligent speculation has led to so many important insights and inspired so many others to follow.

1

THE EARLY YEARS: CHICAGO AND PASADENA

HARRISON BROWN: PROFESSOR AND MODEL
Edward D. Goldberg

I was Harrison Brown's first doctoral student. I hold this association with pride. The collision I had with him in the last several years of the 1940s was nearly elastic—I have seen him only several dozen times since then. This lack of contact has come about unintentionally; we occupy distinct niches in science. Still, the impact of those early years is evident in my pursuits today. The thirty-five years that have elapsed since my scientific apprenticeship at the University of Chicago have dulled the details of our interactions. I simply do not recall any dramatic incidents that can be used to illustrate our friendship. There were a number of moods in our respective roles as student and professor, however, that have provided a base for me to direct my own graduate students (with whom I have had similar elastic collisions) and to pursue my researches.

THE LIGHT TOUCH

Harrison set the stage for a student to carry out independent research, for his involvements in physical and social sciences made him absent from the University of Chicago for long periods of time. Although he had well defined the problem I was to work on (the slow neutron activation analyses of iron meteorites for trace elements), I was essentially a free agent after our initial discussions. This sense that a doctorate is given for demonstrated ability to carry out independent research, free of entanglements with the major professor or other investigators, has

7

largely disappeared from many major institutions. The faculty rely upon
students for survival and for advancement. Both goals often depend
upon the successful gaining and completion of research grants and
contracts. Even when he or she is away from the home institution, the
professor will often very intimately and demandingly direct the project
of a student. As a consequence, students are often involved in satisfying
the needs of the researcher-sponsor rather than allowing their own ideas
and intuitions to guide their research. Harrison, in contrast, displayed
a light touch, guiding me through difficult periods and inspiring me to
more difficult tasks during the calm. I really never knew much about
the financing of my research. It was one less worry in the troublesome
and vulnerable life of a graduate student.

A SENSE OF VALUE

I did gain a most important concept of values in scientific research—
values that for my subsequent life in science would often be in conflict
with the perceptions of those who administer science.

A not-typical interaction of an administrator with a student occurred
when Harrison was absent from the University of Chicago. I needed
platinum metal in the form of wire and foil for my activities. These
supplies were maintained by the business officer of the Institute of
Nuclear Studies at the university. I would request my materials, which
he kept in a safe, from him. While he opened the safe, I was required
to turn my back to the operation so that I would not ever be in a
position to steal platinum and other valuables held by him. I was
somewhat baffled by all of this intrigue inasmuch as I had purchased
through his secretaries the metal rhenium, which was clearly more valuable
than the small bits of platinum foil and platinum wire that he dispensed
to me. I decided not to make him aware of this situation because among
the administrators I have dealt with, a little knowledge is more unusual
than dangerous. At that time—in the late 1940s—I must have been
fearful as to what end he might have put such knowledge.

There was an experience with Harrison that did give me a springboard
to evaluate what is important and what is unimportant in scientific
activities. This involved the irradiation of yellow diamonds, of small
commercial value, in a slow neutron pile to which I had access. The
action converted the rather unattractive yellow diamonds to exotic dark
colors—blacks, blues, and greens. No radioactivity developed in the
gems following irradiation if the surfaces had been scrupulously cleaned
with strong acid. Diamonds are forms of elemental carbon with few
impurities. We had a reasonable technique to transform worthless industrial quality minerals to rather exquisite jewels.

But my strongest impression of the venture was the way in which Harrison husbanded the diamonds. He gave them to me in a beat-up envelope. There were perhaps twenty or thirty individual stones cut as if for mounting in jewelry. I was rather proud of my involvement in this experiment and at the beginning showed the gems to my friends. They were rather stunned at the way I carried them about—much as Harrison did in a beat-up envelope. What if I had lost one? But this was not the concern of Harrison. Would we be able to produce an interesting object that would be attractive to the public? The value was in the outcome of the experiment, not in the worth of the gems, before or afterwards. I was deeply impressed with his nonchalance about some little cut pieces of carbon. To me, his student, he had "style."

In my subsequent career as a marine chemist, I have often been questioned by associates and others as to which minerals in seawaters and marine sediments are financially valuable. To these people's disappointment, I have always been concerned about which minerals in seawaters and marine sediments are scientifically interesting.

A SENSE OF RESPONSIBILITY

Graduate students in science sometimes approach their investigations with a near-religious fervor. I suspect that I was no exception and regarded activities outside the pursuit of scientific knowledge suspiciously. Thus I was taken aback when I realized the deep and intensive involvement of Harrison in the problems of mankind—survival, food supply, standard of living, population, disease, among others. In the late 1940s, I was skeptical about the value of all of these activities. I knew that many distinguished scientists, such as Harold Urey and Willard Libby, had left purely basic investigations for applied research. Most of us felt that their involvement in the development of nuclear weapons had turned them against pure science. But the wanderings of Harrison into social science were difficult to fathom.

Upon leaving the University of Chicago, I totally changed direction in science. Instead of studying the properties of meteorites, I turned to marine chemistry. My interests were in the compositions of seawaters, marine organisms, and sediments. But it was not long before I drifted into societal problems. My director at the Scripps Institution of Oceanography was Dr. Roger Revelle, who felt that the resources of the oceans might be threatened by the promiscuous releases of artificial radionuclides from energy facilities to the environment. He gathered U.S. scientists to his fold to ascertain the amounts of these radioactivities that the oceans could accommodate before such benefits from the marine environment as edible foods, transportation, recreation, and aesthetics might be lost or limited. My shift to this sort of involvement was easy because I had seen a precedent. Subsequently, I have been more deeply associated with waste management, ocean pollution, and water husbandry.

Although I do not think that there was any intention on Harrison's part to exert such a strong influence nor was there on my part to accept some of his ways of life, my apprenticeship with him conditioned me for a satisfying life in science and in public policy.

HARRISON BROWN'S INFLUENCE ON TWENTIETH-CENTURY DEVELOPMENTS IN GEOCHRONOLOGY
Clair Patterson

Extraordinary developments that gave rise to much of our present nuclear geochemical knowledge in the earth and planetary sciences were initiated at the University of Chicago after World War II. A young member of the faculty at that time, Harrison Brown, a highly creative scientist fresh from the laboratories of the Manhattan Project, was influential in these developments. World-renowned scientists were among his faculty colleagues in the fields of radiochemistry, inorganic chemistry, organic chemistry, geology, physics, and astrophysics. Those in nuclear geochemistry included Nobel laureate Harold Urey, who with his co-workers was working out the $^{16}O/^{18}O$ method for determining paleo-temperatures, stable isotopic fractionations of carbon, and the biochemical origin of life on earth; Nobel laureate Willard Libby, who with his coworkers was establishing the ^{14}C dating method; Hans Suess, who was working on the cosmic abundances of the elements and with Nobel laureate Maria Geppert Mayer was developing models for energy levels in atomic nuclei from these cosmic abundances; Gerald Kuiper, who was developing theories for the origin of the solar system; and Mark Inghram, who with coworkers was studying the isotopic and geochronometric occurrences of rare gases in terrestrial and meteoritic materials.

These peers created a challenging environment that enabled Harrison to flourish and realize his full potential as an outstanding scientist who ranks as one of the most stimulating on a world scale. His worthy and exciting ideas and his flair for obtaining positive responses from people influenced both the research aims in a number of major fields in nuclear geochemistry, chemical oceanography, and astrophysics and the development of governmental funding for such investigations. He never wanted people to attack solid, reassuring problems infused with an aura of certainty that acceptable solutions would be ground out if the crank were turned. Instead, he enticed people into striving for splendid new views of our world and got them irretrievably committed to such efforts before they began to sense, too late, the costs associated with cantilevering out into the lonely voids of protoknowledge. He automatically dismissed costs as being unworthy of consideration in assessing priorities that might govern directions of research. In this way he served as a distinguished pioneer on the frontier of science, igniting the passions of the unfulfilled, making the unobtainable appear within reach, and thus inaugurating discoveries that, but for him, might still be hidden.

Included in Harrison's range of interests and work was his concern for the origin of meteorites and their geochronology, and I was involved in these studies as one of his graduate students. I had obtained a B.S. in chemistry at Grinnell and an M.S. at the University of Iowa investigating molecular spectra with George Glockler and had then worked as a spectrographic analyst and mass spectrometrist in the Manhattan Project during the war. My supposed expertise in these matters apparently served to qualify me as a likely graduate student in Harrison's eyes. To initiate my studies he put me to work carrying out literature research on the elemental composition of meteorites. His aim was to develop a model for their origin by hypothesizing the formation of parent bodies in the planetary gap between Mars and Jupiter, which possessed gravitational fields sufficient to segregate iron from silicates. Later collisions between these supposed parent bodies were assumed to have dispersed the smaller fragments now existing as asteroids and meteorites. I ferreted out analytical data on meteorites from seldom-used volumes in the catacombs of the Rosenwald Library and tabulated the results for his consideration. The changing pattern of Harrison's interpretations of these data stimulated me and taught me to consider all avenues of approach to a problem. In this process I was continually confronted with the difficulty of disposing of the remains of a previous interpretation that only a short while before had seemed to have been the final word in the matter. The relentless slaughter by Harrison of these ideas, excitingly formed and savored in application to provide nourishment for their successors, made a lasting impression and helped me establish rigorous standards for carrying out my research in coming decades.

Harrison wanted to investigate the trace metal composition of meteorites as part of his study of the formation of the solar system, and he directed three graduate students in this matter at the University of Chicago. He advised Edward Goldberg in thermal neutron activation analysis of trace metals such as gold in meteorites. This work was the first of its kind in the field and was a natural outgrowth of Harrison's familiarity with the technique gained during the war years. Goldberg and Harrison's meteorite study was important in defining the composition of cosmic matter and related to both the origin of the solar system and nuclear structure. Ed later continued Harrison's interest in geochronology by developing with his students ^{210}Pb and ^{228}Th/^{232}Th dating methods for glacial ice and sediments, methods that were to become widely used.

Harrison advised George Tilton in the measurement of uranium and thorium and advised me in the measurement of lead in microminerals, using isotopic dilution mass spectrometric techniques. Our development and application of these analytical methods to geological materials were also the first to be carried out in the field. Harrison believed that the age of the solar system could be determined from the ages at which meteorites were formed, and he set me to work studying lead in meteorites as part of a program dealing with uranium-lead ages of meteorites. I was supposed to measure the concentration and isotopic composition of lead in an iron meteorite, a task Harrison claimed should be "duck soup." It would be an enormous understatement to say that this was not the case. Contamination problems proved so severe I managed at Chicago only to discover that lead concentrations reported in the literature by previous investigators were excessively high because of lead contamination. George Tilton had also encountered uranium contamination difficulties that originated from residues left in the laboratory by previous investigators who had worked there with milligram quantities of uranium. George solved his problem by carrying out clean-laboratory techniques in a different building where uranium had not been previously used, but the use of lead in our environment was so ubiquitous it took me many years to solve the problem of lead contamination control in determining lead in meteorites.

Setting this matter aside for a while, George and I attacked the problem of determining uranium and lead in microminerals from common igneous rocks. The quantities of lead encountered in these minerals were considerably larger than were the quantities of lead in iron meteorites, so contamination problems were less severe and it was possible to carry out the studies with some success. This latter work was an outgrowth of Harrison's interests in terrestrial geochronology. His involvement with radioactive decay systems in the Manhattan Project led him, after the war, to a collaboration with Esper Larsen, Jr., at Harvard, one of a group of geologists concerned with devising ways of dating geological strata and events. Before World War II geologists had available to them accurate dates placed in only a small handful of stratigraphic locations scattered over the world. Until then, methods for measuring accurate radioactive ages applied only to large gram-sized pegmatitic orelike minerals, which were rare. Larsen belonged to a group of geologists who believed that microscopic uranium-rich, lead-poor minerals occurring ubiquitously in trace quantities in igneous rocks could be used for accurate dating purposes. If this could be done, a geologic breakthrough of enormous importance would be achieved, because it would lead to the accurate dating of common rocks occurring throughout the geologic column on earth. The dating technique would provide a vital parameter to earth scientists and enable them to decipher the complex geologic history of the earth. Geologists had been prevented from doing this because previously used paleontological methods gave only ordinal time arrangements, not the actual span of time. These relative ages embodied two additional fatal geochronometric flaws: They were not necessarily unique for cross-correlations between scattered stratigraphies, and they failed to apply to the 90 percent of the geological record that was virtually fossil-free. Paleontology required prolific and detailed absolute chronometric data of the kind that could be provided by radioactive clocks in order that models explaining biological evolution might be properly developed.

Larsen and his colleagues had crushed and ground igneous rocks, physically separating small quantities of different types of microscopic radioactive minerals from them. They had worked out primitive methods for measuring crystalline ages of these minerals that involved alpha and beta emission counting for their uranium contents and involved emission spectrographic analyses for their lead contents. Harrison wanted George and me to use ultraclean microchemical and mass spectrometric techniques to determine trustworthy and accurate ages for Larsen's mineral separates by measuring uranium, thorium, and lead concentrations and isotopic compositions of lead in them. George, Harrison, and I published the results of our geochronometric studies in a pioneering paper, which did indeed open up the field of uranium-lead dating of common igneous rocks and inaugurate major developments in geological knowledge.

During the following decades George and his students participated in the extension of geochronometric investigations to provide a basis for much of present knowledge of the magmatic evolution of the earth's crust and mantle as well as of the origin and nature of tektites and meteorites.

Harrison's work in geochemistry was recognized by members of the geology division at the California Institute of Technology, and they invited him there to initiate a new program in geochemistry. He did so in an exceptional manner by providing ideas and guidance along innovative avenues of research and instruction, by bringing outstanding people to the division, and by using entrepreneurial skill to secure large funding grants. My collaboration with Harrison continued at Caltech, where I built my first ultraclean lead laboratory, using some of the funds that Harrison had secured for the division. It was in this laboratory that I successfully isolated lead from iron meteorites and, since my mass spectrometer at Caltech was not yet completely built, I had to use Mark Inghram's mass spectrometer at the Argonne National Laboratory to isotopically analyze the lead. These data enabled me to determine the first accurate age of meteorites and the earth. This successful solution of difficult lead contamination problems at Caltech later allowed coworkers and me to explore the natural occurrences of lead in the earth's oceans and biosphere, to discover perturbations of these occurrences caused by engineering technologies, and to probe into reasons for this state of affairs. Harrison's influence on my research career was significant, teaching me, in some inexplicable but effective manner that seems rare among educators, to seek the hidden splendors of science, damning the risks.

I have written only about that facet of Harrison's influence on the development of nuclear geochemistry with which I am personally familiar, but this covers only a small part of his contributions. He left the geology-planetary science division at Caltech a rich legacy of ideas, procedures, and attitudes that serve it well even to the present day.

Some thirty years after Harrison arrived at Caltech, Robert Sharp, who was chairman for fifteen years during part of Harrison's tenure, recalled his influence on developments in the geology division. He said that Harrison lifted our eyes to higher and more distant horizons, prying us out of entrenched ruts. He was instrumental, through his Washington, D.C., connections, in introducing a planetary research program and faculty into the division long before other universities recognized its importance in contemporary research. He was instrumental in bringing many of the present division faculty to the institute and in securing funds with which to initiate their research programs. Harrison also helped install a new proposition-type of Ph.D. examination that greatly improved the quality of our candidates. Harrison endowed the division with ideas, attitudes, and endeavors that helped make it become recognized by the scientific community as one of the outstanding university geology departments in the world.

HARRISON BROWN'S INFLUENCE
ON PLANETARY SCIENCE AT CALTECH
Bruce Murray

Ed Goldberg and Clair Patterson have traced Harrison's role in the flowering of geochronology at Chicago and then at Caltech. Let me pick up the story at that point and relate how Harrison's remarkable instinct for the right problem at the right time and his great entrepreneurial and catalytic skills directly led to major developments in planetary science at Caltech. The National Aeronautics and Space Administration (NASA) was formed in 1958, and Harrison obviously recognized early the great potential for planetary and, ultimately, earth science. He obtained a substantial NASA grant in late 1959, intended to finance extensive meteorite studies, including the examination of the patterns of falls versus compositional class. Ultimately, he also studied extensively the orbital properties of asteroids (with Irene Vidziunas Goddard) in a prescient, but premature, attempt to infer the composition of asteroid families.

At that point I was completing a two-year tour as an officer in the United States Air Force. I had become excited about the potential for planetary research from research activities of the air force and thus wrote to Caltech indicating my desire and availability to pursue planetary research, I hoped, by taking advantage of Caltech's associations with the Mount Wilson and Palomar observatories and with the Jet Propulsion Laboratory (JPL).

Because Harrison had already obtained NASA funding and because he recognized the importance of developing new observational programs, he arranged for me to come and work for him as a postdoctoral research fellow in the Division of Geological Sciences. Initially, Harrison and I, along with graduate student Kenneth Watson, established that water-ice is stable indefinitely in the permanently shaded areas of the polar regions of the moon. Subsequently, we analyzed the stability of common volatiles throughout the solar system, a study that later provided good background when Mariner spacecraft observations of Mars in 1965 and 1969 opened up the exciting issue of the behavior of volatiles on Mars.

The principal focus of the early work, however, was telescopic, made possible first by Harrison's meeting on my behalf with Ike Bowen, then director of the Mount Wilson and Palomar observatories. By October 1960 I was carrying out studies of the moon on the 60-inch telescope on Mount Wilson. Harrison's ability to introduce me—a geologist—into the (at that time) tightly controlled telescopic community, permitted a special opportunity. An extraordinarily talented—but then unrecognized—experimentalist named James Westphal fortuitously was working at Caltech on seismic instrumentation under the auspices of Hewitt Dix, professor of geophysics. Westphal and I formed a telescopic collaboration. Simultaneously, because of my air force experiences, I was able to gain access to state-of-the-art, mid-infrared mercury-doped germanium detectors, which were just being declassified by the military. Jim Westphal and I rapidly developed a new infrared photometer that, by the summer of 1962, enabled us (along with Robert Wildey) to observe the star Alpha Orionis, the first object outside the solar system ever observed in the 10-micron atmospheric "window." That observation helped initiate the field of infrared astronomy.

By fall 1962 we were using the 200-inch telescope at Mount Palomar to observe Venus and Jupiter in the 10-micron region. These were the first modern infrared measurements of the planets and established a new observational tool for their remote study. By 1963 I was made a member of the professorial staff, and a Ph.D. option in planetary science was established at Caltech. Additional new faculty followed closely, along with a growing group of extremely capable graduate students.

All of this could have happened only because Harrison Brown (1) recognized early the great potential of cross-disciplinary planetary studies stimulated by an emerging U.S. space program; (2) raised funds in anticipation of the opportunity; and (3) provided "infrastructure management" so that I and others, inexperienced in academic affairs, could proceed effectively in a new interdisciplinary field.

Additional spin-offs also flowed from Harrison's original commitment to planetary science at Caltech. A long-term collaboration developed among Caltech professors Robert P. Sharp and Robert Leighton and me as investigators for the Mariner television programs. Jim Westphal pursued new instrumentation developments for large telescopes, including pioneering the use of cold cathode detectors (CCDs). These successes, in turn, led to his role as principal investigator for the wide-field planetary camera for the space telescope, in conjunction with technical support at JPL.

In addition, the geochemical group at Caltech played a key role in the analysis of the Apollo lunar samples, starting in 1969. This group had evolved from Harrison's original geochronology efforts. Thus, Harrison Brown was the progenitor in the fullest sense of an extraordinary blossoming of planetary science at Caltech, with its special affiliations with Mount Wilson and Palomar observatories and with the Jet Propulsion Laboratory. It would not have happened nearly so successfully, I believe, without Harrison Brown's pushing, pointing, and pioneering.

Looking back twenty-five years, my respect for and appreciation of Harrison Brown have only increased. I was already beyond the Ph.D. level when our association began, and thus his impact on me was more professional than educational. He recognized the important fields before others and knew the scientific policymakers and funding agencies. Most important, he was willing to help me and others proceed vigorously into an exciting new scientific era, even though his own personal interests and energies were shifting progressively into the problems of the world, especially those arising from uncontrolled growth of population and nuclear weapons. By his own example, he constantly emphasized the scientist's responsibility for understanding and articulating the impact of science on society, even if this activity does not fit into narrow academic disciplines. He made it respectable for a scientist to aspire to be an intellectual at a time when many felt that "scientists ought to stick to their science."

Harrison's instincts for the right problem at the right time, both narrowly within physical science and, more broadly, involving science, technology, and the human condition have been unexcelled. It was a special privilege to have shared with Harrison Brown the unique confluence of Caltech with the expanding U.S. space program of the 1960s.

2

HARRISON BROWN
AND THE ASTRONOMERS

JESSE L. GREENSTEIN

As an astronomer-astrophysicist, I will review two major areas in which some of Harrison's many careers had significant impact, foreshadowing future trends. One is the implication of the composition of our planetary system and sun for stars and the universe. The other is the importance of solids outside the solar system. The rapid advance of atomic and nuclear physics during the 1920s and 1930s had permitted astrophysical progress, in depth, in understanding the atmospheres and interiors of the stars. Because space missions have since provided us with greatly expanded knowledge about planets and their satellites, we may forget how scientifically unfashionable the solar system was in 1950. Furthermore, there was a natural scientific prejudice that links between astronomy and physics were more "important" than links between astronomy and chemistry or geology.

Between 1937 and 1948, I was on the University of Chicago faculty, stationed at the Yerkes Observatory, 80 miles from the university. Harrison worked on the Manhattan Project, about which I knew nothing. After the bomb, my friends at Chicago (notably W. H. Zachariesen) educated me quickly; one of the new phenomena revealed was Harrison Brown. Our interests were related; we became friends. I left Chicago to head the new astronomy group at Caltech in 1948, formed in conjunction with the completion of the 200-inch telescope. Within two years Caltech felt the need for a new venture in geochemistry, within the Division of Geological Sciences. Beno Gutenberg, the distinguished seismologist-geophysicist, wholeheartedly pressed for Harrison's appointment. I was glad to offer Gutenberg encouragement and to help inform the hard-rock geologists how important to the astronomers at Mounts Wilson and Palomar observatories was Harrison's work on elemental and isotopic composition of meteorites. His entrepreneurship, his interest in a broad range of new technologies, and his personal flair resulted in the successful and explosive growth of geochemistry. We really had no clear vision of how broadly significant the knowledge of meteoritic, solar, and stellar compositions would become. In 1983, Caltech's low-energy nuclear physicist, W. A. Fowler, received the Nobel Prize for the study of nuclear fusion reactions that produce stellar energy. These reactions also alter the star's composition. On this road toward a deep understanding of the unity of nature, geochemists like Gerald Wasserburg and astronomers like my colleagues and me played an important part. Provision of accurate ages, e.g., of meteorites or terrestrial minerals by Clair Patterson and others, gave cosmology a firm backbone.

THE MEANING OF THE COMPOSITION OF THE EARTH AND STARS

Harrison used mass-spectrometry and neutron-activation techniques to obtain isotope ratios and elemental compositions in meteorites, at that time the only accessible sample of nonterrestrial material. He also compiled older and new chemical analyses to make important generalizations about abundances in various chemical phases. Together with the analysis of terrestrial minerals, these provided early useful tables (e.g., Brown, 1949) of the solar system abundances of elements present in the solid phase. The special study of the isotopes of uranium and lead later gave ages of the oldest minerals. Regularity in the patterns of abundances had been noted by Harkins in 1917; they reflected then unknown aspects of nuclear stability. The nuclear shell model of M. Mayer (1948) and of Haxel, Jensen, and Suess (1949) made these regularities less mysterious and permitted Suess and Urey (1956) to extend Harrison's work. Suess and Urey provided a table of abundances of some three hundred isotopes. The stability of various isotopes is an essential feature of nuclear reaction chains; the processes that synthesized these nuclei are illuminated by frozen-in patterns of abundances. Various studies showed that no single process could account for the abundance patterns, if nuclei were all to be built from the simplest element, hydrogen, either in the "big bang," or in stellar interiors. The concentration of a nucleus involved in a steady-state chain of reactions is inversely proportional to its cross section for destruction.

On earth and in the meteorites we inherit these concentrations as they were established over the approximately 10 billion years that passed before the solar system was born. Unfortunately they have been altered by chemistry, and detailed geochemical and mineralogical study is needed to reverse the effects of the last 4.5 billion years. But what and where were the nuclear furnaces? How much did chemical differentiation alter the primordial solar system abundances? We see only the integrated effects. The first question requires a model for the evolution of the stars (relatively easy) and the origin of the universe (a hard question, indeed). The second question is a geochemical and thermodynamic problem, best left to experts.

In the easy world of the stars, chemistry played little role; the metals of which the earth is made are only trace impurities in stars. About 70 percent of the mass of the universe is hydrogen; 28 percent, helium; 2 percent, mostly C, O, Ne, Si, and Fe. But H, C, and O are gases, retained on earth where chemically bound in minerals. These elements are seen in comets, derived from more complex, cold, solid compounds, and their compounds are common in space. Molecular hydrogen is found in dense regions of interstellar space. The gravitational pull of the earth is insufficient to retain H, H_2, or He in its atmosphere; cold, massive planets (Jupiter and Saturn) contain H and He, as well as compounds of other elements, retained by their more intense gravity. Thus, the earth and meteorites are poor samples of the matter of which the universe is made; the good samples are still inaccessible. We believe that the sun is a good sample. Although much is known about the composition of its atmosphere, its isotope ratios are mostly unknown, as is its radial gradient of composition. The idea that the stars contain nuclear furnaces makes the study of stellar composition an important check on the theory of nuclear reactions. The isotopic ratios both of heavy elements in meteorites and among the radioactive elements proved to be important clues to the formation of the heavy elements at elevated temperatures in stellar explosive nucleosynthesis (in supernovae). That subject is unfortunately quite technical and complex. But to understand the logic required, let us study the nucleosynthesis accompanying stellar energy generation in normal stars.

The mean temperature in stellar interiors is above $10^7°$K, density about 1 gm cm^{-3}; surface temperatures are in the range 2,000 to 50,000°K. Under conditions in the interior, hydrogen is ionized (broken down to protons and electrons). Such a gas is nearly "perfect"; it is mixed with photons, which maintain the surface temperature and radiation as they diffuse outward. The theory of stellar interiors is well developed. The photons, originally created in particle-particle collisions, near the center of the star, are typically 1 or 2 MeV gamma rays, from radiative capture. The most common reaction chain is the carbon cycle, involving four successive proton captures on an original carbon nucleus, two beta-decays, and the formation of an alpha particle, with rebirth of the original catalyzing carbon. The hard gamma rays and the kinetic energy of reacting nuclei are absorbed in the surrounding gas; the photons degrade to the energy proper to the local temperature. About 0.7 percent of the mass is destroyed, 0.1 percent is lost as neutrinos. In a steady state the reaction chain predicts an isotope ratio, $^{13}C/^{12}C = 1/4$, $^{14}N/^{12}C = 30$. The predicted isotope ratio is 20 times that on earth (or its value at the solar surface). The predicted nitrogen abundance is 50 times the average found in the stars. What is wrong with these predictions is the assumption that the earth and stellar surfaces reflect the composition of the reacting stellar interior. In a stable star, the outer layers are shielded from the nuclear furnace. As in the earth, the nature of the accessible sample requires understanding. While there is no chemical differentiation, there may be gravitational stability against hydrodynamic mixing. We must look at a more sophisticated model.

We have reached a more sophisticated picture in which the universe started mostly as hydrogen and helium, with negligible heavy elements; massive short-lived stars burned hydrogen to helium, helium to carbon, and exploded, mixing such exhausted material into unprocessed interstellar hydrogen. There is a fortunate trick of nature, by which a ^{13}C nucleus captures an alpha particle and makes oxygen and a neutron. The neutrons, though short-lived, are essential for production of heavier elements and neutron-rich isotopes. Further carbon and oxygen burning produced elements like silicon and magnesium in stars that explode. In later generations of stars formed from this complex interstellar gas, with sufficient neutron exposure, we can produce nearly all elements and isotopes. Among elements heavier than iron, the terrestrial pattern of isotope abundances indicates that very extreme conditions existed, i.e., temperatures near 3 or 4 billion degrees and enormous neutron fluxes. It is believed that these conditions exist briefly in massive stellar explosions, blast waves in stellar envelopes, as the star's core collapses into a neutron star or black hole. We are "blessed" with uranium as a result of such explosive events—supernovae—which radiate as much energy in a few days as the sun produces in its life of 10 billion years.

Many intermediate steps with observable consequences give us some confidence in this model; some stars lose mass gradually, exposing a carbon-rich core; many are helium-rich, or have the predicted $^{13}C/^{12}C$ ratio of $1/4$. An unstable element, technetium, is seen in some stars, formed by neutron capture in the last 100,000 years. Such stars are returning nuclear-processed matter to space by strong stellar winds that peel away 80 percent of their mass, without explosion. Because our sun was formed 10 billion years after our galaxy, it is made of inherited material that has passed through many nuclear furnaces. The model is one of an organic growth, an evolution of the residual gas out of which later stars can form, toward a more heavy-element rich, more complex composition. It must be remembered that the solar system is one-third the age of the galaxy; furthermore, the rate of heavy-element formation was more rapid early in the galaxy's history. The oldest stars have about one-thousandth as much metal content as our sun. They cannot have produced rocky planets.

I was heavily involved for nearly thirty years in the spectroscopic analysis of stars, especially those of peculiar composition that could shed light on stellar-interior nuclear processes. About forty elements and a few isotopes can be so studied. In the first analysis of the sun by H. N. Russell (1929), results were compared to those of the chemical analyses of meteorites. By 1950 we used Harrison's results, based on newer techniques. An important novelty was the lead-free laboratory at Caltech; here Patterson's work gave a sharply defined age of the earth, using lead and uranium. Much slower radioactive decays have interest for cosmology. Age dating at relatively short time scales, between 10 million and 1 billion years, can illuminate time sequences in the early history of the solar system. The useful tracers are short-lived, extinct radioactivities found in certain minerals by Wasserburg and others, e.g., ^{107}Pd, ^{129}I, and especially ^{26}Al (Wasserburg and Hayden, 1955). With the existence of plutonium fission products, these have exciting implications. An explosion of a nearby supernova seems to have triggered compression and then cooling of the interstellar gas and possibly even supplied solids in its radioactive debris. From these, plus normal matter, a gas and dust nebula formed, preceding the solar system. Strong evidence exists that short-lived isotopes were present when the meteoritic minerals were condensing. Thus, because of development of very precise new techniques, including study of lunar samples, the insignificant amounts of matter falling on the earth have had enormous implications for cosmogony; Harrison's early work helped start many such exciting reconstructions of our past.

SMALL PARTICLES AND SOLIDS IN THE UNIVERSE

In the current big bang cosmology, most of the important physics is supposed to have occurred in the first few 10^{-43} seconds; only a few minutes later the primordial synthesis of helium from hydrogen was complete, and the universe coasted as galaxies, stars, and our solar system formed. The sun, earth, planets, satellites, asteroids, and interplanetary debris are secondary products of accretion under gravity and of involved chemistry. For two hundred years speculation on cosmogony was a quasi-philosophical question, lacking enough scientific data to attain scientific respectability. Too many unknown initial conditions were the problem. Sizes, masses, densities of planets were known, but not their composition. The atmospheres of planets (earth, Venus, Jupiter, Saturn) were studied spectroscopically, and the evolution of these atmospheres studied theoretically. Brown (1952) was among the pioneers in the study of the rare gases in our own atmosphere; their escape probabilities had been a classical problem. The earth cannot have retained any primitive atmosphere with which it formed; in its secondary atmosphere, now modified by living organisms, the terrestrial sources of helium and the ^{3}He$/^4$He ratio are significant.

Harrison also studied (Brown, 1950) the pattern shown by the density of planets of different mass and distance from the sun (which regulates their temperatures and therefore escape of light atmospheric gases). Adopting cosmic abundances, he studied the high densities of inner planets, a function of the compressibility of solids. The outer planets, with low density near that of water, gave him an incorrectly high He$/$H ratio, probably because of the unknown equation of state of H and He. At that time we did not know the masses and the low densities of Jupiter and Saturn's satellites, which interplanetary probes have shown also to be ice balls. But what of the meteorites, which we know only if they survive our atmosphere and their landings? These are complex stones and irons, probably derived from the asteroids. They are quite different from comets, which yield icy, low-density, fragile meteors that never land. What is the nature of the dust that causes the zodiacal light? How much mass exists in the form of small solids? In an amusing article (Brown, 1960), Harrison studies the frequency of meteorites that fall on earth. He finds their number to increase with decreasing mass, m, as $m^{-0.8}$. He also notes that Kuiper had found the same law to describe the frequency of the asteroids; in the latter, one must correct for discovery probability. One must also allow for the destruction of the meteorites in the atmosphere. It appears reasonable that both types of objects survive as a result of a competition between their rates of growth and their destruction by collision. It might be expected that a more or less similar power-law dependence on mass would result for solids everywhere. In private speculation Harrison generalized this to planets and stars.

For the astronomer, small solids have recently become quite important. In space between the stars in our galaxy are found interstellar dust or smoke grains, with relative frequency dependent on mass. In the winds that blow off dying red giants, dust is formed too. Complex molecules are found by radio astronomers in dense interstellar clouds, in which dust also grows rapidly. Dust and molecules characterize dense regions, where stars are born. Such a protostar is often located in what is called a dense molecular cloud. Within this, largely by infrared observation, powerful infrared signals indicate a new luminous star, often visually obscured by small solids formed as the gases compress, streaming into the protostar. A characteristic toroidal ring of dust may also be seen, suggesting a presolar system nebula. The size distribution of particles also affects the absorption and reddening of light in space; this same size distribution seems to hold in other galaxies. Because of the rarity of elements that can form solids, the dust in space has only about 1 percent the mass of hydrogen.

How are solids formed in space, at densities so low that chemical combination is terribly slow? It is conjectured that at temperatures of 3 to 30°K and typical densities of 1 hydrogen atom per cubic centimeter, molecules grow first by radiative combination of H and C, leading to an unstable radical that captures further hydrogen atoms. Until the molecule is fairly complex it lacks sufficient modes of radiating away the heat of successive captures. But once it is large enough, it may be treated as a solid. Once a solid, growth of the molecules, including surface chemical combinations, even at 30°K, may be rapid. The time for typical dust grains to form, before they are destroyed by collisions or evaporation by passage near a star, is about 100 million years. Water-ice, solid methane, ammonia, carbon dioxide, graphite, and silicates are likely primeval solids. The radio astronomers have found about a hundred complex molecules and ions, most of them in dense molecular clouds. In the infrared, the signatures of emission of light by silicates are seen; graphite is detected by its ultraviolet absorption of light. Combining the theory of agglutinative growth with that of destruction, the typical distribution of grain masses corresponds to about $m^{-1.2}$, which resembles that Harrison found for meteorites fallen on earth. These particles, however, are near the wavelength of light, far smaller than those that land on earth.

Another change for astrophysics, indicated by the last paragraph, is a forcible entry into chemistry (low temperature and surface). Solids are produced in a wide variety of relatively violent events. Even a red-giant wind starts from a surface near 2,000°K, where gases are expelled during late stages of stellar evolution. As such a wind expands it cools below the condensation temperature, and solids may form; in an interesting case, a carbon-rich red giant has enveloped itself in an opaque cocoon of graphite. But stars being born often do similar things, with dust of normal composition. In the birth of stars, however, events are quite violent; the energy of rotation and trapped magnetic field must be dissipated—cosmic rays are accelerated, and flare-like emission is detected at radio frequencies. Somehow dust still is formed. The Infrared Astronomical Satellite (IRAS) has seen and resolved infrared-emitting, very large dust rings near stars. It detected large (solar system–sized) rings of dust around a few stars near the sun and a cool ring of dust in our own solar system. The growing importance of solids in astronomical environments is just being realized.

Perhaps the least understood solids are the nuclei of comets. These are about 1 km in diameter, composed of frozen gases, with some metals. They have the typically high cosmic abundance of hydrogen and hydrogen-rich compounds. The breakdown products of these ices pour out when heated by the sun and include H_2O, OH, NH, NH_2, CN, C_2, and C_3. Their true parent molecules are not yet known but may resemble the material of our giant planets, Jupiter and Saturn. Their history may provide us glimpses into the early history of our solar system or of large objects condensing in the dense molecular clouds.

Finally, no discussion of unsolved astrophysical problems is now complete without reference to the so-called missing mass in the universe. For reasons of elegance, theoretical physicists tend to hope that there is sufficient gravitational mass in the universe to decelerate and eventually reverse the expansion of the universe. There is unfortunately a theological taint on a universe that had a beginning in time. Some weak arguments also suggest that formation of galaxies is difficult if the initial expansion was very rapid and not slowed by gravity. The presently known mass in stars, gas, and dust is too small by a factor between ten and thirty; furthermore there is direct observational evidence that the mean ratio of starlight to mass is far lower than we would expect—especially in outer halos surrounding galaxies and in clusters or superclusters of galaxies. For a while, it was suggested that we lived in a universe dominated by enormous numbers of neutrinos, important if neutrinos had nonzero mass.

These speculations seem to have had short lives; the astronomical evidence from the dynamics of large aggregates of matter has only strengthened. There seems to be about five times more mass than we can account for by stars that emit light. Since stars less than 5 percent as massive as the sun cannot ignite nuclear fuel sources, there could be enormous numbers of undiscovered black dwarfs, with low surface temperatures and negligible optical radiation. As they cool they could be seen in the far infrared, if sufficiently nearby. But IRAS saw none. In many ways a black dwarf resembles Jupiter, which is still radiating weakly, after 4.5 billion years. If black dwarfs are companions of known stars, they might be found by the gravitational wobble of their more massive companions. If their mass is to close the universe, however, the number of black dwarfs required is so large that we should look for some feature to explain this in the early expansion of the universe. We need conditions greatly favoring production of myriads of Jupiters, rather than of galaxies and stars. No such conditions have been found, even in wild speculations. We might imagine smaller solids, too large to produce much absorption of light, too small to radiate light. Unfortunately, the elements that can make solid rocks are rare in the universe, and it is improbable that small solid hydrogen or helium balls are stable anywhere. The laws that regulate the growth and destruction of small solids are largely unknown, although the process seems universal. And the solar system gives us a guideline in that its total mass of small solids is negligible compared to that of the sun or Jupiter. Nevertheless, the problem of missing mass remains.

I hope to have given glimpses into topics that are still current in which Harrison Brown was a pioneer—their present status and some unanswered questions. He chose to work later on problems of more directly human application—peace, the future of the human race, and the future of earth's resources. It was stimulating to know him and to recall here a few subjects in which his own research formed a significant part of science history.

REFERENCES

Brown, H., 1949. A table of relative abundances of nuclear species. *Reviews of Modern Physics* 21(4):625–634.

———, 1950. On the compositions and structures of the planets. *Astrophysical Journal* 111:641.

———, 1952. Rare gases and the formation of the earth's atmosphere. In *The Atmospheres of the Earth and Planets*, ed. G. P. Kuiper, 2d ed. (University of Chicago Press, Chicago), pp. 258–266.

———, 1957. Age of the solar system. *Scientific American* 102 (April):2–11.

———, 1960. The density and mass distribution of meteoritic bodies in the neighborhood of the earth's orbit. In *Space Research*, Proceedings of the First International Space Science Symposium, ed. H. K. Kallmann Bijl. (North-Holland Publishing Co., Amsterdam), pp. 1063–1070.

Brown, H., and E. Goldberg, 1949. The neutron pile as a tool in quantitative analysis; the gallium and palladium content of iron meteorites. *Science* 109:347–353.

Brown, H., and C. Patterson, 1948. The composition of meteoritic matter. III. Phase equilibria, genetic relationships and plant structure. *The Journal Geology* 56(2):85–111.

Clarke, F. W., 1889. *Bulletin of the Philosophical Society of Washington* 11:131.

Goldberg, E., and H. Brown, 1950. Radiometric determination of gold and rhenium. *Analytical Chemistry* 22(2):308–311.

Goldschmidt, V. M., 1959. *Geochemistry* (Clarendon Press, Oxford). 750 pp.

Harkins, W. D., 1917. The evolution of the elements and the stability of complex atoms. A new periodic system which shows a relation between the abundance of the elements and the structure of the nuclei of atoms. *Journal of the American Chemical Society* 39(5):856–879.

Haxel, O., J.H.D. Jensen, and H. E. Suess, 1949. On the "magic numbers" in nuclear structure. *Physics Review* 75(11):1766.

Mayer, M. G., 1948. On closed shells in nuclei. *Physics Review* 74(3):235–239.

Russell, H. N., 1929. On the composition of the sun's atmosphere. *Astrophysical Journal* 70(1):11–82.

Suess, H. E., and H. C. Urey, 1956. Abundances of the elements. *Reviews of Modern Physics* 28(1):53–74.

Wasserburg, G. J., and R. J. Hayden, 1955. A^{40}–K^{40} dating. *Geochim. et Cosmochim. Acta* 7(1–2):51–60.

3

THE ABUNDANCES OF THE ELEMENTS AND SOME REFLECTIONS ON THE COSMOGONY OF THE SOLAR SYSTEM

FRED HOYLE

My interest in the problem of the origin of the chemical elements began in the late 1930s, with the publication of a paper by Bethe and Critchfield on the proton-proton chain and then of Bethe's famous papers on the carbon-nitrogen cycle (1938; 1939). World War II intervened to drive all such thoughts from one's head. But in 1945, with the war at last at an end, I turned to the possibility that *all* the chemical elements might be generated inside stars, not simply helium from hydrogen—a problem that I mistakenly thought to be disposable within a few months, but that was to occupy a considerable fraction of my attention over many years and that is still today occupying the attention of a younger generation.

In retrospect I find it curious that my thinking in those early years was entirely nuclear in its orientation. I took the data on abundances to be sufficiently well known for the purposes of a physicist or an astronomer. It never occurred to me that better data based on a synthesis of chemical determinations for the Earth and for meteorites, and on astrophysical determinations for stars, might provide vital clues relating to the nuclear processes I was seeking to investigate. The first perceptions I had on this matter came when I read Harrison Brown's paper "A Table of Relative Abundances of Nuclear Species" (1949b). The most striking point for me was the combination of volatile and refractory elements into a single table of abundances. Previously I had been keenly aware of the high peak of abundances in the iron group elements and of course of Harkins's rule—that nuclei of even atomic weight are more abundant than neighboring nuclei of odd atomic weight—but the dominance among the lighter elements of those that can be considered to be made up of alpha-particles had largely escaped my attention to this point. In effect, this was a pointer toward helium burning, by what Geoffrey and Margaret Burbidge, Willy Fowler, and I were later to call the alpha-process (1957).

When I look back at the actual numbers given in Harrison Brown's table, distant memories of trials and tribulations come flooding back to me. It was no reflection on the author of the table that the nitrogen abundance was given about five times too high because this was the way that astronomers said it was in stars. What agonies of mind this astronomical error caused for those of us on the nuclear side because it seemed to demand that most of the CNO group had been through the carbon-nitrogen cycle, in which case it seemed impossible (nearly!) to understand the small value of the terrestrial $^{13}C/^{12}C$ ratio. Many were the hours of discussion, and many were the times that Willy Fowler's blackboard in his office at the Kellogg Radiation Laboratory was smothered in symbols, in an attempt to resolve this apparent difficulty.

Another trial and tribulation involved the lead abundance. Harrison Brown had an abundance distribution among the heavy elements that rose to a pronounced peak at lead, which was fine from a nuclear point of view because lead is the ultimate reservoir of what we called the s-process. The trouble was that Hans Suess and Harold Urey in their rediscussion of the abundance table (1956) felt the lead abundance should be much smaller, to a point where it contradicted the requirements of the s-process quite severely. If my memory serves me correctly, this issue was eventually resolved in favor of the higher value on the strength of an astronomical determination of the lead abundance in the sun. How far the latter determination might have been influenced by the considerable strength of the theoretical argument I never really cared or dared to enquire.

Although Harrison Brown gained much from joining the geochemical data to the astronomical data, he suffered from it too. If one judges the Fe/Si ratio from the iron and silicon abundances in the Earth, the value comes out quite a bit higher than if abundances in meteorites are used. In favor of the meteoritic value, one can argue that meteorites are more primitive than the Earth. In favor of the terrestrial value, one can argue that the Earth is a far more substantial sample of the original material of the solar system. So which view was correct? Harrison Brown had the sensible idea of appealing to the spectroscopic determination of the Fe/Si ratio in the sun for resolving this dilemma. Unfortunately, in 1949 the astronomers had a wrong determination. If the wrong determination had been quite unlike the geochemical values, its suspect nature would have been apparent. Unfortunately again, the wrong astronomical value agreed with the terrestrial determination. By the mid-1950s the astronomical value was much improved, however, and then it agreed with the meteoritic determination. Bad luck!

Actually, I have never been entirely satisfied about this business. It is hard to see why silicon should have been depleted relative to iron in the Earth. Moreover, the oscillator strengths for silicon lines in the solar spectrum are notoriously insecure. On the other hand, the Fe/Si ratio is considerably variable among the terrestrial planets, so that some process for differentiating these two refractory elements must certainly have existed. This brings me to the question of the differentiation of materials in the solar system and thus to the second of Harrison Brown's papers that I wish to discuss in this chapter, namely, "Rare Gases and the Formation of the Earth's Atmosphere," a paper presented at the fiftieth anniversary symposium of the Yerkes Observatory (1949a).

This second paper stands in remarkable contrast to the first. The first belonged to several published in the late 1940s and in the 1950s dealing with the abundances and genesis of the elements, a subject that has become standard lore, even to the extent that particular words and phrases that we coined thirty years ago have become the everyday small change of conversation among a younger generation of astronomers and geochemists. When one looks back on the papers of this first category one is struck by the extent to which details have changed but ideas have survived and broadened. The situation with "Rare Gases and the Formation of the Earth's Atmosphere" is opposite. The details survive essentially unchanged, whereas its crucial idea—lesson might be a better word—has not yet been properly assimilated into cosmogonical theories of the solar system. The reason is probably that the lesson contradicts the emotional beliefs of astronomers. Unlike nuclear physics, where emotion is at a discount, theories of the origin of the solar system have been an emotional battleground for almost two centuries, a battleground akin to that which exists currently with respect to theories of the origin of the universe.

What Harrison Brown's paper did was to set a constraint that any theory of the origin of the planets must satisfy if it is to have a chance of being correct. Figure 3.1 reproduces the original Figure 62 given in the paper. The meaning of the ordinate in the figure is that the rare gases He, Ne, Kr, and Xe have been depleted on the Earth relative to Si by this "fractionation" factor, the two sets of points being calculated as maximum and minimum values for the amounts of the rare gases.

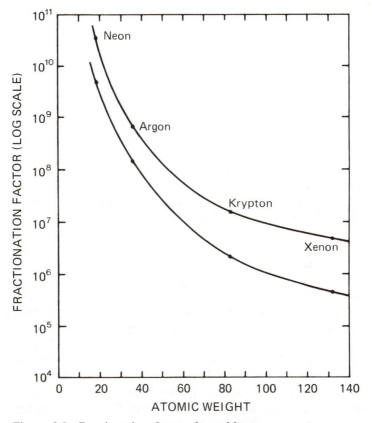

Figure 3.1. Fractionation factors for noble gases.

SOURCE: H. Brown, "Rare Gases and the Formation of the Earth's Atmosphere" (in *The Atmospheres of the Earth and Planets,* ed. G. P. Kuiper, University of Chicago Press, 1949, p. 264).

Minimum values were obtained from the concentrations of the rare gases in the terrestrial atmosphere, and maximum values obtained by assuming the rare gas content of the whole of the Earth's mantle to be given by the average amounts measured in the surface rocks. The latter determinations rest on the physical argument that it is harder for gases to remain occluded in rocks at very high pressures than in rocks at low pressure. Even if a critic were to contend that this argument may not be quite secure, it would be hard to believe that the lower rocks of the mantle could contain amounts of gas that exceeded the amounts in the surface rocks by as much as a factor of $\sim 10^6$, the order of the fractionation factor for xenon.

The atomic weights of krypton and xenon are so high that the fractionation factors for these heavier rare gases cannot be explained by simple thermal evaporation, once the Earth had accumulated sufficiently for the resulting protoplanet to possess an appreciable gravitational field. Thus the protoplanet that eventually became the Earth did not have a solar mix of the elements and the protoplanet was not a glob of material of solar composition, as most theories of the solar nebula variety would like it to have been. The krypton and xenon, and likely enough all elements existing in the gaseous phase, had already been separated out when the protoplanet formed. As Harrison Brown said it (with original italics): "In view of the large fractionation factors, it would appear that *during the process of Earth formation the mechanism was such as to prohibit the retention of an appreciable fraction of any substance that existed at that time primarily in the gaseous state.*" (p. 263)

SOME ANECDOTAL REMARKS

I wish I could remember the precise year and time of year when Harrison Brown organized a weekly seminar at Caltech, held in the eastern block of the Mudd Building—on the left as you walked toward Robinson from the north. I think the era was 1955–1956, but it could be fixed exactly because the seminars coincided with an extended visit to Caltech by F. Houtermans, the father of the lead-uranium dating method. I remember Houtermans partly because of the two seminars he gave and partly because the presence of Houtermans, or even the mention of his name, always moved Walter Baade to laughter. Walter would tell how they had both been young men-in-research at Göttingen and how Houtermans had been a great fellow for burning the midnight oil. His ideas and suggestions became ever more imaginative, wild, or preposterous it seemed (depending on how you saw it) as the late hours advanced into still later hours, to a point where the father of lead-uranium dating became universally known to the young men of the day as "Eine-Kleine-Nachtmusik" Houtermans. By 1955-1956, however, Houtermans had become a thoroughly revered figure, and it was in this spirit of course that we listened to him with due reverence and awe.

My own seminar in that series was on the problem of the origin of the solar system. My approach to it was heavily conditioned by a Cambridge mathematical background with its emphasis on planetary dynamics rather than on chemistry. Just as Harrison Brown's discussion of the depletions of rare gases in the terrestrial atmosphere is an argument from chemistry with far-reaching implications, so there is a simple fact of planetary dynamics with far-reaching implications. Although the combined masses of all the planets is only a little over 0.1 percent of the mass of the sun, the planets have combined angular momenta about the center of the solar system that is ~100 times greater than the angular momentum of the sun. Gram for gram, planetary material has on the average ~10^5 times more angular momentum than solar material. This curious fact led the Cambridge school of cosmogonists—James Jeans, Harold Jeffreys and Ray Lyttleton—to investigate theories of a catastrophic kind, the close approach of another star to a one-time binary companion of the sun. It was in this intellectual atmosphere that I began thinking about planets and their origins, and an early remark of mine was that the sun would have been more likely to have lost an original binary companion through catastrophic mass loss from the companion than through a close encounter with a third star.

In the 1940s I was doubtful of rival theories that sought to explain the origin of planets in terms of the turbulent development of a rotating solar nebula. Due to Carl von Weizsäcker, such a theory was widely and sympathetically discussed, but for me it was an unconvincing attempt to add flesh to the bones of the old Laplace theory. The reason for the sympathetic discussion, as I eventually came to realize, was that the von Weizsäcker theory fitted very well with the astronomical fashion of the day. The first fashion I encountered in astronomy was radiation pressure. Back in the 1930s radiation pressure was supposed to be responsible for 99 percent of the mysteries in the universe. As long as you said a phenomenon was due to radiation pressure you could get away with a vague argument, without supplying details or working anything out in accordance with the more rigorous standards that were required when radiation pressure was not involved. Radiation pressure died as a fad, though not of course as a valid dominant process in a few cases, sometime before 1945. Turbulence was the fad from 1945 to about 1950. The running was then taken up by magnetic fields. The current fad is black holes. Relativistic beaming is currently a subsidiary fad, and gravitational lensing threatened a year or two ago to become another subsidiary fad. Each fad has a component of truth in it, but a component with a scale that is modest compared with all the grandiose claims. The majority of my successes in astronomy are unpublished and unsung. They come from adopting the simple precept that whatever is attributed to the current fad is wrong. Experience shows that one is then eventually proved to be correct in better than nine cases out of ten, a success rate superior to anything I have ever been able to achieve by even the most determined burning of midnight oil.

Fads do have their uses, however, in an inverted kind of way, by forcing one to examine critically one's own antifad point of view. As I was thinking about the development of a rotating nebula of the kind that was being contemplated in the von Weizsäcker theory, it seemed to me that the effect of a turbulent transfer of angular momentum between different parts of the nebula would be to produce not a star and planets, but two stars, one of them—the central star as one might call it—two or three times more massive than the other. The likely outcome would be a close binary similar to an actual class of binaries, the W Ursa Majoris stars. Both components of W Ursa Majoris binaries are in rapid rotation, a fact that then led me to wonder why the sun was not in rapid rotation.

I have never timed explicitly how long it takes for sudden shifts to take place in one's point of view. In my experience I would say no longer than a few seconds. What I suddenly saw in this instance was that the preoccupation of the Cambridge school with the large angular momenta of the planets had tended to conceal a significant and important question: Why was the angular momentum of the sun itself so small? To this point, I would probably have answered that most dwarf main-sequence stars rotate slowly, so that as a member of its class the sun was quite normal. It was rapid rotators like the W Ursa Majoris stars that were abnormal. This was a matter of empirical experience, I would have argued. But why then was empirical experience the way it was? Every condensation occurring within clouds of interstellar gas would be likely to possess sufficient initial angular momentum to produce a rapidly rotating star—unless a large fraction of the initial angular momentum were lost in some way. These considerations created a dilemma that could be resolved only if some process of angular momentum loss existed for most dwarf stars or for the protostars from which dwarf stars were eventually formed.

Since angular momentum is a conserved quantity, the angular momentum that had been lost by the sun was not destroyed. It had to go somewhere, and the next question was evidently where. If it were returned back to the interstellar gas from whence it came, well and good. The arguments of the Cambridge school could then survive largely unaffected. But what if most of the angular momentum of the sun were passed to the material that eventually formed into the planets? One would then understand why the planets have so much angular momentum and the sun so little, and disastrously the Cambridge position would collapse at a stroke, almost without a shot being fired. This would occur because it had always been assumed implicitly in this position that no internal process of angular momentum transfer from the sun to planets could exist, a supposition I felt to be correct insofar as the turbulence of the von Weizsäcker theory was concerned. The crucial point was that to explain the facts (a slowly rotating sun with planets orbiting it at distances large compared with the solar radius), it was essential for the angular momentum to be transferred across more or less empty space, not through a continuous medium as with turbulence. This was the nub of the matter, the empty space. How could angular momentum go across empty space?

The years immediately following World War II was the time when Hannes Alfvén emphasized the importance of magnetic fields in astronomy. Alfvén had a magnetic theory of the origin of the planetary system, according to which neutral atoms falling toward the sun became ionized by solar radiation, whereupon they were subjected to the influence of the magnetic field of the sun. The latter would cause the ions and the electrons to rotate with the same angular velocity as the sun, imparting to the ionized atoms an angular momentum increased by a factor $\sim d/R$ above the angular momentum of a similar atom within the sun, where d was the distance from the sun at which ionization took place, with R the solar radius. Because values for d of order $10^4 R$ could be contemplated, the excess angular momentum acquired by ionized atoms at large d would be of planetary order, assuming the planets to have condensed from a multitude of such ionized atoms. It was here, however, that I disagreed with Alfvén. I well remember arguing at length with him in Cambridge that one could not apply to matter in bulk (such as was needed to form the planets) considerations that were applicable only to single atoms. If matter in bulk fell into the weak solar magnetic field at $d >> R$ it would simply continue to fall, pushing the field inward, instead of acquiring significant angular momentum in the manner of a single atom.

Although I could not feel that Alfvén's argument in terms of single atoms had come to grips with the essentials of the problem, the introduction of a magnetic field certainly opened up a new train of ideas. Suppose one began with a rapidly rotating protosun around which there was a toroidally shaped disk of gas, with each element of the disk in nearly Keplerian motion around the protosun (leaving aside for the moment how such a situation had come about in the first place). One could conceive of gas in the disk as having initial distances d not much larger than R. Was there a process that could transfer angular momentum from protosun to toroidal disk, across the gap between them?

One could see from the known facts of solar physics that the answer to this question was quite likely affirmative for the following reasons. From solar physics one knew there is indeed a magnetic field in the present-day sun, with an intensity in sunspots rising at least to hundreds or even to thousands of Gauss. From solar physics one also knew that flares near sunspots cause chromospheric material to be expelled more or less radially outward from the sun at speeds of order $1,000$ km s^{-1}. Such expelled ionized material carries with it a magnetic field that expands outward into a loop or lobe, the magnetic lines of force remaining connected to roots beneath the solar photosphere. In such a situation the magnetic field acts to transfer angular momentum from the sun to the material expelled by the flare, a process that tends to maintain the expelled material in corotation with the sun. If the field is strong enough in relation to the amount of the expelled material, the angular momentum so transferred can be very considerable on a gram-for-gram basis, essentially because in this form of the theory the intensity of the field falls as the inverse square of the distance d, rather as the inverse cube for a dipole. Suppose now that such expelled flare material, instead of being ejected entirely from the solar system, were to encounter a rotating disk of gas and to become incorporated therein. The effect would be to transfer angular momentum from the sun to the disk, just the process we are seeking. Angular momentum does not go by itself across the gap between sun and disk. It is carried across the gap by the expelled material, which, however, remains comparatively small in its total amount.

In order to store angular momentum from a protosun in rapid rotation initially, the toroidally shaped disk of gas must move outward to distances that can easily be shown to be $\sim R(M/m)^2$, where R is the radius of the protosun, M is its mass, and m is the mass of the disk. Thus for $M/m \gg 1$ the disk of gas must retreat to large values of d, if it comes through some such process as that described above to acquire most of the initial angular momentum of the protosun. The outcome of the process, if it were maintained sufficiently, would be a slowly rotating central star accompanied by a toroidal distribution at comparatively large d of rotating protoplanetary material, the kind of situation needed to explain the situation in the solar system. With M essentially fixed at the solar mass, the order of magnitude of d, and hence the order of magnitude of the radii of the orbits of the main planets of the system, turns on the disk mass m. To obtain a case like the solar system, m is required to be a few percent of M.

Consider now what happens during the process of angular momentum transfer as the distance of the protoplanetary gas increases from an initial value of order R to an eventual value of order $R(M/m)^2$. The temperature of the gas falls from an initial value of, let us say, 4,000°K to a value of order $4,000°(m/M)$, which for $m = M/40$, for example, is only 100°K, far below the thermodynamic condensation points of refractory materials and even below the condensation point of water. Although most of the protoplanetary material will remain gaseous, largely H_2 and He, condensable substances will form as solids suspended within the outward-moving gas. Refractory substances with thermodynamic condensation temperatures above 1,000°K will come out of the gas as solid grains and chunks while the gas is still comparatively close to the protostar, but volatile substances like water will come out of the gas only as the most distant regions of the eventual system are reached. In short, variations of thermodynamic condensation temperatures among substances with differing degrees of refractivity and volatility are reflected in a segregation process from the gas.

If all the solid particles were tiny grains that were carried along by the outward-moving gas, this segregation process with respect to condensation temperatures would have no significant eventual effect because all the particles would then be carried to the outer regions of the system, where they would be mixed in proportions that were the same as in the original gaseous phase. But if some of the solids grow to hunks—planetesimals—large enough to resist being carried along by the gas, refractory solids would be left behind in the inner regions of the system as the gas continued to acquire angular momentum from the central protostar and thus expanded more and more to large values of d. The segregation process from the gas would then be reflected in a system of planetesimals moving around the protostar in nearly Keplerian orbits, planetesimals that had been left behind by the outward-moving gas, left behind in an ordered sequence with respect to condensation temperatures, the highest temperatures nearest to the center.

Three important correspondences with our actual solar system now emerge. We see why the innermost planets are very largely composed of materials of the higher refractivity. We see why the masses of these planets are small compared with the masses of the outer planets—because the original gas contained only a small fraction of refractory substances. And as long as the time scale for the planetesimals to aggregate into planets was longer than the time scale for the process of angular momentum transfer, the gas would necessarily be gone before the newly forming inner planets acquired gravitational fields of appreciable strength. Thus there would be an absence of gas as the planetesimals aggregated into planets, except for a tiny amount that occluded itself at temperatures $\sim1,000°K$ within the solid planetesimals. So we understand Harrison Brown's conclusion: "*[D]uring the process of Earth formation the mechanism was such as to prohibit the retention of an appreciable fraction of any substance that existed at that time primarily in the gaseous state.*" (p. 263)

Chemistry and dynamics thus join together. This was the substance of my contribution when I gave one of the seminars in Harrison Brown's weekly series in 1955-1956 at Caltech. The broad picture as I have now described it has survived essentially unchanged in my mind ever since that time. Such changes as there have been are mostly additions, some of which may be worth mentioning here—in the following section.

FURTHER CONSIDERATIONS

Let us pick up the discussion of the previous section at the early stage, where a protostar surrounded by a toroidally shaped disk of protoplanetary gas was taken as the starting configuration (for the process of angular momentum transfer from star to disk). One can ask how such a situation arose. There is no difficulty in answering this question in general terms. The angular momentum acquired by a protostar from the interstellar cloud in which it condenses is likely to be amply large enough for it to spin up during condensation to a point of rotational instability, a condition that occurs when rotary forces at the star's equator become comparable with gravity. A disk of gas then emerges at the equator, and provided the process of angular momentum begins immediately so as to relieve the incipient instability of the star, the mass m of the disk can remain small compared to M, as it is required to do in order to explain the situation in the solar system. If, on the other hand, the process of angular momentum transfer worked too slowly to prevent m from becoming comparable with M, a double-star system like W Ursa Majoris, not a planetary system, would be the outcome.

At first sight one might think from these straightforward considerations that scooping together all the present-day planets, conserving their angular momenta in the process, and dumping them into the present-day sun would necessarily have the effect of making the sun rotationally unstable. It comes as a minor shock to one's sense of logic that this is not the case—the sun would then be spun up to an equatorial rotational speed of about 100 km s^{-1}, which is not sufficient to cause instability (300 to 400 km s^{-1} are required for that).

One then notices, however, that an important component of the original protoplanetary material is missing from the present-day planets. This is the H_2 and He gas that must have accompanied the material from the planets Uranus and Neptune. From their densities, about 1.6 g cm^{-3}, it is clear that these two planets can contain little H_2 and He compared with what must have originally been present. How much must originally have been present? Calculating on the basis that the masses of Uranus and Neptune are largely made up from the next most abundant group of elements, namely, C, N, and O, the present-day masses have to be multiplied by the abundance ratio (by mass) of H, He to C, N, O, which is a factor ~50, assuming the original protoplanetary material to have been of normal cosmic composition. This leads to the surprise that the original quantity of gas in the region of Uranus and Neptune must have been ~1,500 Earth masses, about four times greater than the combined masses of Jupiter and Saturn. With an extra factor of about 2 also appearing in the angular momentum contribution, due to the large radii of the orbits of Uranus and Neptune, the original angular momentum of the protoplanetary material had to be greater than the present-day angular momentum—mostly contributed by Jupiter and Saturn—by a factor of order 10, amply sufficient if dumped into the sun to endow the resulting body with rotational instability.

Although one's sense of logic thus survives unimpaired, a new problem evidently arises, for how did essentially all of the H_2 and He that originally accompanied the material of Uranus and Neptune contrive to escape from the periphery of the solar system? The answer is clear in principle, if not in detail. As the toroidal disk of gas moved outward to greater and greater distances from the protosun, a stage was eventually reached at which the holding power of solar gravity weakened sufficiently for H_2 and He, the gaseous particles of least mass, to evaporate thermally from the disk back to interstellar space. The main uncertainty concerns the source of heating in the gas, for which there are several contenders: radiation from the protosun, the kinetic energy of a wind of particles from the protosun, and a relative motion of the whole solar system with respect to the gas of the cloud in which it condensed. It is still unclear which of these processes was the dominant one.

It is also necessary to face up to an old problem that is still not solved in detail. Given that there is a swarm of planetesimals in nearly Keplerian orbits around the protosun, how do the planetesimals aggregate together into a number of full-blown planets? One can make quick progress in this problem if the orbits have negligible eccentricities to begin with, for then even the small mutual gravitational fields between the bodies are sufficient to bring planetesimals in adjacent orbits into a gentle juxtaposition with each other, permitting them to join together into larger and larger bodies, a process that can be shown to continue until sizes of the order of the satellites of planets are attained. Mutual gravitational forces between neighboring bodies then become too weak to overcome the shearing effect of the gravitational field of the central star.

At this stage of the aggregation process one needs an opposite dynamical situation in which a quite large number of bodies of lunar dimensions initially in nearly circular orbits contrive to develop orbits of considerable eccentricity, so that the orbits of adjacent bodies then interlace each other when collisions occur at random between them. Such collisions lead to an aggregation of the inner planets on a time scale of ~ 10 million years and to an aggregation of the outermost large planets on a time scale of ~ 500 million years.

The big question here is whether as a matter of celestial mechanics such a system of bodies really does evolve from nearly circular to considerably eccentric orbits. I have for long had the intention to try to resolve this problem by a computer calculation, but a recollection of the subtleties that can arise in such calculations—subtleties dating from Isaac Newton's discussion of the motion of the moon and clearly demonstrated in the work of Pierre-Simon Laplace—caused me to desist. So I have tended to make do with the old saw that wherever entropy can increase it will do so. Without inflexible intelligent control, physical systems always seem to develop toward increasing disorder, whether in classic thermodynamic situations or in one's personal filing system.

If it could be demonstrated that sufficiently eccentric orbits do *not* develop, there is still a remaining recourse, an encounter at a distance of $\sim 10^{15}$ cm with a passing star, which would certainly change nearly circular orbits into eccentric ones. Under present-day circumstances, with the solar system moving through the general galactic star field, the chance of such a close encounter would be small, perhaps $\sim 10^{-4}$ taken over the whole history of our system. The chance could have been higher, however, with the solar system still embedded in the dense cloud in which it condensed—which presumably gave rise to a whole cluster of stars having comparatively small separations between them. If it should eventually turn out that this recourse is essential for solving the planetary aggregation problem, the old catastrophic form of theory would have reasserted itself in a novel form.

BACK TO CHEMISTRY

As well as calculating fractionation factors for the rare gases, Harrison Brown also made calculations of the terrestrial amounts of water, nitrogen, and carbon dioxide, obtaining terrestrial depletions relative to silicon of $\sim 10^{-4}$, $\sim 10^{-5}$, and $\sim 10^{-4}$, respectively, from which he concluded, *"The Earth's atmosphere is almost entirely of secondary origin, and it was formed as the result of chemical processes that took place subsequent to the formation of the planets."* (p. 266)

The first part of this statement accords with the above discussion. The second part of the statement concerning "chemical processes" requires further discussion, however. Because the fractionation factors for H_2O, N_2, and CO_2 are smaller than those for the rare gases by some two to three orders of magnitude, we can conclude that the Earth acquired H_2O, N_2, and CO_2 in a manner different from the rare gases. If the latter were occluded within the planetesimals that went to form the Earth, then H_2O, N_2, and CO_2 were not occluded—they were obtained in some other way. The way that appealed to Harrison Brown was through chemical bonding (as for instance in water of hydration, or CO_2 in $CaCO_3$) within the material of the planetesimals. One would then seek to argue that H_2O, N_2, and CO_2 have appeared at the Earth's surface through a process of outgassing, which has taken place subsequent to the formation of our planet, a point of view that had a good run for its money in the 1950s and 1960s. As always, I was doubtful of this popular view, not only because it was popular but because I did not believe that weak chemical bondings like CO_2 in $CaCO_3$ would arise thermochemically in a condensation process at temperatures in excess of 1,000°K. So from 1960 or thereabouts I have gone a different way, which I will now describe.

Materials built from C, N, O, probably in combination with hydrogen, were dominant in the outer regions of the solar system, and it is there, it seems to me, that one should look for the source of the volatiles that are so important nowadays in the terrestrial biosphere. As well as many bodies with the sizes of satellites and small planets moving in approximately circular orbits around the sun, there would also be a great swarm of smaller objects of cometary sizes present in the outer regions over the first ~500 million years in the history of our system. Suppose these smaller bodies to have acquired eccentric orbits either through internal dynamical effects or through the stirring effect of an encounter of our system with a passing star in the manner discussed in the preceding section. A highly eccentric orbit can be obtained from a circular orbit either by adding energy or by subtracting it. Those smaller bodies that obtained highly eccentric orbits through additions of energy would move in orbits with distances from the sun at perihelion of the order of the radii of their original circular orbits, which is to say radii of the same order as those of the present-day planets Uranus and Neptune. The aphelion distances, on the other hand, could be much larger, depending on the amounts of the energy additions. Bodies could even have aphelion distances approaching the distances of the nearest stars, and some may well have acquired positive total energy and thus have lost permanent connection with our system. Small bodies that maintained connection, but with large aphelion distances, form the present-day Oort cloud of comets, or so it seems to me.

Bodies that acquired highly eccentric orbits by losing energy would move in orbits with aphelion distances comparable with the radii of their original circular orbits. Depending on the amounts of energy lost, perihelion distances would be reduced, bringing a fraction of the bodies to the inner regions of the solar system. Those that interlaced the orbit of the primitive Earth would be subject on a random basis to collision with the Earth, and similarly for the other terrestrial planets. Since the swarm of small bodies must have been very large, perhaps ~10^{12} bodies of cometary scale, collisions with the Earth, moon, and other inner planets could have been frequent. These collisions could have resulted in the addition of the required volatile materials, accompanied by a heavy cratering such as must certainly have happened. This cratering would explain the severe scarring of the surfaces of the moon and of Mercury that have persisted to this day.

THE GREAT WATER MYSTERY

Until the last decade it was taken as axiomatic by astronomers that, because of the exceptionally strong binding of the CO molecule ($\sim$11eV), all the available carbon present in a sample of cosmic material cooling from high temperature would become locked up as CO. This would leave about a half of the O, a minor fraction of which would become incorporated into refractory metal oxides, with the major fraction joining H_2 as H_2O. This would make the CO abundance (by number) equal to the original C abundance, with H_2O about equal to the CO. Aside from the great abundance of H_2, CO and H_2O would then be by far the most common molecules in the universe, with the possibility that in some situations at temperatures below $\sim$500°K the thermochemical balance would lead to $CO + H_2O \longrightarrow CO_2 + H_2$. This picture has turned out to be entirely wrong. Less than 10 percent of the C available in the interstellar medium is locked up as CO (for example, P. M. Solomon and D. B. Sanders, 1980). Nor is the bulk of the C present as atomic carbon in the gas phase, or as CO_2. The carbon is mainly present as solid particles together with some form of dielectric solid, likely of an organic nature. It is also likely that the solid particles arose from the degeneration of the organics by a process analogous to coalification.

Astronomers are at present in the process of accommodating themselves to this drastically changed situation for CO. What very few have yet accommodated themselves to is that H_2O is still more rare than CO, even though the proof of this statement is simple and decisive. Water-ice has an extremely strong absorption bond near 3 microns, giving an extinction at this wavelength that is clearly comparable to the visual extinction. The visual extinction through the Galaxy from the Earth to the galactic center has been estimated to be about 35 magnitudes, along the particular line to the infrared source GC-IRS7, the spectrum of which shows no characteristic extinction due to water-ice near 3 microns. This is at a sensitivity better than 0.1 magnitudes. At most then, water-ice grains in the general interstellar medium cannot be more than a fraction of a percent of all the grains. Since free molecules of H_2O would easily be disrupted by ultraviolet light, H_2O is evidently almost completely absent from the general interstellar medium.

There are absorptions near 3 microns in the spectrum of infrared sources embedded in molecular clouds, typically with extinctions of 1 to 2 magnitudes, compared to visual extinctions for the clouds of perhaps 30 to 100 magnitudes. If these absorptions are really due to water-ice grains, then the water-ice still amounts to only ~5 percent of all the grains within the clouds. Even this very limited amount may be questioned, however, since the shape of the observed absorption band near 3 microns is much too broad to be explained by the basic water-ice absorption itself, as it is measured in thin films or for very small grains. What has to be done is to consider grains so large that interference effects occur between one part of a particular grain and another, which makes an explanation of the shapes of the observed bands contingent on the choice of special size distributions for the grains. By carefully finagling the size distributions, the observed bands can be fitted with a correspondence that is still only barely tolerable.

Another approach is to argue from basic principles. Absorptions near 3 microns are found in many substances, and they arise typically from longitudinal oscillations (so-called stretching) of OH groups. Whereas the OH groups in water-ice have a similar relation to each other, OH groups in complex organic solids vary considerably, one OH group to another, in their relationships to neighboring atoms, thereby producing a spread in their oscillation frequencies. Thus the absorption band produced by a complex organic solid is characteristically broad, whereas that from H_2O is characteristically narrow. Since the observed bands are broad, the natural inference from first principles is that organics, not H_2O, are likely to be the source material for the 3-micron band.

The old argument concerning CO and H_2O, as outlined at the beginning of this section, was not a bad argument. It was sufficiently good to convince generations of astronomers and geochemists, even to the point where many have still not come to terms with the crucially changed situation demanded by the facts. It is a part of my own scientific philosophy, when good arguments turn out to be wrong, to think that something of great consequence must have been overlooked. Good arguments are not wrong for vague reasons. The unexpected in this case appears to be connected with a possible biological origin of organic materials and with microorganisms playing a role in the behavior of molecular clouds and of star formation, with possible effects on planet formation, and therefore on the history of our own solar system.

REFERENCES

Bethe, Hans A. 1939. "Energy Production in Stars." *Physical Review* 55:434. March 1.

Bethe, Hans A., and C. L. Critchfield. 1938. "The Formation of Deuterons by Proton Combination." *Physical Review* 54:248–254, 862.

Brown, Harrison. 1949a. "Rare Gases and the Formation of the Earth's Atmosphere," in G. P. Kuiper, ed. *The Atmospheres of the Earth and Planets.* Chicago: University of Chicago Press.

———. 1949b. "A Table of Relative Abundances of Nuclear Species." *Reviews of Modern Physics* 21 (4):625–634. October.

Burbidge, Geoffrey, M. Burbidge, W. Fowler, and F. Hoyle. 1957. "Synthesis of the Elements." *Reviews of Modern Physics* 29:547–650. October.

Suess, Hans, and Harold Urey. 1956. "Abundance of the Elements." *Reviews of Modern Physics* 28 (1):53–74. January.

Solomon, P. M., and D. B. Sanders. 1980. "Giant Molecular Clouds as a Component of the Interstellar Medium of the Galaxy," in P. M. Solomon and M. G. Edmunds, eds. *Giant Molecular Clouds in the Galaxy.* Oxford: Pergamon Press. Pp. 41–73.

4

EVIDENCE FOR RING SYSTEMS ORBITING EARTH IN THE GEOLOGIC PAST

RICHARD P. SHELDON

The intellectual, scientific pursuits of Harrison Brown have ranged from studies of atoms to stars, meteorites, planetary atmospheres, geochemistry, mineral resources, and international science and resource systems, with a bit of science fiction thrown in for fun. Although this may appear at first glance to be a collection of disparate subjects, to Harrison they are all related by the natural environment in which men and women live and by their efforts to understand and thoughtfully harvest the fruits of this environment. My path crossed Harrison's at conferences on long-range mineral resources and growth at the Institut de la Vie in France. Our paths were to follow the same course for several years at the Resource Systems Institute of the East-West Center. One cannot know Harrison without having some of his universal viewpoint rub off, and I consider myself fortunate to have been so affected. This is not to put a portion of the blame on Harrison for any scientific mischief I might be guilty of, as I have no idea whether or not he would subscribe to the conclusions of this chapter. He would not find it strange, however, for a scientist to go from iron ore, petroleum and phosphate rock geology and resources, to fertilizer raw material resource systems, and finally to ancient orbiting ring systems, although he might have a pithy remark on the sequence. He does, like it or not, have to share some of the blame for inspiring one to think universally.

*   *   *

The astronomic and astrogeologic mainstream literature is mute on the possibility of ancient ring systems orbiting the Earth. This is understandable, in that no observational geologic data have been presented requiring the presence of ancient rings, and no theory on the origin of the solar system postulates an Earth ring system.[1] However, three workers (Ives, 1940; O'Keefe, 1980, in press; Sheldon, 1984, 1985) have advanced ring system hypotheses, which are discussed below. In each case, the observational data and paleoclimatic interpretations allow a ring system hypothesis, but do not require it. The possibility of ancient ring systems is not generally accepted, because it is easier and simpler philosophically to accept the present climate processes operating in some unknown fashion to account for unusual paleoclimatic and paleontologic data— a standard practice since the days of Charles Lyell—than to hypothesize a ring system shadow process to account for these data.

The recent discovery, however, of a unique type of stratification in some sedimentary rocks may change this. The stratification consists of cyclic banding that in turn is made up of about eleven sets of four microlaminae each, whose upper three microlaminae commonly form a doublet.[2]

The stratification appears to be observational data that can be explained only by a ring system hypothesis. If these observations and their interpretations can run the scientific gauntlet, it will become necessary to consider the ring system hypothesis in the Earth's geologic history.

HYPOTHETICAL EARTH RING SYSTEMS

The idea that the Earth had a ring system in ancient times was first advanced in 1940 by Ronald L. Ives. At that time there was debate about the stability of the continents over geologic time, with the majority of U.S. geologists (in contrast to European geologists) not accepting the hypothesis of continental drift. Assuming the continents were always in their present position, Ives identified a climatic problem for Permian time. Permian glacial deposits (some of which were later disproved to be of glacial origin) had been found in southern Asia, Australia, Africa, South America, and the United States. These glacial deposits occur on both sides of the equator between latitudes 35°N and 30°S. Ives concluded that if the continents were stable, these data could not satisfactorily be explained by the present climate system. He proposed the "ring hypothesis" that the Earth had a second smaller moon, either captured from space or formed at the origin of the solar system. This satellite, which he named Ephemeron, orbited closer to the Earth with time until just prior to Permian time when it came within the Roche limit and broke into pieces, forming a ring around the Earth in the plane normal to the Earth's rotational axis. The shadow of this ring caused a low-latitude, cold climate, which in turn caused low-latitude glaciation. Ives concluded, "This explanation seems to account for all the major features of the Early Permian, and to be in general accord with current astronomical theories." A decade later, studies of remnant magnetism in Permian rocks yielded evidence that the Permian glacial sediments were originally deposited at high, not low, latitudes. About a decade after that, the theory of plate tectonics provided the process for movement of crustal plates on the Earth's surface. Thus, the occurrence of Permian glacial deposits at present-day low latitudes was explained by the present Earth climate system acting on continents with a different distribution. There was no need for Ives's ring hypothesis, and it was forgotten (almost).

In 1980, a ring system hypothesis was advanced by John A. O'Keefe to account for observational data in rocks of transitional age between the late Eocene and early Oligocene time, about 34 million years before the present. These data included extinction of a number of radiolarian (a unicellular silica-secreting animal) species in the Caribbean Sea at the same stratigraphic horizon that contained abundant tektites in North America. O'Keefe reasoned similarly to Ives that the shadow on the Earth of the ring system would cause a low-latitude, cold climate. This would account for the faunal extinction. The ring system was composed of tektites, and the origin of the tektites was from lunar silicic volcanism, driven by hydrogen gas (O'Keefe, 1976).

In a later paper (in press), O'Keefe extended this process to the transitional time between the Cretaceous and the Tertiary to explain the biotal extinctions at the time. The lunar volcanic material captured by the Earth's gravitational field would partly impact directly on the Earth, giving meteorite craters with lunar glass meteorites, such as the Aouelloul crater glass found in the immediate vicinity of the 250-meter crater of Aouelloul in the Mauritanian Adrar (Sahara) (O'Keefe, 1976, p. 34) and would partly give tektite-strewn fields when the lunar ejecta were composed of smaller particles. Also, part of the volcanic material would go into orbit, resulting in the formation of a ring system. If the trajectory of the lunar volcanic material were even wider off the mark, the material would miss the Earth and go off into space. O'Keefe analyzed the alternative origins of tektites, which include lunar meteorite impact, Earth volcanism and meteorite impact, and material from outer space. He rejected lunar impact for insufficient energy source, Earth volcanism for lack of any Earth volcanic source that matches the chemistry of tektites, and outer space for a number of reasons including lack of evidence of extensive bombardment of primary cosmic rays.

Most (but not all) astronomers and astrogeologists agree on these exclusions, but an acceptable hypothesis still exists that the tektites possibly had an origin from meteorite impact on Earth. However, if this were true, no ring system could be formed, according to O'Keefe, because Earth material impacted into space would return to Earth at the point of initial impact and not go into orbit. Additional objections raised by O'Keefe on a meteorite impact on Earth origin are based on the petrology of tektite glass, on consideration of the ballistics of material blown from the surface by meteorite impact in relation to the distribution of tektite-strewn fields, and on consideration of the chemistry of the tektites of individual strewn fields, one of which is made up of two events with chemical differences between the two levels. A significant piece of data is the widely accepted identification of the Allen Hills sample 8001 from an Antarctic ice field as a Moon rock meteorite (Lunar Planetary Institute, 1983), indicating that Moon material does on occasion reach the Earth. O'Keefe's hypothesis of ring systems orbiting the Earth to explain extinctions of the Eocene-Oligocene transition time would seem to be correct if the tektites that are associated with that time are of lunar volcanic origin. The alternative hypothesis being advanced at present is a meteorite impact raising a global dust cloud (Alvarez and others, 1983). If the associated tektites are proved to be volcanic, it would mean that the fall of lunar tektites on Earth would coincide with an unrelated meteorite impact, which would be improbable. No direct evidence of a ring system has been shown by O'Keefe, and its existence is supported by logical deduction alone. This is not to detract from O'Keefe's logic, as the geologic data for that period of time appear to be well explained by his ring system hypothesis.

A third ring system hypothesis was formu....ed in 1980 and 1981 by me to explain the occurrence on all continents of low paleolatitude glacial deposits of upper Proterozoic age, which are interbedded with warm climate, marine chemical sediments including limestone and dolomite (Sheldon, 1984, 1985). Other chemical sediments occurring in association with the glacial deposits and also probably low-latitude deposition are major deposits of chert (SiO_2), phosphorite (calcium fluorophosphate), and banded iron formation (iron oxides, carbonates, and silicates). The association at low paleolatitudes of warm climate, marine, chemical sedimentation alternating with glaciation at the same locality is an anomaly in relation to the Earth's present climate system. Something is wrong! The geologic data stand up well, I believe, and are duplicated in six continents. If true, the backward extrapolation of the present climate system would have to fall. To replace it, a ring system hypothesis was advanced, using Saturn's ice rings as an analogue. The ice rings were hypothesized to have come either originally at the formation of the solar system or subsequently from ice moons that approached the Earth to within the Roche limit. It was hypothesized that episodes of ice-ring shadows caused episodes of glaciation and equatorial oceanic upwelling with concurrent sedimentation of phosphorite, iron formation, and other thalassophilic metal deposits. During periods of weak or no ring shadows, climates were more like the present one, and low-latitude, warm climate sedimentation occurred. From this hypothesis, a number of deductions were made that were not essential to the climate anomaly solution but that seemed possible and logical consequences of the hypothesis. One was that the Earth's ocean and atmosphere had their origins from ice rings. Another was that metazoan evolution was inhibited by an atmospheric oxygen cycle.

One major problem of the ice-ring hypothesis is that present evidence indicates that the Sun has always been too hot to allow ice rings to exist for any significant length of time. The Sun's luminosity is thought by solar physicists to have originally had only 60 to 70 percent of the present luminosity and to have increased linearly to the present. If so, the Sun's luminosity was too high in the Proterozoic to have allowed long-lived ice rings. Another major problem was that no direct evidence could be adduced for the ring system, which is also a failing of the Ives and the O'Keefe hypotheses.

RING SHADOW DYNAMICS

Direct evidence of an ancient ring system around the Earth could come from recognition in the geologic record of a phenomenon uniquely resulting from the shadow of the ring system. Ring shadow dynamics have been discussed by both Ives and O'Keefe. The rings of Saturn, which has about the same axial tilt as Earth, are taken as an analogue (except for composition) for Earth rings. The rings were formed in the plane normal to the axis of rotation at the equator, as required by the physics of the formation. The rings were formed of innumerable small satellites, each in an orbit around the Earth according to its velocity. The drag of Earth's atmosphere would cause ring material to slow and fall to Earth, so that the inner radius of the ring must have been at least beyond the outer limit of the atmosphere. Beyond the Roche limit, matter could form moons by gravitational attraction, but within the Roche limit, Earth's tidal forces would have overcome gravitational attraction and broken moons into smaller pieces, forming rings. Thus, the maximum outer radius of the ring would have corresponded to the Roche limit, which depends on the Earth's gravity and the density of the ring material.

Because of the tilt of the rotational axis of the Earth to the plane of the ecliptic, the shadow of the ring on the Earth's surface would have swept from one pole to the other and back each year as the Earth circled the Sun. At the autumnal equinox, the width of the ring shadow would have been equal to the thickness of the ring, which probably was no more than a few kilometers, and the ring shadow would have been quite dark. As the Earth moved away from the equinox position, the shadow would have swept poleward, widened, and become less dark. At the winter solstice, the shadow would have been at its maximum poleward position, and from the winter solstice to the vernal equinox, the shadow would have swept equatorward in a reverse fashion. These dynamics are shown in Figure 4.1.

As the Earth circled the Sun and the ring shadow migrated annually from one polar region to the other and back, the shadow would pass over any point at low to intermediate latitudes twice between the autumnal and vernal equinoxes (Figure 4.1). At the equator the time between shadows was six months, but at higher latitudes the time between the fall arrival and the winter departure of the shadow midpoint would become less. As the shadow broadened, the length of time when a point was under the shadow would increase directly with the latitude of the point. Thus at higher latitudes the time between shadow passes was shorter and the duration of the shadow longer until at some high latitude no winter solstice break in the shadow would have occurred. The exact latitude where this would occur would depend on the width and position of the ring around the Earth.

RING SHADOW CLIMATIC EFFECTS

Possible climatic effects of a migrating ring shadow would have been strong. The shadow itself would not be perfectly latitudinal because it would be the result of a parabolic projection of the arc of the ring on the nearly spherical surface of the Earth. The rotation of the Earth would average the shadow out into latitudinal zones of equal hours of insolation. Atmospheric circulation cells would probably form by air masses rising in sunlit areas and descending in areas of shadow. Zonal winds would be set up by these vertical circulation cells and the rotation of the Earth. Climates would be stormy as the cold air masses formed under the shadow would flow under the warm air masses of the sunlit areas. The continental effect on climate would be strong. It seems likely that conditions of high rates of precipitation would occur close to the edges of the shadow zone. At lower annual Earth temperatures, caused by a combination of lower solar luminosity, low atmospheric CO_2 content, and a broad, dense ring system, conditions would be favorable for

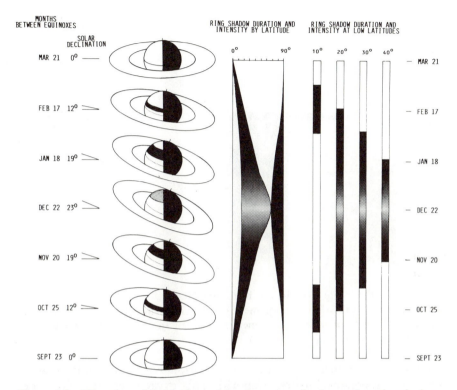

MONTHS
BETWEEN EQUINOXES

SOLAR
DECLINATION

RING SHADOW DURATION AND
INTENSITY BY LATITUDE

RING SHADOW DURATION AND
INTENSITY AT LOW LATITUDES

Figure 4.1. Migration of the shadow of the ring system in the northern hemisphere between the autumnal and vernal equinoxes. The seasonal variation of the solar declination and its effect on the ring and polar shadows are shown at left. The seasonal variations of the intensity and latitudinal extent of the shadows are shown in the middle figure, and the seasonal duration and intensity of the ring shadow at 10, 20, 30, and 40 degrees of latitude north are shown in the figure on the right. The axis of rotation of the Earth is indicated by the ticks at the poles, and the equator is shown by the dotted line. This model arbitrarily assumes a ring system of one size, but no sound basis other than the Roche outer limit exists for this particular choice.

development of low-latitude glaciers. At high average Earth temperatures, caused by higher atmospheric CO_2 and a narrow, scattered ring system, glaciers would be unstable, and the warmer conditions would allow deposition of low-latitude, laminated, chemical sediments.

CYCLIC-DOUBLET LAMINATION

Climate-laminated sediments occur both in cold and temperate climates. In cold climates, annual laminations are caused by ice formation on

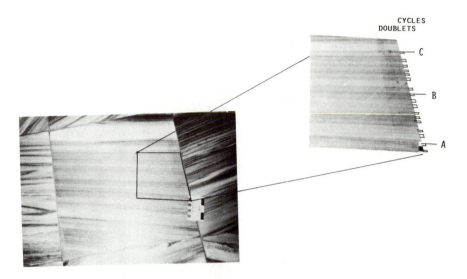

Figure 4.2. Floor tile T-11 in the Kunming Hotel, Kunming, China, showing cyclic-doublet lamination. Enlargement on the right shows details of microlamination. Left side of scale in centimeters, right in inches. Cycle boundaries, A, B, and C are same as in Figure 4.4.

bodies of water that affect the sedimentation rate and sediment grain size. In temperate climates, evaporitic and oxygen-depleted sediments can be laminated. In the modern Earth climate system, only one annual cold season occurs. Analysis of ring shadow effect predicts that a ring shadow climate would show two cold seasons between autumnal and vernal equinoxes at low and intermediate latitudes, and it seemed possible that this might show up in sediment lamination and could be distinguishable from lamination produced by the present climate system.

In 1982, the International Geological Correlations Programme, Project 156 (Phosphorites) Seminar was held at the Kunming Hotel in Kunming, China. An unusual banded marble is used as floor tiling in the lobby of the hotel (Figure 4.2). This banded marble was quarried from a single locality at Da Li, a village about a hundred kilometers west of Kunming from a Proterozoic, low-grade metamorphic sequence (Prof. Yeh Lien-Tsun, Institute of Geology, Academia Sinica, written communication, 1983). The marble is laminated by alternating laminae of organic-rich and organic-poor, medium crystalline, calcite marble, containing the organic matter as black specks between calcite crystals. Although metamorphism has recrystallized the original limestone and in some tiles contorted and squeezed it, the original lamination is generally, but not always, present. In some tiles, the marble is uncontorted, and the laminations are well enough preserved to be suitable for study. Eighty of the Kunming Hotel floor tiles were photographed, and five of these were selected for detailed study, including the tile shown in Figure 4.2.

The lamination of the Da Li marble shows two prominent features. The first is a cyclic banding of light and dark bands two to ten centimeters thick. This is the feature that has led to the beauty of the Da Li marble and its value as an ornamental stone. The second feature is a doublet microlamination of the bands (Figure 4.2). The microlaminae are up to several millimeters thick and consist of alternating light and dark microlaminae. The light-colored microlaminae tend to alternate systematically from thick to thin microlaminae. This gives the effect, if one concentrates on the dark microlaminae, of doublets of dark microlaminae. A set of four microlaminae, made up of a doublet of two dark microlaminae separated by one thin, light microlamina and overlying a thicker, light microlamina, constitutes a sedimentary unit that is repeated. The sets vary in both color and thickness, and, in general, the lighter the set is, the thicker it is. In some sets, the dark microlaminae are nearly the same shade as the light microlaminae and are difficult to distinguish. In other sets, the thin, light microlamina is absent, and the doublet of dark microlaminae becomes a singlet microlamina, so that two thick, light-colored microlaminae occur on each side of the dark singlet microlamina. When this happens, the dark-colored microlamina is commonly thicker than usual. The sets can be classified objectively into six classes on the basis of thickness and shade, as shown in Figure 4.3.

The class of 251 microlaminae sets from 5 tiles was determined according to the classification shown in Figure 4.3 and was plotted as histograms in Figure 4.4. The thickness of each set was normalized to unity and plotted in stratigraphic sequences from the tiles. A curve of the running average of 5 sets for each sequence is also plotted and shows a cyclicity that is the same as the banding of the marble. The boundaries of the cycles were taken arbitrarily as the highest of class V or VI sets (in two cases a class III set was chosen) in those parts of the curves composed of dominantly higher class sets.[3] Eighteen cycles were thereby defined, and it is found that the cycles contain an average of 11.05 sets. The 18 cycles contain 199 microlaminae sets, of which 50 percent contain definite doublet microlaminae and an additional 36 percent contain probable doublet microlaminae.

The cyclic-doublet lamination of the Da Li marble can best and perhaps only be interpreted as resulting from sedimentation climatically controlled by an annually migrating shadow of a ring system. It is interpreted that the Da Li was deposited at low latitudes as a laminated, organic-rich calcium carbonate sediment below wave base in a shallow body of water. No burrowing organisms existed in the Proterozoic to destroy the

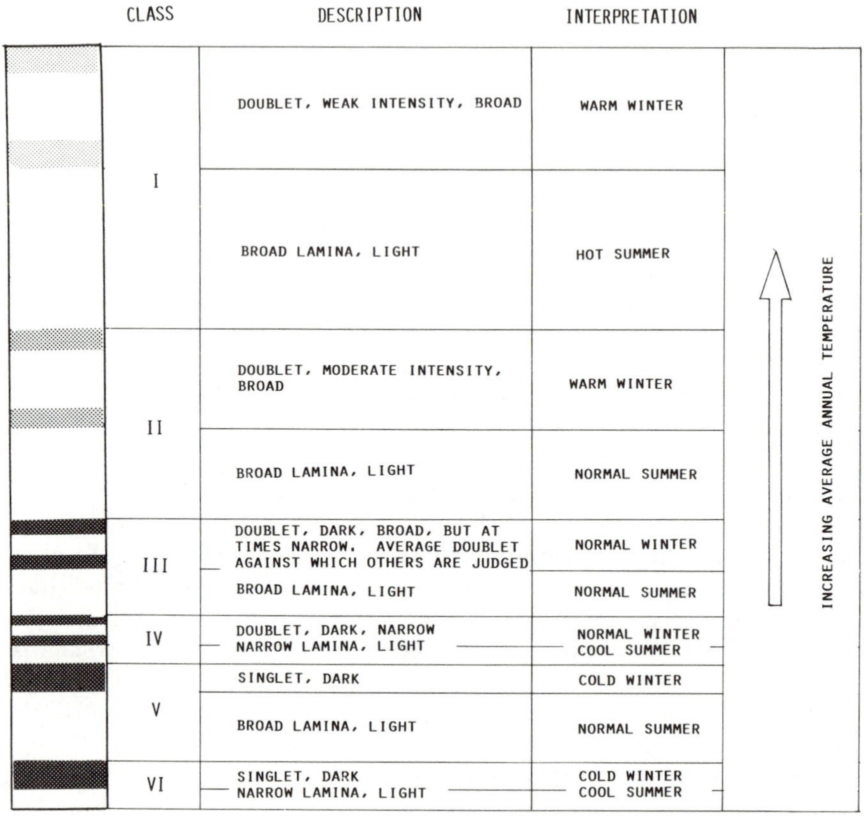

Richard P. Sheldon

CLASS	DESCRIPTION	INTERPRETATION	
I	DOUBLET, WEAK INTENSITY, BROAD	WARM WINTER	
	BROAD LAMINA, LIGHT	HOT SUMMER	
II	DOUBLET, MODERATE INTENSITY, BROAD	WARM WINTER	
	BROAD LAMINA, LIGHT	NORMAL SUMMER	
III	DOUBLET, DARK, BROAD, BUT AT TIMES NARROW. AVERAGE DOUBLET AGAINST WHICH OTHERS ARE JUDGED	NORMAL WINTER	
	BROAD LAMINA, LIGHT	NORMAL SUMMER	
IV	DOUBLET, DARK, NARROW / NARROW LAMINA, LIGHT	NORMAL WINTER / COOL SUMMER	
V	SINGLET, DARK	COLD WINTER	
	BROAD LAMINA, LIGHT	NORMAL SUMMER	
VI	SINGLET, DARK / NARROW LAMINA, LIGHT	COLD WINTER / COOL SUMMER	

INCREASING AVERAGE ANNUAL TEMPERATURE ↑

Figure 4.3. Classification and interpretation of doublet-lamination sets of Da Li banded marble.

lamination, so the body of water did not have to be continually euxinic for the preservation of laminations. The deposition of the organic matter was caused by planktonic algal blooms at times of vertical circulation of the water column and abundant sunlight. In modern lakes and oceans in temperate climates, this occurs after the winter cold has destroyed the thermal stratification of the water body and when spring days have lengthened to give more hours of sunshine and warmer temperatures. In mid-fall a second, minor bloom occurs due to nutrient increase from the breakdown of organic matter (Russell-Hunter, 1970, p. 42).

One might expect that winter doublet lamination of organic matter sedimentation should occur by this process (although none has been reported to my knowledge), but they should be recognizable by a minor nature of the lower laminae compared to the upper laminae of the doublets. Also, one would not expect carbonate sedimentation in the

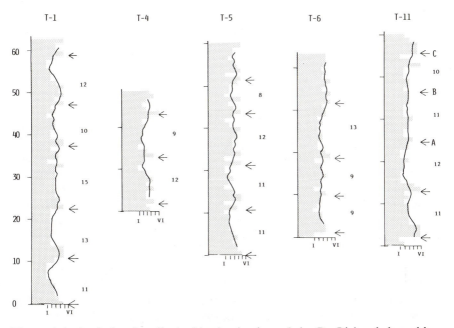

Figure 4.4. Analysis of cyclic-doublet lamination of the Da Li banded marble. Arrows show boundaries of cycles. Number of sets in cycle shown by number between arrow. Histogram shows set class, illustrated in Figure 4.3. Curve is a running average of five sets. Set thicknesses are normalized to unity.

winter laminae separating the doublets in cool temperate climates. The Da Li does not have doublet microlamination of this nature; instead, the dark microlaminae of each doublet tend to be about the same color and thickness and separated by a thin carbonate microlamina. The doublet microlamination is interpreted to be caused by a vertical circulation of the water column due to surface water cooling when the shadow of the ring was over the water area. Return of sunlight following the passage of the shadow would cause a planktonic algal bloom that would be brought to a close when thermal stratification was reestablished and the nutrient level of surface water decreased. The overturn would occur twice between the autumnal and vernal equinoxes. The continued deposition of alternating summer solstice singlet microlaminae and winter solstice doublet microlaminae would lead to a sequence of doublet-laminated chemical sediments. The Da Li with its strong cyclic-doublet microlamination is interpreted to have been deposited at low latitudes, because at higher latitudes where no ring shadow–free period would have occurred at the time of the winter solstice, the only ring shadow effect would have been the decreasing intensity of the shadow close to the time of the winter solstice. Thus one would expect the cyclic-doublet signal in the lamination to become weaker with higher latitudes, and at polar latitudes no shadow effect other than colder winters could be expected.

Multiyear cycles would be apparent by cyclic variations between the sets of microlaminae. During colder years, the winter doublet could be replaced by a single microlamina if the winter solstice warming was insufficient to produce a significant warm-climate microlamina. Or during warmer years, the winter microlaminae could be suppressed. Thus the six classes of microlaminae sets that were defined on thickness and darkness criteria can be interpreted on the basis of origin as differing sedimentation depending on the average summer and/or winter temperatures (Figure 4.3). The cycles composed of about eleven microlaminae sets can be interpreted as being caused by the eleven-year sunspot cycle of increasing and decreasing solar insolation.

OCCURRENCES OF CYCLIC-DOUBLET LAMINATION

Cyclic-doublet lamination, which on a genetic basis could be called ring shadow lamination, has been found in Proterozoic banded iron formation, Proterozoic laminated shale associated with glacial tillites, Cambrian shales associated with phosphorites and banded carbonate rocks, and Eocene oil shale.[4] These occurrences are discussed below.

The banded iron formation of the Hamersley Group of Western Australia of early Proterozoic age was shown to be laminated at several scales by Trendall (1973). Considering only the chemical sediments, three scales of lamination occur. The largest, called mesobanding, consists of alternating chert (SiO_2)-rich and iron-rich beds of about 10 centimeters thickness. The next smallest scale is striping of the chert mesobands by iron-rich and chert-rich beds on a scale of about 5 millimeters. Finally, the stripes are made up of iron-rich and chert-rich microlaminae on a scale of about one-half millimeter or smaller. Trendall and Blockley (1970) argue on sedimentologic grounds that the microlaminae were annual and that the average 23.3 microlaminae content of the stripes suggested its origin from the 20- to 24-year double sunspot or Hale cycle. Trendall (1973, Fig. 3) remarked on "doubling or bifurcations" of the hematite (Fe_2O_3) laminae. Examination of Figure 4.5 shows the lateral transition of hematitic laminae into doublets where the relative amount of chert in the rock increases. Trendall and Blockley (1970) are able to correlate sequences of these laminated rocks over large areas. In particular, their Figure 15 shows the evidence for the remarkable lateral continuity of microlaminations on the Dales Gorge member over an area of 5,000 square miles. The lamination of the Hamersley Group is

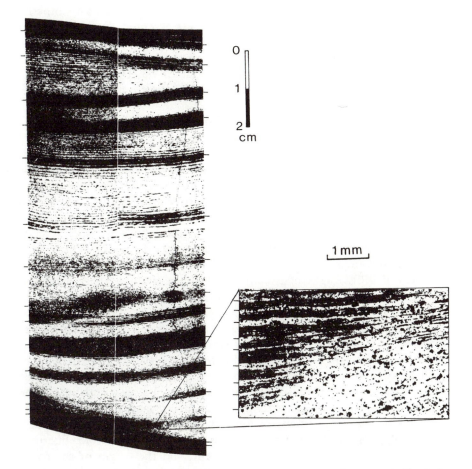

Figure 4.5. Cyclic-doublet lamination in the Weeli Wolli Formation of the Hamersley Group, Western Australia. Figure modified from Trendall (1973, Figures 4 and 5). Cycle boundaries indicated by ticks on left photograph; microlaminae sets indicated by ticks on detail enlargement on right.

complex mineralogically and is the result of postsedimentation mineralogic changes superimposed on the original sediments, and therefore the processes of sedimentation are difficult to interpret.

Holland (1973) suggested that the origin of the iron in banded iron formations may have been from upwelling of deeper iron-rich ocean water onto a shallow shelf. Such a process would be the same as that advanced for phosphorites by Kazakov in 1937 (reviewed by Sheldon, 1981). The upwelling process at low latitudes during periods of low equator-to-pole temperature gradients has been postulated by Sheldon

(1985) to be caused by ring shadows acting on the oceans. This hypothesis is far from being generally known, much less accepted, but despite the uncertainties in oceanographic interpretation, the cyclic-doublet lamination of the silica-rich beds seems clear in the Hamersley Group. The 23.3-year cyclicity is more than double that of the Da Li marble and also of the other examples discussed below. The reason for this difference is unknown.

The Mount Rogers Formation of late Proterozoic age in the Appalachian Mountains of southwestern Virginia is made up of a sequence of sandstone, shale, and volcanic rock. The upper member of the Mount Rogers Formation contains a unit of conglomerate and microlaminated sandy shale (Rankin, Espenshade, and Neuman, 1972; Schwab, 1981). The microlaminated sandy shale is composed of thin laminae of reddish-brown claystone alternating with somewhat thicker beds of light-colored, well-sorted sandstone. The microlaminae of some beds are only several millimeters in thickness but in other beds are as thick as a centimeter. Many beds contain much larger, erratic, poorly rounded pebbles and boulders of lithic fragments, many of which are granitic. These pebbles are dropstones, that is, ice-rafted debris dropped into deeper water laminated sediments. Analysis of the microlamination shows clearly that it is unlike the annually laminated clay of ice-dammed lakes of Pleistocene and Holocene times. Whereas these young lakes contain annually laminated sediments that show a random thickness distribution of winter clay layers and summer sand-silt layers, the microlaminated Mount Rogers rocks show clear doublets of red clay microlaminae separated by a thin quartz sand-silt lamina and overlying a thick quartz sand-silt microlaminae (Figure 4.6). The dropstones are contained in the silt-sand microlaminae.

The microlaminae sequence is similar to the Da Li marble, but the composition of the rock is totally different, and the origin of the rock is different. The Mount Rogers sediment was formed in an ice-dominated environment, giving the alternating silt-sand and hematitic clay microlaminae. The doublet microlamination is interpreted as due to the double passing of a ring shadow before and after each winter solstice. This caused surface ice formation during the shadow on the water body in which the microlaminated sediments were deposited. During the warm season, coarser clastic material was brought into the basin by the increased water flow, and icebergs rafted coarser material to the parts of the basin where the microlaminated sediments were being deposited. At times of roll-overs, the icebergs dumped clastic residuum on their tops into the water, where it fell through the water column into the sediment (Oven-shine, 1970). The warm season at the time of the winter solstice was shorter than the warm season at the time of the summer solstice, giving the doublet microlamination. Although there is a variation of thickness

DOUBLETS

Figure 4.6. Doublet microlamination in glacially laminated sediment of tillite
member of Mount Rogers
Formation, Virginia. Doublets indicated by ticks at right.

and geometry from one microlaminae set to the next, no cyclicity was
obvious. If present, it would have to be proved by careful study of many
stratigraphic sections, followed by statistical analysis.

On the north flank of Montagne Noire, to the south of the Massif
Central in southern France, a laminated greenish-gray schist (a slightly
metamorphosed shale) occurs (Prian, 1980). The schist is early Middle
Cambrian in age and overlies a dolomite unit of late Early Cambrian
age, which is phosphatic at its base. The sequence occurs in the Peux-
Couffouleux area of Aveyron Department, and the schist occurs in a
road-cut about 300 meters south of Couffouleux. The schist shows a
cyclic banding, which in turn is composed of microlaminations (Figure
4.7). Although this rock has not been studied in detail, doublet microlamination is apparent. The phosphorite and associated dolomite below
also are laminated and may be cyclic-doublet laminated. Other Cambrian
and upper Proterozoic phosphorites exhibit possible cyclic-doublet laminations and include the lowermost Cambrian–uppermost Proterozoic
phosphorite of Mongolia and China and the Middle Cambrian phosphorite
of Queensland, Australia. Although these occurrences of laminated rock
need more study, these preliminary data suggest that the study may
prove fruitful.

CYCLES

DOUBLETS

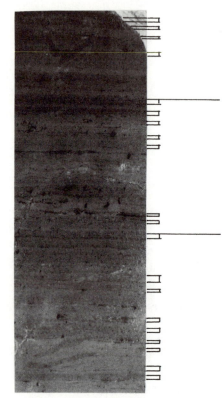

Figure 4.7. Cyclic-doublet lamination in Middle Cambrian rocks near Couffouleux, Aveyron, France. Cycle boundaries and doublet microlamination are indicated on right by ticks.

The oil shale of the Green River Formation of Eocene age occurring in the Piceance Creek Basin of Colorado contains definite cyclic-doublet lamination (Figure 4.8). This lamination has been interpreted as ring shadow lamination (Sheldon, 1985) and is collaborative evidence of O'Keefe's hypothesis of Eocene ring system shadow (O'Keefe, 1980). The doublet microlaminations of organic-rich microlaminae were interpreted to have formed by algal blooms stimulated by the sunlight when it had returned after the ring shadow passed. The blooms were fertilized by nutrients brought to the surface by lake water mixing during the period of shadow. Cycles of microlaminations are well developed and exhibit a likely eleven-year sunspot cycle, as originally recognized by Bradley (1929).

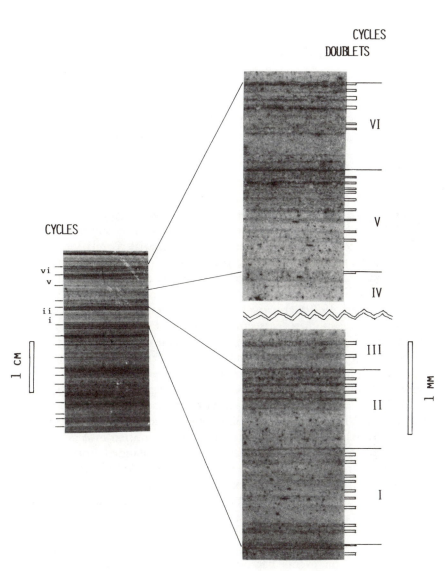

Figure 4.8. Cyclic-doublet lamination in the Green River oil shale, Colorado. Cycle boundaries are shown by tick marks on left of left photograph and on right of detail enlargement on right. Definite doublet microlamination is indicated on enlargement on right.

CORRELATION OF RING SHADOW–RELATED PHENOMENA

There appears to be a correlation between certain kinds of sedimentologic, biologic, and extraterrestrial phenomena. The sedimentologic phenomena include low-latitude deposition of banded carbonate rock, banded iron formation, phosphorites of the equatorial family (Sheldon, 1980), and rocks of glacial origin. The biologic phenomena include mass extinction, major evolution, and species migrations. The extraterrestrial phenomena include meteorite and tektite falls and unusually high contents of iridium in sedimentary rock beds.

Sedimentologic Phenomena

Phosphorite of the equatorial family, banded carbonate rock, and banded iron formation are themselves closely associated. Cook and McElhinny (1979) showed the temporal and spatial correlation between phosphorites and iron-rich rocks, particularly in the Proterozoic. Phosphorites are commonly intercalated with laminated carbonate rocks. Both phosphorites (Sheldon, 1964; Cook and McElhinny, 1979) and carbonate rocks (Habicht, 1979) are low-latitude sediments. Because of its association with phosphorite, it seems likely that Precambrian banded iron formation also was deposited at low latitudes, although, to my knowledge, no study of paleolatitudes of banded iron formation has been made. Proterozoic glacial deposits are spatially associated with both phosphorite (Cook and McElhinny, 1979) and iron formation (James and Trendall, 1982), but the glacial deposits are not synchronous with at least the phosphorites. Low-latitude glacial deposits occur in the Precambrian (Harland, 1981) and perhaps extend into the Cambrian in Algeria (Caby and Fabre, 1981) and Bolivia (Crowell, 1983). Banded iron formation is largely restricted to the Precambrian and not known in its typical form in younger rocks. The Paleozoic equatorial family of phosphorites are of lower Proterozoic to Cambrian and possibly to Early Ordovician and Upper Cretaceous to Eocene in age.

Biologic Phenomena

Mass extinction events have been studied for many years but have been redefined and reevaluated in the last few years as the result of the highly stimulating and controversial hypothesis of Alvarez and others (1980) that large meteorite impacts were the cause of terminal Cretaceous mass extinction. McClaren (1983) has summarized these studies and shown that correlations, causes, and effects of mass extinctions and extraterrestrial events are far from being satisfactorily resolved. Mass extinctions have been postulated for a number of times in the Phanerozoic and once in the Proterozoic. Knoll and Vidal (1983) have discovered a mass extinction of planktonic algae and protozoans at 650 million years before present, the same time as the last Proterozoic low-latitude glacial episode. Palmer (1982) reported his discovery of biostratigraphic units, which he proposed calling biomeres, with abrupt extinction boundaries at several times in the Cambrian. Major extinctions occurred in the Phanerozoic at least four other times (Raup and Sekoski, 1982), probably as many as seven (Boucot, 1983), and perhaps even more times. Some of these extinctions are associated with periods of polar glaciation, including the Late Ordovician–Early Silurian, the Late Devonian and Late Permian (McClaren, 1983, Figure 4), but others are not. Another type of biologic phenomenon that is not as drastic as mass extinction, but nevertheless shows a strong ecologic stress on the biota, is species migration. Haq (1981) reports six episodes of migrations of cold-water, high-latitude foraminifera and nannoplankton during the early Tertiary in the north Atlantic Ocean. The equatorward migrations of some cold-water species corresponds with extinctions of other species. Periods of increased biologic evolution commonly have followed mass extinctions. For example, Knoll and Vidal (1983) pointed out that evolution of the metazoans followed shortly after the planktonic algae and protozoa mass extinction of the late Proterozoic. Thus, mass extinction, increased biologic evolution, and extensive species migration episodes seem to be related in time and space.

Extraterrestrial Phenomena

Tektite falls and iridium anomalies have been correlated at the end of the Eocene epoch at 34 million years before present (O'Keefe, 1980; Ganapathy, 1982; Glass, 1983). Alvarez and others (1980) have hypothesized that a large meteorite impact occurred at the end of the Cretaceous, but no direct evidence for this in the form of an impact crater has been found. Although there is no question that extraterrestrial bodies greater than 10 km in diameter do impact the Earth with a predictable mean frequency of about once every 50 million years (Shoemaker, 1983), their relationship to tektites is questionable. O'Keefe (1976) has assembled the arguments for and against a large body impact on Earth for the origin of tektites. If large meteorite impacts are responsible for the associated iridium anomalies and tektite falls, then such impacts occurred at the end of the Cretaceous and at the end of the Eocene, an interval of about 31 million years. Keller and others (1983) have shown that multiple tektite-rich layers occur in late Eocene and early and middle Oligocene marine sediments and discount large meteorite impacts as a causal factor in their origin. The Popigai crater in the USSR was formed by a large body at 38 ± 9 my bp (McClaren, 1983), which would mean that large meteorites would have impacted

Earth at 65, 38, and 34 my bp, which is more frequent than would be expected from Shoemaker's calculations. However, if the last two can be shown to have occurred at the same time, the link between a meteorite impact and the terminal Eocene tektite fall would be indicated. On the other hand, if large meteorite impacts are not responsible for tektite and iridium anomalies, they are coincidental and unrelated to the sedimentologic and biologic phenomena discussed in this chapter.

Correlation Between Sedimentologic, Biologic, and Extraterrestrial Phenomena

The correlation between these sets of phenomena is shown in Figure 4.9, along with the known occurrences of cyclic-doublet or doublet only laminations. It should be noted that the time scale used in Figure 4.9 is logarithmic in order to display the data. Because the resolution of dating rocks becomes progressively worse the older the rock is, the correlations become progressively worse also, which is shown in Figure 4.9 only by taking into account the logarithmic scale. In all cases, the uncertainties of dating preclude establishing accurate and precise time correlations. The best evidence for correlation of these phenomena, therefore, lies in observation in single stratigraphic sections, where relative ages are easy to establish, even though accurate ages are not. With these uncertainties in mind, one can say that the data of Figure 4.9 indicate general correlation of the biologic, sedimentologic, and extraterrestrial phenomena.

In the Late Cretaceous to early Tertiary time, extinctions, migrations, equatorial phosphorites, cyclic-doublet laminations, tektites, and iridium anomalies appear to be associated. This suggests the hypothesis that Earth ring systems were the underlying cause of the unusual low-latitude sedimentation involving cooling of both the land and ocean surfaces as well as the underlying cause of unusual stresses on the biota of both land and oceans, also involving surface cooling. If the extraterrestrial phenomena of tektites and iridium anomalies were related to ring system formation, as suggested by O'Keefe (1980), the Late Cretaceous to Eocene rings would have been formed of tektite glass.

In the late Proterozoic to Cambrian time, a correlation exists among banded iron formation, equatorial phosphorite, doublet-laminated carbonate rock, mass extinctions, glacial deposits, cyclic-doublet lamination, and perhaps iridium anomalies (Woo, 1985). Given the present dating uncertainties, the details of this correlation cannot be determined, but the correlation itself seems real because of the rock relations within individual stratigraphic sections and the long period of time preceding and following this period in which none of the phenomena other than extinctions has been observed.

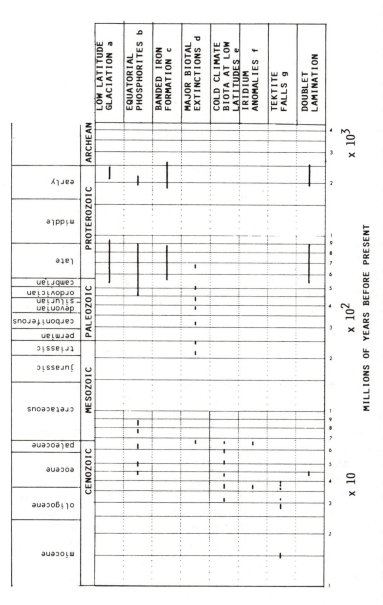

Figure 4.9. Temporal correlation of phenomena possibly related to ring system shadows. Time scale is logarithmic. Notes: (a) Hambrey and Harland (1981); (b) Sheldon (1980 and unpublished data); (c) James and Trendall (1981); (d) Raup and Sepkoski (1982), Boucot (1983), Knoll and Vidal (1983); (e) Haq (1981), data only for the Early Cenozoic; (f) Alvarez and others (1980, 1982), Ganapathy (1982); (g) O'Keefe (1976); Keller and others (1983).

In the early Proterozoic, glacial deposits, banded iron formation, equatorial phosphorites, and cyclic-doublet lamination have been observed. The time interval is several hundred million years, so the correlation is not impressive, except in individual stratigraphic sections, such as the Hamersley Group and related rocks in Western Australia (Trendall, 1973), where all occur.

The early Paleozoic and Precambrian data suggest a hypothesis similar to that used to explain the Late Cretaceous to middle Eocene data. A ring system formed that caused low-latitude cooling, resulting in the deposition of phosphorites, banded iron formation, doublet-laminated carbonate rocks, and, at times when the cooling was great, glacial deposits. The plant and animal life was primitive, but mass extinctions and significant evolution may also have been caused by the low-latitude cooling. The only extraterrestrial evidence for the rocks of this period is the possible iridium anomaly in the Cambrian rocks of China. The composition of the rings is not indicated by any known data at present. If they were formed from primordial material first collected into moons outside the Roche limit, the material could have been made up of lithophile elements or perhaps atmophile elements. If the rings originated from lunar volcanism, they may have been composed of high-silica volcanic glass.

SUMMARY

In summary, three general periods of ring systems orbiting the Earth appear to have occurred, one in early Proterozoic, one in late Proterozoic to Cambrian, and one in Late Cretaceous to Oligocene. These conclusions are based on data that cannot be explained by the present Earth processes. These include (1) the low-latitude glaciation of Proterozoic time, (2) equatorial oceanic upwelling to give major deposits of iron, phosphorus, and silica-rich sedimentary rocks, (3) sedimentary rocks at low paleolatitudes showing strong seasonality, (4) periods of numerous low-latitude extinctions and migrations of biota both on land and in the oceans in Phanerozoic time. These anomalous events seem to require anomalous low-latitude cooling events that occurred during specific episodes during geologic time. Episodic, ring system–induced climate could explain these episodic anomalous events. Evidence from cyclic-doublet laminations of sediments associated with the anomalous data shows the dynamics of a ring system shadow that screened sunlight from low latitudes in a systematic way. The extraterrestrial nature of these events of the Late Cretaceous to Paleogene is also shown by the presence of tektites and iridium anomalies in the same rocks.

It must be stressed that these conclusions are as tenuous as the data are scarce and uncertain. Nevertheless, an episodic pattern of events seems to emerge. Due to uncertainties of age dating, the time scale on which these episodes can be examined at present is on the order of tens to hundreds of millions of years. However, at individual localities, depositionally continuous sequences of sedimentary rocks show a finer scale episodicity of most of the phenomena on a time scale of hundreds of thousands to a few million years. Further research into this problem would require additional data collection of chemical and glacial sediments, fossils, tektites, and trace-metal distribution and additional synthesis of the ancient distribution of continents and sea-floor sediments. Above all, more precise age dating of events would be needed. Given such research, one can hope to test and refine or discard this model.[5]

NOTES

1. After I completed this chapter, a report was published of the Conference on the Origin of the Moon, convened by William Hartman and Roger Phillips and held in October 1984 at Kona, Hawaii (Kerr, R. A., 1984, Making the Moon from a big splash: *Science* 226, pp. 1060–1061). The hypothesis that the Moon was formed early in Earth's history by an impact of a very large body received attention. The hypothetical impact volatilized the upper levels of both bodies into a material that in part went into orbit around Earth because of prolonged acceleration by expanding gases. Orbital material outside the Roche limit formed the Moon. Although not mentioned in the report, orbital material inside the Roche limit presumably would have formed a ring system.

2. The terminology of lamination used in this chapter is as follows: The finest scale lamination is called microlamination. If it includes prominent doublets, it is called doublet microlamination. Cyclic sequences of microlamination are called cyclic banding. The combination is called cyclic-doublet lamination. If no cyclic banding occurs, the term doublet lamination is used.

3. It was not possible to identify true tops and bottoms of the tiles from sedimentologic criteria, so the "lowest" set was not necessarily the lowest stratigraphically.

4. After completing this chapter, I had the opportunity in 1983 to study the Upper Cretaceous, marine, cyclic sequence of phosphorite, chert, black shale, carbonate rock, and sandstone of the Cordillera Oriental, Colombia. The chert beds exhibit well-developed, microlaminated, cyclic bedding, which appears to be cyclic-doublet lamination. A later study in 1984 of the Upper Cretaceous evaporite deposits of the Khorat Plateau, Thailand, showed similar lamination. Also in 1984, study of the Lower Proterozoic Bijawar Series near Hirapur, Madhya Pradesh, India, showed similar laminations in intercalated beds of chert, dolomite, iron-rich sedimentary rocks and phosphorite.

5. Many scientists have helped in the formulation of this working hypothesis on ancient ring systems through discussions—with reactions ranging from

thoughtful encouragement to healthy skepticism to constructive disbelief. They include William Burnett, Peter Cook, John Denoyer, Eric Force, Gerald North, John O'Keefe, Stanley Riggs, Kirk Smith, Kenneth Towe, Newell Trask, and Malcolm Walter.

REFERENCES

Alvarez, Luis W., Walter Alvarez, Frank Asaro, and Helen V. Michel, 1980, Extraterritorial cause for the Cretaceous-Tertiary extinction: *Science* 208, pp. 1095–1109.

Alvarez, Walter, Frank Asaro, H. V. Michel, and L. S. Alvarez, 1982, Iridium anomaly approximately synchronous with terminal Eocene extinctions: *Science* 216, pp. 886–888.

Boucot, A. J., 1983, Does evolution take place in an ecologic vacuum? II: *Journal of Paleontology* 57, no. 1, pp. 1–30.

Bradley, W. H., 1929, The varves and climate of the Green River epoch: U.S. Geol. Surv. Prof. Paper 158, pp. 87–110.

Caby, R., and J. Fabre, 1981, Late Proterozoic to Early Paleozoic diamictites, tillites and associated glacigenic sediments in the Serie Pourpree of western Hoggar, Algeria: in Hambrey and Harland, 1981, pp. 140–145.

Cook, P. J., and M. W. McElhinny, 1979, A re-evaluation of the spatial and temporal distribution of phosphorites in the light of plate tectonics: *Economic Geology* 74, pp. 315–330.

Crowell, John E., 1983, Ice ages recorded on Gondwanan continents: *Transactions of the Geological Society of South Africa* 86, no. 3, pp. 237–262.

Ganapathy, R., 1982, Evidence for a major meteorite impact on the Earth 34 million years ago: implication for Eocene extinctions: *Science* 216, pp. 885–886.

Glass, B. P., 1983, Upper Eocene North American microtektite layer: associated radiolarian extinctions, climatic change, and iridium anomaly, abs.: *American Association of Petroleum Geologists Bull.* 67, no. 3, p. 470.

Habicht, J.K.A., 1979, Paleoclimate, paleomagnetism, and continental drift: American Association of Petroleum Geologists, *Studies in Geology*, no. 9, 31 pp.

Hambrey, M. J., and W. B. Harland, 1981, *Earth's pre-Pleistocene glacial record:* Cambridge University Press, London, 1004 pp.

Haq, B. U., 1981, Paleogene paleoceanography: early Cenozoic oceans revisited: Oceanol. Acta, *Proceedings 26th International Geological Congress, Geology of Ocean Symposium,* Paris, July 7–17, 1980, pp. 71–82.

Harland, W. B., 1981, Chronology of Earth's glacial and tectonic record: *Journal, Geological Society of London* 13, pp. 197–203.

Holland, Heinrich D., 1973, The oceans: a possible source of iron in iron-formations: *Economic Geology* 68, no. 7, pp. 1169–1172.

Ives, Ronald L., 1940, An astronomical hypothesis to explain Permian glaciation: *Journal of the Franklin Institute* 230, no. 1, pp. 45–74.

James, H. L., and A. F. Trendall, 1982, Banded iron-formation: distribution in time and paleoenvironmental significance: in H. D. Holland and M. Schidlowski, eds., *Mineral deposits and the evolution of the biosphere:* Springer-Verlag, Berlin, 332 pp.

Kazakov, A. V., 1937, The phosphorite facies and the genesis of phosphorites: in Geological investigations of agricultural ores, Leningrad, *Sci. Inst. Fert. and Insecto-fungicides Trans.* 142, pp. 95–113.

Keller, Gerta, Steven D'Hondt, and T. L. Vallier, 1983, Multiple microtektite horizons in Upper Eocene marine sediments: no evidence for mass extinctions: *Science* 221, pp. 150–152.

Knoll, A. H., and G. Vidal, 1983, Press release of National Science Foundation, April 1983.

Lunar Planetary Institute, 1983, 14th Lunar Science Conference, Abstracts of papers: Houston, Texas, vols. 1 and 2, pp. 55, 164, 179, 361, 472, 828.

McClaren, Digby J., 1983, Bolides and biostratigraphy: *Geological Society of America* 94, pp. 313–324.

O'Keefe, John A., 1976, *Tektites and their origin:* Elsevier, New York, p. 254.

——— , 1980, The terminal Eocene event: formation of a ring system around the Earth?: *Nature* 285, pp. 309–311.

——— , in press, The terminal Cretaceous event: circumterrestrial rings of tektite glass particles?: *Cretaceous Research.*

Ovenshine, A. T., 1970, Observations on iceberg rafting in Glacier Bay, Alaska, and the identification of ancient ice-rafted deposits: *Geological Society of America Bull.* 81, pp. 891–894.

Palmer, A. R., 1982, Biomere boundaries: a possible test for extraterrestrial perturbation of the biosphere: Geological Society of America, Spec. Paper 190, pp. 469–474.

Prian, J. P., 1980, Caractérisation des paléoenvironnements des phosphorites cambriennes du versant septentrional de la Montagne Noire (Sud du Massif central français): in Géologie comparée des gisements de phosphates et de pétrole, Bureau de Recherches Géologiques et Minières, document de BRGM no. 24.

Rankin, D. W., G. H. Espenshade, and R. B. Neuman, 1972, Geologic map of the west half of the Winston-Salem quadrangle, North Carolina, Virginia, and Tennessee: U.S. Geological Survey, Misc., Geol. Invest. Map I–709–A.

Raup, D. M., and J. J. Sepkoski, Jr., 1982, Mass extinctions in the marine fossil record: *Science* 215, pp. 1501–1503.

Russell-Hunter, W. D., 1970, *Aquatic productivity:* Macmillan Company, London, p. 42.

Schwab, R. L., 1981, Late Precambrian tillites of the Appalachians: in Hambrey and Harland, 1981, pp. 751–755.

Sheldon, Richard P., 1964, Paleolatitudinal and paleogeographic distribution of phosphorite: U.S. Geol. Surv. Prof. Paper 501-C, pp. 106–113.

——— , 1980, Episodicity of phosphate deposition and deep ocean circulation— a hypothesis: Society of Economic Paleontologists and Mineralogists Spec. Publ. no. 29, pp. 239–247.

———, 1981, Ancient marine phosphorites: *Annual Review of Earth and Planetary Science*, pp. 251–284.

———, 1984, Ice-ring origin of the Earth's atmosphere and hydrosphere and late Proterozoic-Cambrian phosphogenesis, in Phosphorite: Geological Survey of India Spec. Publ. no. 17, pp. 17–22.

———, 1985, The Precambrian Earth ice-ring model to account for changes in exogenic regimes from Proterozoic to Phanerozoic eras: *Proceedings of Symposium of Fifth International Field Workshop and Seminar*, Geological Publishing House: Beijing, China, pp. 227–243.

———, 1985, Equatorial upwelling origin of the Eocene–Late Cretaceous equatorial-belt family of phosphorites—were they caused by the shadow of a tektite ring system orbiting the Earth?: Sciences geologiques, Mem 77, Université Louis Pasteur de Strasbourg, pp. 99–104.

Shoemaker, E. M., 1983, Asteroid and comet bombardment of the Earth: *Annual Review of Earth and Planetary Science* 11, pp. 461–494.

Trendall, A. F., 1973, Varve cycles in the Weeli Wolli Formation of the Precambrian Hamersley Group, Western Australia: *Economic Geology* 68, no. 7, pp. 1089–1097.

Trendall, A. F., and J. G. Blockley, 1970, The iron formations of the Precambrian Hamersley Group, Western Australia: *Geological Survey of Western Australia Bull.* 119, 347 pp.

Woo, C. C., 1985, Are iridium anomalies in a Lower Cambrian polymetallic deposit extraterrigenic?: *Proceedings of Symposium of Fifth International Field Workshop and Seminar:* Geological Publishing House, Beijing, China, pp. 253–254.

PART TWO

DIMENSIONS OF THE HUMAN PREDICAMENT: POPULATION, RESOURCES, AND ENVIRONMENT

INTRODUCTION

JOHN P. HOLDREN

Harrison Brown's most remarkable book, *The Challenge of Man's Future* (Viking, 1954; reprinted by Westview, 1984), was published more than three decades ago. By the time I read it as a high school student a few years later, the book had been widely acclaimed as a monumental survey of the human prospect, illuminated through analysis of the interaction of population, technology, and the resources of the physical world. I knew even before high school that science and technology held special interest for me, and I suppose I also had some prior interest in the larger human condition. But *The Challenge of Man's Future* pulled these interests together for me in a way that transformed my thinking about the world and about the sort of career I wanted to pursue. I have always suspected that I am not the only member of my generation whose aspirations and subsequent career were changed by this book of Harrison Brown's.

What was so special about the book? Perhaps most impressive at the time was the combination of audacity and erudition with which Brown wove together insights from anthropology, history, economics, geochemistry, biology, and the study of technology to provide a coherent, multidimensional picture of his subject—how humans have provided themselves with the physical ingredients of existence in the past, their prospects for doing so in the future, and the connections between these matters and the sociopolitical dimensions of the human condition. As a demonstration of the power of (and necessity for) an interdisciplinary approach to global problems, the book was a tour de force.

The Challenge of Man's Future was notable, too, for the balance of its treatment of both the potential and the limitations of technology. As a highly accomplished scientist and technologist himself, Brown could write with authority and conviction about the benefits for human well-being that wise application of these tools might deliver. But unlike so many enthusiasts (then and now), Harrison Brown also was aware of—indeed, preoccupied with—the many dimensions of the human predicament that are highly resistant to technological "fixes" (hence the need for solutions rooted in human attitudes and behavior) and the potential for misuse of science and technology when power grows faster than wisdom.

The central theses that Brown developed in *The Challenge of Man's Future* can be summarized with deceptive simplicity:

- The division of human society into a set of industrialized nations containing a relatively prosperous minority of the world's population and a set of primarily agrarian nations containing an impoverished majority is not only unsatisfactory in humanitarian terms, it is fundamentally unstable.
- In the long run, either the agrarian regions will achieve a substantial degree of industrialization, producing a wholly industrialized world with a degree of material prosperity for all, or the collapse of "machine civilization" will produce a wholly agrarian world where poverty is the norm.
- Which of these outcomes prevails will depend on several interrelated factors: the rate of growth of the human population; the level of food production that can be attained and sustained without "consuming" the environmental resources on which agricultural productivity ultimately depends; whether the implementation of affordable technologies to exploit low-grade resources can outpace the depletion of high-grade ones; and success or failure in the avoidance of major wars.
- Even if these factors develop in a way conducive to the continuation of industrial civilization, a pleasant existence for our descendants is by no means assured. Their lives may be impoverished by the absence of environmental diversity for which global industrialization left no room, their freedoms constrained by a rigid centralization of authority that efficient management of scarce resources seemed to require.
- It is possible to envision a pathway through these perils to a sustainable world in which a stable human population, in harmony with its environment, enjoys peace and substantial measures of prosperity, human dignity, and individual freedom; but this outcome is of low a priori probability, and achieving it will require a cooperative human effort unprecedented in its comprehensiveness, intensity, duration, and demands on wise leadership.

Thirty years after Harrison Brown elaborated these positions, it remains difficult to improve on them as a coherent depiction of the perils and challenges we face.

Brown's accomplishment in writing *The Challenge of Man's Future,* of course, was not simply the construction of this sweeping schema for understanding the human predicament; more remarkable was (and is) the combination of logic, thoroughness, clarity, and force with which he marshalled data and argumentation on every element of the problem and on their interconnections. It is a book, in short, that should have reshaped permanently the perceptions of all serious analysts about the interactions of the demographic, biological, geophysical, technological, economic, and sociopolitical dimensions of contemporary problems. That it failed to do so—that the world is still full of analysts who are generally regarded as serious despite their insistence that problems of population, resources, the rich-poor gap, and the prospects for war or peace are all separate issues—must be an even greater disappointment to Harrison Brown than to those of us who have been restating his points (usually less eloquently) in the three decades since he first made them.

The Challenge of Man's Future was not Harrison Brown's first book on the human predicament, nor, of course, was it his last. By December 1945, when many of his colleagues in the Manhattan Project had barely begun to try to sort out the ultimate significance of the new weapons that had resulted from their work, Harrison Brown had already completed a compelling and lucid little book on that topic, *Must Destruction Be Our Destiny?* (Simon and Schuster, 1946). In its 160 pages are developed a surprising number of the major themes that have shaped the subsequent four-decade debate about the control of nuclear weapons, as well as a set of specific predictions that have proven astonishingly accurate.

Brown predicted (in December 1945, remember) that the U.S. monopoly on nuclear weapons was unlikely to last much more than three years (the first Soviet atomic bomb was exploded in August 1949); that bombs a thousand times more powerful than those that destroyed Hiroshima and Nagasaki would be constructed (this had happened by 1954); and that the means of delivery of these weapons would include large fleets of accurate ballistic missiles of intercontinental range (a prediction that, like the others, was disputed by many other scientists at the time). He explained the impracticality of perfect defense against weapons at once so small and so destructive; elucidated the technologic and economic advantages accruing to the offense in an offense-defense arms race involving nuclear weapons; discussed the difficulties of deterrence as a long-term strategy; argued that major conventional conflicts between nuclear powers would almost certainly become nuclear and, once nuclear, would probably escalate to the total destruction of industrial civilization; pointed out the deep dilemma posed by the incompatibility of widespread access to peaceful uses of nuclear technology and tight controls on the production of nuclear bombs; and warned of the threat to both national security and civil liberties that would be posed by the possibility of nuclear attack "from within, using bombs concealed in our cities." (Nearly forty years later, the last problem still has not really penetrated the public consciousness. The first explosion of a clandestine nuclear bomb will change that in a most painful way.)

Perhaps by getting off his chest so early so much of what could sensibly be said about the problem of nuclear weapons per se, Harrison Brown was intentionally freeing himself to devote a major part of his subsequent efforts to the broader dimensions of the human predicament—population, resources, the application of science and technology for good or ill, competition and cooperation in East-West and North-South relations—which he saw as related to the long-term prospects for avoiding the major conflict that would cause those weapons to be used. (This is not to say that he has since neglected nuclear weapons issues: As an early and vigorous exponent of the social responsibilities of the scientists who had created nuclear weapons, Brown for many years played important roles in the Federation of American Scientists, the *Bulletin of the Atomic Scientists,* and the Pugwash Conferences on Science and World Affairs [for a discussion of Pugwash, see Chapter 10]. In the 1980s, he has been increasing his involvement in war and peace issues once again, and in late 1984 he accepted one of the most respected "chairs" in the field—that of editor-in-chief of the *Bulletin of the Atomic Scientists.*)

On the issues of population, resources, technology, and international cooperation, Harrison's book *The Challenge of Man's Future* was followed by *The Next Hundred Years* (with James Bonner and John Weir, Viking, 1957); *The Next Ninety Years* (with James Bonner, John Weir, George Harrar, Norman Brooks, Thayer Scudder, and Athelstan Spilhaus, California Institute of Technology, 1967); *Population: Perspective 1971* (edited with Alan Sweezy, Freeman-Cooper, 1971); *Population: Perspective 1972* (edited with Alan Sweezy, Freeman-Cooper, 1972); *Are Our Descendants Doomed? Population Growth and Technological Change* (edited with Edward Hutchings, Viking, 1972); *Population: Perspective 1973* (edited with John Holdren, Alan Sweezy, and Barbara West, Freeman-Cooper, 1973); *Learning to Live in a Technological Society* (The First Ishizaka Lectures, Simul Press, Tokyo, 1978); *The Human Future Revisited* (Norton, 1978); *China Among the Nations of the Pacific* (edited, Westview, 1982); and *Critical Energy Issues in Asia and the Pacific: The Next Twenty Years* (with Fereidun Fesharaki, Corazon Siddayao, Toufiq Siddiqi, Kirk R. Smith, and Kim Woodard, Westview, 1982). These books of Harrison's, plus the much larger number of his articles and individual chapters on the same topics, represent a body of work that none of us engaged in the preparation of this section of his festschrift could realistically undertake to summarize.

The five chapters in this section provide, therefore, not a summary but a sampler of some issues that have concerned Harrison Brown under the broad heading of "Dimensions of the Human Predicament." The authors had complete independence and flexibility in deciding how to approach their topics—there was no attempt at coordination save in the initial assignment of general subject areas.

In the first of these chapters, "Harrison Brown's Role in the Manhattan Project," Glenn T. Seaborg draws on the daily journal he has maintained throughout his long career to provide a picture of the early development of nuclear chemistry and the role Harrison played in it, starting in 1938 with Brown's undergraduate days as a chemistry major at Berkeley. The bulk of the chapter deals with Brown's work in the chemical-separation group of the Plutonium Project at the University of Chicago, which he joined at Seaborg's invitation in mid-1942. Seaborg's journal, which intermingles an account of the solution of a set of difficult problems in chemistry with excerpts from news accounts of the war on the European and Pacific fronts, conveys a vivid impression of the scientific excitement and sense of urgency that pervaded this effort—a phase of the Manhattan Project less heralded but no less important than the design and fabrication of the first weapons at Los Alamos.

Alvin M. Weinberg's chapter, "Burning the Rocks Forty Years Later," begins where Seaborg's leaves off, with Harrison Brown's move from Chicago to the Oak Ridge Laboratory in the fall of 1943. Interest had already been expressed by some of the Manhattan Project scientists in the peaceful applications of nuclear energy, and Weinberg suggests that it was in this environment that the seed of Brown's postwar work on the extraction of uranium from common rock was planted. As one of the most energetic and articulate advocates of nuclear power from the early postwar period onward, Weinberg does not dwell here on the deep feelings and concerns that must have driven many of the Manhattan Project participants to seek constructive applications for their discoveries to offset the obvious destructive ones. It is clear from other evidence, however, that Harrison Brown at first considered the early fascination with nuclear energy's peaceful potential an unfortunate diversion from the needed facing up to the implications of the bomb. In late 1945, Brown wrote (in *Must Destruction Be Our Destiny?*):

We should not permit our sense of values to be warped by irresponsible speculation as to the future of atomic power as a practical source of energy. Important applications will most certainly appear, but they will appear slowly. Coal and oil will not be replaced during the next ten years. Ten years from now our cars and airplanes will probably continue to be powered by ordinary chemical energy as they are today. But ten years from now will we still be alive? Will our cities still exist? The practical application of atomic energy as a destructive force is a reality. That fact should be our main concern and interest at the present time.

It was not until the early 1950s, by which time he had moved to Caltech, that Harrison Brown allowed himself the "luxury" of doing some work on the long-term fuel supply for peaceful uses of nuclear energy. As Alvin Weinberg's chapter relates, the work Brown did then with Leon Silver was instrumental in establishing that the uranium resources in common rock really could run an energy-hungry, fission-powered civilization for millennia. Most of the rest of Weinberg's chapter deals with the diverse issues and controversies that bear on whether doing so is likely to prove desirable.

The next chapter, "Energy and the Human Predicament," is mine. Harrison Brown's ability to see both sides of these "technology and society" issues—the grounds for optimism and the grounds for pessimism—makes it especially appropriate that his festschrift contain some contributions emphasizing the most difficult aspects of contemporary problems. In its focus on the interactions of energy supply with the problems of the poor, environmental disruption, the probability of war, and human population growth, my chapter inevitably has a somewhat pessimistic flavor. I should emphasize, therefore, that my contribution is written in what I take to be the spirit in which Harrison wrote *The Challenge of Man's Future*—that is, the conviction that it is necessary to dwell on the perils in order to stimulate timely action to avoid or minimize them. Those who think a rosy future is assured and those who find disaster inevitable can meet at the bar; the rest of us will keep working to improve the odds in what we assume to be an uncertain world.

Roger Revelle is a scientist who has been doing just that—working to improve the odds—for more than fifty years. Trained and highly accomplished as an oceanographer, he is also internationally known for his work on the subject matter of his chapter in this section: the assessment and management of water resources, soils, nutrients, plants, and animals to cope with the demands of a growing human population for food, fiber, and energy. In its sweep, its use of quantitative data and illustrative "back of the envelope" calculations, and its dual stress on the potential and on the problems of sustainable resource supply, Revelle's chapter is appropriately reminiscent of Harrison Brown's treatment of similar subject matter in *The Challenge of Man's Future* thirty years earlier.

In the concluding chapter of this section, "Speculating on the Global Resource Future," the distinguished geographer Gilbert White undertakes an informative retrospective on the successes and failures of midcentury prognostications about the human future. Having recently served as coeditor of a major United Nations Environment Programme (UNEP) report on the world environment in the decade 1972–1982, White is in a better position than most to tackle such a task. I will not spoil the suspense by summarizing here how *The Challenge of Man's Future* fares in White's evaluation, but I will mention one extraordinarily successful prognostication that he overlooks. On page 162 of *The Challenge of Man's Future,* Harrison Brown estimated that in 1975 the United States would be "consuming energy at a rate equivalent to burning 2.3 billion tons of coal per year—nearly the present rate of consumption for the whole world." The actual U.S. figure for 1975 turned out to be 2.4 billion tons of coal equivalent.

To put too much emphasis on the correctness or incorrectness of particular predictions, however, is to miss the main point of writing usefully about the future. The idea is not to be "right," but to illuminate the possibilities in a way that both stimulates sensible debate about the sort of future we want and facilitates sound decisions about getting from here to there. This philosophy has informed Harrison Brown's writing about the human future throughout the four decades in which he has been doing it. Our understanding of the dimensions of the human predicament—and of what might be done to alleviate it—is much the better for his effort.

5

HARRISON BROWN'S ROLE IN THE MANHATTAN PROJECT

GLENN T. SEABORG

My contribution to this festschrift for Harrison Brown involves a little known aspect of his career, his first job after leaving Johns Hopkins University, where he obtained his Ph.D. degree. Brown went directly to the Metallurgical Laboratory of the University of Chicago to throw his energy, expertise, and exuberance into solving the chemical extraction problems connected with the wartime Plutonium Project, whose aim was to produce a nuclear weapon before Adolf Hitler and his Nazi war machine could do so. At the time there was an uneasy perception among members of the project that we were behind in this race. Harrison joined my chemistry group, which had the responsibility for conceiving and developing the chemical processes required for isolation of plutonium to be produced in large nuclear piles (as they were called then). He began almost immediately to function as one of the leaders of my group of chemists. And, I believe, his work on the processes for producing the nuclear weapon, even though for wartime use against a dangerous enemy, colored his outlook and furnished the background of experience that led later to a lifetime dedicated to the achievement of arms control and arms limitation measures.

In order to try to capture the essence of Harrison's venture into this early phase of his life, I shall quote from sections of my journal that relate to his activities during his "Met Lab" days in 1942 and 1943 and the immediately preceding years when I knew him as a student.

My first encounter with Harrison was at the Wednesday evening seminars in nuclear chemistry at Berkeley during the spring of 1938, when I was serving as a research assistant to Professor Gilbert Newton

81

Lewis and Harrison was doing undergraduate research with Professor George Ernest Gibson. These seminars were attended by several chemistry faculty members, postdoctoral fellows, graduate students, and some especially talented undergraduate students, like Harrison Brown. I recall specifically a report Harrison made one evening on a rule he and Professor Gibson had formulated, largely as a result of Harrison's innovative spirit, for predicting the range of mass numbers of the stable isotopes of elements:

Wednesday, April 6, 1938
    In the evening I went to the Nuclear Seminar in Gilman Hall and heard Harrison Brown, a bright undergraduate student who works with Professor G. E. Gibson, report on his observations on the range of occurrence of stable isotopes and the relation between atomic masses among stable isotopes.

By analogy with an old rule of organic chemistry, known as the Crum-Brown-Gibson rule, this became known among our seminar members as the crummy Brown-Gibson rule.

    After graduating from Berkeley in the spring of 1938, Harrison went to Johns Hopkins University for graduate work in nuclear chemistry under the direction of a former Berkeley faculty member, Robert Dudley Fowler. I saw him there in early July 1940, when a young colleague of mine, Joe Kennedy, and I visited Johns Hopkins as part of a nationwide tour of nuclear laboratories. In a conversation at this time I expressed my doubts, based on my work with Jack Livingood on the radioactive isotopes of cobalt, that Co^{57} exists as a stable isotope. My journal records my subsequent correspondence with Harrison on this:

Monday, November 25, 1940
    A letter, dated November 22, arrived from Harrison Brown at Johns Hopkins University. Since he is considering making a study of cobalt, he asked that I refresh his mind about the existence of Co^{57}, recalling that I had said last July that there was some doubt about the validity of Bleakney's work. Brown mentioned that he is presently measuring some thermal diffusion coefficients. . . .
    "Raf Hammers the Axis from Berlin to Turin" reads today's headline.

Wednesday, April 16, 1941
    A long letter, dated April 5, had also arrived from Harrison Brown, who described the mass spectrometer work that he, Mitchell, and Fowler have done on the isotopic constitution of cobalt. He said, "It can definitely be said that if Co^{57} exists it must exist to less than 1 part in 6000 of Co^{59}." He went on to say that Bleakney's result must have been due either to a reflection of some sort or to an impurity. Brown mentioned that he

has just measured the coefficient of thermal diffusion of argon and that he plans to visit California in August. . . .

Today's paper reports that the Allies have been driven back.

Monday, September 1, 1941

There are no classes today because this is Labor Day, but I had a long talk with Hamaker about his research program. I feel very strongly about introducing techniques of microchemistry into our program. I also spent some time in the library, where I noted a "Letter to the Editor" of *The Physical Review* by John J. Mitchell, Harrison S. Brown, and Robert D. Fowler. In the "Letter" "On the Isotopic Constitution of Cobalt" they report the absence of stable Co^{57} and set an upper limit of less than 1 part Co^{57} in 30,000 parts of Co^{59}. This is important to Jack Livingood and me in our mass assignments of cobalt radioactivities.

"RUSSO-FINN PEACE TALKS REPORTED!" reads this morning's headline.

When I moved to Chicago in April 1942, it had already occurred to a number of people that it would be desirable to produce a pure fissionable isotope, undiluted with inactive isotopes, because of the difficulties inherent in isotope separation as is necessary in the case of U^{235}. Such a nucleus is Pu^{239}, which had been shown to be fissionable with thermal neutrons and with a cross section greater than that of U^{235}. The Plutonium Project had as its objectives (1) the large-scale production of plutonium (element number 94), utilizing a nuclear chain reaction in uranium; and (2) the chemical separation of it from the unreacted uranium and fission products.

During the work at Berkeley we had developed the lanthanum fluoride oxidation-reduction cycle for separating plutonium from uranium and fission products. In this method lanthanum fluoride was used to carry plutonium in its lower oxidation state to separate it from uranium and some fission products; next the carrier and the plutonium were dissolved, the plutonium oxidized to its higher oxidation state, and lanthanum fluoride precipitated again, leaving plutonium in solution—this cycle could then be repeated to effect further separation of the plutonium from fission products. This became known as the "wet fluoride process" and was the leading candidate, because it was known to work on the laboratory scale, for development as a plant-scale chemical separation process. It was thought advisable, however, to investigate other possibilities. One of the suggestions of a process for the separation of plutonium from neutron-irradiated uranium involved fluorination to produce a plutonium hexafluoride—the "dry fluoride" volatility method. In the course of staffing the group at Chicago, I wrote a number of recruiting letters, including one to Harrison Brown. Brown was not only brilliant

Figure 5.1. Herbert A. Jones Laboratory, University of Chicago campus. Our laboratory space on top (fourth floor) on wing at left. In addition, we used top work area at right end of right wing.

but also had experience with fluorine chemistry and Fowler's fluorine generator at Johns Hopkins. At the end of April Brown wrote that his contract at Johns Hopkins would be over on June 30 and he would be interested in joining my group.

Harrison started to work in my chemistry group, whose laboratories were then located on the fourth floor of Jones Laboratory (Figure 5.1), on June 1, 1942, while I was away on a trip to California and Nevada getting married. I found him on the job when I returned:

Tuesday, June 9, 1942

Brown started work here as a Research Associate, as scheduled, on June 1 and has been outlining methods of separation of 94 from uranium and fission products by volatility methods. In talking with him today, I see that he is already convinced that this is the way to go into production, everything scaled up and using remote control. His argument is that the non-volatile 94 higher fluoride can be separated not only from the volatile uranium hexafluoride but also from a large proportion of the fission products due to the fact that the non-volatile higher fluorides of the fission products, in general, are water insoluble, whereas the non-volatile 94 higher fluoride is water soluble.

Although we had already, in March of 1942, suggesed that the element with atomic number 94 be given the name "plutonium" (with the chemical symbol Pu), we still had the habit of referring to it as simply "94."

My wife, Helen, and I met Harrison's wife, Adele, under rather rushed circumstances. (Harrison had married Adele Scrimger of San Francisco shortly after he graduated from Berkeley in May 1938.) This was Helen's first meeting with Harrison also. I had spent the afternoon with Metallurgical Project Director Arthur H. Compton and other members of the Engineering Council in a meeting that ran later than expected:

Thursday, June 11, 1942
Compton presented a chart listing 16 factors that should be considered before choosing between Chicago (Dunes area) and the Tennessee Valley (Elza area) as the site of the atomic power piles. According to Compton's weighing of the factors, Chicago is favored slightly; it was agreed, however, that it is difficult to make a stronger case for one as compared with the other. He outlined as a proposed schedule the building of piles of the following power levels: (1) 100 watts, (2) 100 kilowatts, (3) 100–100,000 kilowatts (helium-cooled power plant), (4) up to 1,000,000 kilowatts. There was general agreement that plants 2, 3, and 4 should be at the same site.

The afternoon meeting ran so late that Helen and I were terribly late to dinner at Harry and Adele Brown's apartment in nearby Hyde Park (5542 Blackstone Avenue). Then Harry and I had to rush off to our regular Thursday evening Research Associates meeting. Later we rejoined our wives, bringing along some other guests.

Adele was a most gracious hostess and showed no irritation at this rather unorthodox introduction to Harrison's new colleagues.

Brown vigorously attacked the problems associated with his volatility method for separating element 94 from uranium and fission products with the aid of Orville Hill, another new, young chemist who had just received his master's degree from the University of Illinois.

Tuesday, June 16, 1942
Brown and Hill have completed construction of their fluorine generator and started their first experiment today in the fume hoods in the entry area of Room 404 and just outside Room 403. Their aim is to test the fluorine volatility method for separating 94, outlined in our last weekly report. They fluorinated, at about 250°–350°C, a mixture of uranium and

fission product elements (tellurium, barium, lanthanum, cerium, selenium, antimony, silver, rubidium) containing tracer 50-year 94, to test the behavior of the fission product elements and whether the unvolatilized 94 higher fluoride can be separated, by leaching with aqueous solution, from the non-volatile fission product elements. They find, however, that the unvolatilized 94 fluoride does not leach out in a 6 N HF solution. As their working space in Room 404 they are using laboratory bench no. 3, and Brown has set up his desk against the wall at the south end of the area between laboratory benches 2 and 3.

Figure 5.2 shows the room assignments of the members of our group corresponding to a later date (October 1942) when our laboratory space was fully occupied to the point of crowding. Spofford English and Ralph James, and Isadore Perlman and William Knox, who preceded Brown in joining my research group, were assigned laboratory benches 1 and 2 in the large laboratory room 404 (Bertrand Goldschmidt joined us somewhat later, in July). Harrison Brown (joined later by Orville Hill) was assigned to laboratory bench 3; and Ted Magel, John Willard, and Elton Turk, who started later, worked at bench 4. Arthur Jaffey and Stanley Thompson, who also began later, worked at bench 5. (Dan Koshland, who was among the earliest to join us, worked at bench 4.) The others worked in smaller rooms as shown in Figure 5.2.

Wednesday, June 17, 1942
   Continuing their experiment of yesterday Brown and Hill leached the non-volatile 94 fluoride residue with a solution of potassium peroxydisulfate plus silver ion, and again they find that the 94 remains behind with the non-volatile fission product elements. This indicates that either the 94 is reduced rapidly by water or has a peculiar higher fluoride that is water insoluble. In order to check the previous results (the experiment Brown performed while still at Johns Hopkins University in which he and Perlman found that 94 does not volatilize with fluorine at 450°C), Brown and Hill fluorinated the same UF_4–UF_{4-94} mixture at 250° and at 750°C and they find again that the 94 does not volatilize. The fluoride volatility process can, of course, be modified to recover the 94 from the non-volatile fluoride residue by dissolving it in acid and using the lanthanum fluoride oxidation-reduction cycle.

Friday, June 26, 1942
   In experiments today, yesterday, and the day before Brown and Hill have tested the behavior of short-lived fission products in their volatility process. In a number of experiments they bombarded uranium tetrafluoride for about an hour with slow neutrons at the University of Chicago cyclotron. They then fluorinated the neutron-irradiated uranium tetrafluoride and found that about 50% of the fission product beta-particle radioactivity is removed with the volatile uranium hexafluoride. . . .

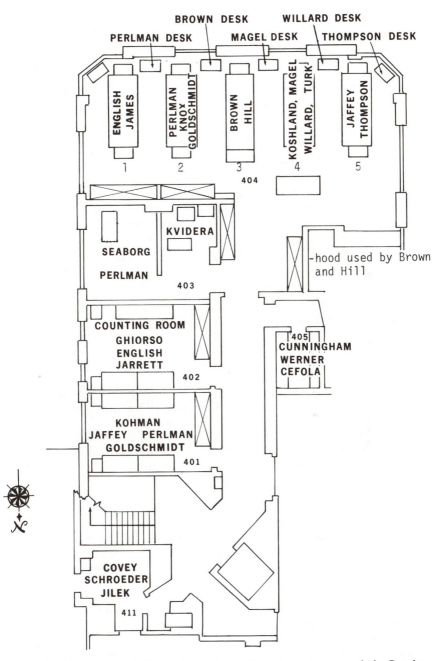

Figure 5.2. Space occupied by individual members of our group, early in October 1942, in Jones Laboratory, University of Chicago campus.

An article in today's newspaper says that the United States is advancing plans for a second front in Europe by establishing a European theater of operations, led by Major General Dwight D. Eisenhower, considered the ablest young officer in the U.S. Army. This new conduct of the war is thought to be the outcome of Prime Minister Churchill's current visit here with President Roosevelt.

Another possible nuclear fuel was U^{233}, which Raymond W. Stoughton, John W. Gofman, and I had proved earlier was also fissionable with slow neutrons. Again there was the problem of the chemical separation from fission products and from thorium, from which the U^{233} is produced by irradiation with neutrons via the reaction sequence: $Th^{232} \longrightarrow Th^{233} \longrightarrow Pa^{233} \longrightarrow U^{233}$. (In this case the U^{233} must be produced in conjunction with a nuclear chain reaction operating with uranium since thorium cannot sustain a chain reaction with slow neutrons.) When I was in Berkeley in early June, Ray Stoughton and I discussed the possible development of a method utilizing the fluorination method; I suggested he prepare some thorium fluoride incorporating 7-day U^{237} tracer and then send it to us for fluorination. We would then return it to him so that he could identify the U^{237} to see whether it would be found in the volatile uranium hexafluoride fraction as expected.

Monday, June 29, 1942

Stoughton wrote from Berkeley notifying me that he is sending two samples of thorium fluoride (containing 7-day U^{237} as tracer) for use in testing the U^{233}-thorium fluoride volatility separation process which we discussed when I was in Berkeley the first of this month. Shortly after receiving the letter, the samples themselves were delivered and Brown and Hill set to work fluorinating them. They finished tonight and we airmailed the fractions back to Stoughton.

This method of transferring radioactive samples by mail, although not acceptable today, was rather commonplace in 1942. Stoughton wrote in July about the results of these efforts:

Friday, July 17, 1942

He described the results of working up the two neutron-irradiated samples of thorium-fluoride he sent us June 29 for fluorination for his thorium-uranium separation and which we returned the same day. The distillate from the fluorination yielded 25–35% of the uranium, and that which remained in the thorium fluoride residue was successfully extracted by digestion with fuming sulfuric acid.

Thus this initial experiment yielded somewhat disappointing results. This work, however, was peripheral to our main task, which was to devise a method for separating plutonium (94) from uranium and fission products.

At about this time active consideration was being given to the location of the site near Chicago where a chain-reacting uranium pile might be built as a pilot plant for the production of plutonium. The Metallurgical Laboratory was on a six-day work schedule with only Sunday off. Helen (Seaborg) and I, together with Harrison and Adele Brown, Isadore and Lee Perlman, and Milton and Frances Burton decided to combine a picnic lunch with a search for and inspection of the site:

Sunday, July 5, 1942
    Today we took our regular Sunday holiday. Helen and I, along with the Perlmans, Browns, and Burtons, drove out on State Highway 4A to explore the proposed Argonne Forest Preserve site at Palos Park where it is rumored the experimental chain reacting pile will be built. Compton and his wife discovered it one Saturday afternoon while horseback riding. He said it is an isolated area about five miles northeast of the village of Lemont and twenty miles west of the University of Chicago campus. We had a fine lunch in the general area there but are not sure we found the actual site.

The question of how much of the fission products could be separated from the plutonium was an important one that needed to be answered:

Tuesday, July 14, 1942
    One of the most important problems related to the isolation of 94 by the fluorine method is the determination of the percentage of fission products that will be carried over with the UF_6 and away from the non-volatile 94 fluoride during the fluorination process. Brown's earlier experiments, using fission products of rather short half-lives (about four hours after bombardment) show that, if the fluorination takes place at about 250°C, roughly half of the fission activity will be carried over with the uranium. In today's "Report for the Week Ending July 11, 1942, Group I: Chemistry of 94" (CC–179), I say that further studies now show that the carryover of long-lived fission products is the same under the same conditions. Furthermore, according to experiments last week, if the fluorination process takes place at 450°C, 80% of the fission activity, when fluorination takes place 48 to 96 hours after neutron bombardment, passes over with the volatile UF_6.
    More bad news from the Russian front! The Reds have retreated after a twelve-day battle with their Don River lines ripped.

Wednesday, July 15, 1942

Last week Brown and Hill found that approximately 80% of the fission product activity of UF_4 samples irradiated with neutrons can be volatilized together with the uranium when subjected to a fluorine stream at 450°–500°C. It should be noted that the 20% fraction of fission products left behind could cause serious complications in scaled-up chemical operations because of the intense radiations. Although much information is known about the behavior of individual fission product fluorides in macroscopic amounts, experiments must be performed to determine if minute concentrations in uranium behave in the same way. And what are the elements associated with the volatile fraction and what elements remain behind as non-volatile fluorides? This was the analysis that Brown and Hill attempted to make today. Brown fluorinated a gram of the neutron-bombarded UF_4 at 450°C. The volatile products were collected with uranium hexafluoride in a trap maintained at −78°C. They were then dissolved in water and standard chemical separations were made on the solution without rigorous quantitative separations. The residue was dissolved in nitric acid and then, after adding carriers chemically, analyzed for its constituents by measuring the fission product radiations. . . .

From the war front on the Pacific comes news of a U.S. victory at Midway; eighty Japanese ships were routed.

Harrison's research program for developing his dry fluoride volatility method for separating plutonium from uranium and fission products took an unexpected turn:

Tuesday, July 21, 1942

Brown came into the office this afternoon very excited about the results of an experiment that Hill has just performed under his direction. Until today, their research has shown that 94 cannot be volatilized in a fluorine stream together with UF_6 if the 94 is introduced into the UF_4 (used in preparing the UF_6) by the so-called "wet" method. (In this method the 94 is added to a solution of uranyl sulfate and the solution is reduced with zinc. Hydrofluoric acid is added and the 94 precipitated quantitatively with the UF_4. The UF_4 is dried and then fluorinated.) When this procedure is followed, the 94 remains quantitatively behind and the uranium disappears as a gaseous fluoride, UF_6.

In today's experiment, 94 was introduced into the UF_4 prepared by the "dry" method, i.e., by hydrofluorination of uranium oxide. Several thousand counts/min. of 50-year 94 was added to a solution containing 0.25 gm of uranyl nitrate. This was evaporated to dryness and converted to the oxide (U_3O_8) by heating. The U_3O_8 was treated with hydrogen at 500°C, giving UO_2. The UO_2 was in turn hydrofluorinated (treatment with anhydrous HF) at 500° and thus converted to anhydrous UF_4. Small samples of this UF_4 were weighed to be fluorinated at various temperatures. To their amazement, when they fluorinated the first sample at 500°C, they discovered that both the uranium and 94 volatilized completely. Then, when they fluorinated a sample at 250°C, they learned that element 94 fluoride is somewhat less volatile than the UF_6. This changes the entire aspect of the fluorination method but makes it no less applicable as a potential way of separating 94 from uranium and fission products. Tomorrow, Brown will start a long series of experiments on the neutron-bombarded uranyl nitrate that we received yesterday from Wahl. The purpose is to identify the long-lived fission product elements. Some of the work will be done in collaboration with Perlman. These elements, especially, must be recognized in order to make the final purification of 94 from the pile feasible.

This was big news for it showed that 94 higher fluoride was volatile after all! This changed the process completely, placing the plutonium in the fraction of volatile fluorides, instead of with the non-volatile fluorides, under certain conditions. His continuing research was directed toward defining these conditions:

Wednesday, August 12, 1942
On July 21 I wrote here that Brown and Hill have discovered that the highest fluoride(s) of element 94 can be completely volatilized in a fluorine stream of about 500°C. This volatilization takes place if the lower fluoride is prepared by the anhydrous ("dry") method. At that time they worked with a sample of uranyl nitrate to which 50-year 94 had been added. In an experiment today to confirm more fully the volatility of the higher fluoride of 94, they worked with 0.8 gram of UF_4 that they prepared last week by hydrofluorination from the Berkeley neutron-bombarded UNH that we received from Wahl on July 20. This sample was fluorinated at 500°C, and all of the volatile material was collected in a cold trap. As they hoped and expected, all of the 94^{239} present in the original sample was found to have volatilized and condensed in the trap, together with the UF_6 formed.

Thus, they have shown that the higher fluoride of element 94 can be volatilized completely at about 500°C, this volatilization taking place if the lower fluoride is prepared by the anhydrous method. Uranium can be completely separated from element 94, as the very volatile UF_6 will be quantitatively formed at about 250°–300°C, leaving the 94 behind. When the temperature is raised to 500°C, the 94 will volatilize quantitatively upon fluorination.

Harrison now began to think in terms of the scale-up required to put his fluoride volatility process in operation at a plutonium production site. With his characteristic energy and enthusiasm he visited a number of places where large-scale production of fluorine was underway. A flow sheet for his process was now beginning to take shape:

Saturday, August 15, 1942

A report, "The Present Status of Fluorine Production," by Harrison S. Brown, was issued today. Earlier this month Brown visited several installations where fluorine cells are being used in production. His report covers the Du Pont's two cells, the Harshaw cell, Johns Hopkins' three cells, and Columbia's two cells. He also went to the Hooker plant in Niagara Falls to see the large Hooker type "S" cell used extensively for the production of chlorine. The objective of his visits is to prepare for the eventual design and construction of fluorine generators to be used in the chemical separation of 94.

It is appropriate here for me to give an accounting of experiments on the distibution of long-lived fission products that were conducted by Brown and Hill during the time since they first got a sample of the irradiated UNH on July 20. The advantage of using this particular sample is that it should closely approximate the fission condition of the material from an operating chain-reacting pile one month after shutdown. The beta-particle and gamma-ray activity losses on performing each of the following five steps between July 20 and July 31 were determined:

(1) Convert UNH to U_3O_8

$$UO_2(NO_3)2\ 6H_2O \xrightarrow{700°C} U_3O_8$$

(2) Convert to UO_2 with H_2

$$U_3O_8 + 2H_2 \xrightarrow{600°C} 3UO_2 + 2H_2O$$

(3) Treat with HF (anhydrous)

$$UO_2 + 4HF \xrightarrow{600°C} UF_4 + 2H_2O$$

(4) Remove uranium with F_2

$$UF_4 + F_2 \xrightarrow{300°C} UF_6$$

(5) Remove 94 with F_2, i.e., volatilization of the higher fluoride of 94 at 600°C.

(1) The loss in fission product activity in step (1) was found to be less than 1%, thus indicating that the activity contributions of krypton and xenon are quite small.

(2) A small but detectable loss in activity of about 1% was found in step (2). This is probably due to the iodine and bromine volatilization as HI and HBr.

(3) A marked decrease of both beta and gamma activity was observed on treatment with anhydrous HF. The gamma-ray activity loss as measured through 11.5 grams of lead was about 25–30%. The beta-particle activity losses were about 36% using absorbers from 7.3 to 117 mg/cm². The elements that volatilize are probably columbium, zirconium, antimony, and possibly 43 and tellurium.

(4) On fluorinating the UF_4 formed in step (3) at 300°C the uranium volatilized away completely. No detectable amount (<1%) of the beta-particle activity, however, passed over with it.

(5) On raising the temperature to 600° and refluorinating the reaction vessel, no detectable loss of beta-particle activity was observed. It should be noted that this is the step in which one would volatilize element 94.

The residue contained the balance of the beta-particle activity (about 60%) and the gamma-ray activity (about 70%). This residue consists of rubidium, strontium, yttrium, barium, lanthanum, cerium, and cesium.

The same series of runs was made again (ending this week) on another portion of the Berkeley sample. It was found that in the hydrofluorination step (3) the amount of volatilization of beta-particle activity decreased to about 15% of the total, but that the volatilization of the gamma-ray activity increased to about 60–70% of the total. In all other steps the beta and gamma activity losses were less than 1%.

The Navy announced it is making satisfactory gains in the Solomons, but news from the Russian front remains bleak as the Germans broke through the Soviet lines in two places.

Because Np^{239}, the beta particle–emitting precursor of Pu^{239}, would be present in the uranium from the chain-reacting pile, it was necessary to study its behavior in the chemical separation process:

Monday, August 17, 1942

The determination of the volatility of the higher fluoride of element 93 is of considerable interest, not only from the point of view of knowing its involvement in fluorine treatment of pile uranium, but for the purpose of correlating the chemical properties of elements 92, 93, and 94. Brown and Hill began their experiments this week by doing just this—investigating the volatility of the higher fluoride of element 93. To a solution containing 105 mg of unirradiated UNH, they added about 10,000 beta-counts (counted through a 7.56 mg/cm^2 absorber) of 2.3 day 93^{239}. This was ignited to U_3O_8 and then converted to UO_2 by hydrogenation. Small samples of this were weighed into smaller copper discs and converted to UF_4 by hydrofluorination (treatment with anhydrous HF). No loss of 93 was observed in this step. The UF_4 samples were then fluorinated at 250°–300°C for half an hour. In *all* cases, the 93 volatilized with the uranium. This indicates that the higher fluoride of element 93 is more volatile than that of element 94. Its behavior thus resembles more closely that of uranium. . . .

The Soviets announced the fall of Maikop but said that they had rendered the oil establishment completely unusable. Meanwhile, the United States Marines are fighting on in the Solomons.

Tuesday, August 18, 1942

Brown and Hill had a more successful day. As a check on the results
of the experiment they performed yesterday, they took about 15 mg of
the UO_2 containing 93 tracer and fluorinated it at 250°C for a half hour,
meanwhile collecting the volatile products in a trap maintained at dry ice–
acetone temperature. The volatile products were then dissolved in water,
and the 93 was extracted, after reduction, by co-precipitation with LaF_3
carrier. It was found that all of the 93 that had volatilized had collected
in the trap. . . .

Today's newspaper carried the story of the defeat of the Japanese fleet.

Essential to the development of the process was the need to separate
the volatile fluorides of plutonium and uranium from each other:

Monday, August 24, 1942

Brown and Hill started a series of experiments today to compare the
volatilization of uranium and 94 fluorides as a function of temperature.
In their first run they had difficulty in transferring volatilized 94 fluoride
to a cold trap with UF_6; a substantial fraction of 94 was retained in the
outlet tube of the fluorination reactor. They hope to complete these studies
in about a week. . . .

More bad news from the Russian front! The Germans are driving closer
to Stalingrad.

It was thought that a chloride volatility method might provide an
alternative to the use of fluorine:

Thursday, August 27, 1942

Brown and Hill performed an experiment today on the volatility of
the higher anhydrous chloride of 94. Some 94 tracer (50-year) was added
to a uranyl nitrate solution and the whole was ignited to U_3O_8. This was
thoroughly mixed with charcoal and the mixture in a boat was treated
with chlorine at 350–450°C. The reaction that took place was as follows:

$$2U_3O_8 + 8C + 15Cl_2 \rightarrow 6UCl_5 + 8CO_2.$$

The UCl_5 left the boat and condensed in the cooler portions of the
reaction vessel. At the end of the reaction, the boat was weighed and
analyzed for element 94. The UCl_5 in the cool portion of the vessel was
dissolved in water and also analyzed for 94. It was found that 92% of
the uranium had volatilized, but at the most only 7% of the 94 had
volatilized with it. Thus this preliminary experiment indicates that 94 does
not have a very volatile higher chloride. Further experiments, however,
should be undertaken in order to test the volatility under various other
conditions. . . .

News today is the reverse of yesterday—news from Moscow good and
from the Pacific bad. The Russians advanced on the Moscow front and

slew 45,000 Germans. But in the Pacific the Japanese invaded Guinea again.

Additional experiments on the relative volatility and stability of the plutonium and uranium higher fluorides were performed.

Monday, August 31, 1942
Brown and Hill concluded their experiments started last Monday on the volatilization of fluorides of uranium and 94 as a function of temperature. Several samples of UF_4 containing 94 tracer incorporated by the anhydrous method were fluorinated at various temperatures for an arbitrary interval of 30 minutes and the percent of element 94 volatilizing at a given temperature was measured. They find they can remove the uranium UF_6 and leave the 94 behind at fluorination temperatures up to about 300°C, then remove the 94 as a volatile higher fluoride by fluorination at a higher temperature. Their experiments, however, do not indicate whether the higher temperature is required for the 94 fluoride in order to volatilize it or merely in order to synthesize it. Experiments on passing the 94 higher fluoride through copper tubing (175°C) show that it condenses; this might be due either to low volatility or to instability.

Work on the scale-up of the process and the separation of the higher fluorides of plutonium, neptunium, and uranium continued:

Monday, September 28, 1942
Brown and Hill have been working with Donald S. Webster, one of the Du Pont chemical engineers assigned to our program, to test the possible practical application of their volatility separation process. Last week, using a vertical column, they worked on the production of UF_4 through hydrogen reduction of U_3O_8 to UO_2 and subsequent hydrofluorination. They encountered considerable "caking" of the UF_4 produced in this manner. The technique they finally developed is one in which the gases are actually bubbled through the solid uranium oxide powder, and this seems to work quite well.

They also performed a series of experiments to test the volatility of element 93 in the form of the higher fluoride. A known quantity of 93^{239} tracer was added to some uranium nitrate, and this was then converted to UF_4 by hydrofluorination. Samples of this were then heated in a fluorine stream for a half-hour at various temperatures between about 140°C and 300°C and higher. Their experiments showed that the volatilization of element 93 in fluorine is much like that of uranium and unlike that of element 94, whose fluoride volatilizes at higher temperatures. These experiments indicate that 93 would be readily separated from 94 in the fluoride volatility separation process. . . .

Fighting continues in Guinea, and the Allies have swept the Japanese back for two days in a row. The seesaw fighting in Stalingrad favors the Soviets today; they are beating off the Nazis.

Brown and Hill performed experiments to test the feasibility of a new type of pile for the production of plutonium:

Friday, November 6, 1942
Today Brown and Hill performed an interesting experiment. The aim was to see whether or not UF_6 when evaporated from its solid or liquid state can be freed from tracer amounts of nonvolatile activity. A tank of UF_6, which is quite old (about seven months) so that it contains an equilibrium amount of UX_1 (thorium), was opened; and the UF_6 that distilled out was dissolved in water. This was evaporated to dryness and then weighed and counted. It was found that the UF_6 distilled was 100 times less beta active (i.e., UX_1 activity) than the UF_6 present in the tank. In view of the fact that the distillation method used was so simple, it would appear that direct fractional distillation of neutron-bombarded UF_6 would be a rapid way of separating element 94 and fission products from uranium. It would also appear the UF_6 might be a feasible material for use in a continuously operating pile, in which liquid UF_6 could be circulated, and then evaporated from the fission products and 94 in an evaporator on the outside. Such a scheme might well offer definite advantages. . . .
The headline today says "'Complete Victory' in Egypt!"

Early in November a crisis arose on the Plutonium Project. It was realized that the plutonium would have to be purified to an extraordinary degree from light elements (lithium, beryllium, boron, carbon, nitrogen, oxygen, fluorine) in order for it to be suitable for use as the explosive ingredient of the nuclear weapon. The feasibility of such a chemical purification procedure, and indeed the feasibility of the plutonium approach, was under serious question and a committee including Du Pont chemists and chemical engineers came to the Metallurgical Laboratory to conduct an investigation. The committee concluded that the plutonium route should continue to be pursued and recommended to Project Director Arthur H. Compton that work on the Wet Fluoride Process be emphasized and that work on other chemical separation methods, such as the Dry Fluoride Process, should also be continued. This also marked the entry of the Du Pont Company into the Plutonium Project, with the responsibility for designing and building the plutonium production plants.
Although the outline of a chemical separation process could be obtained by tracer-scale investigations, the process could not be defined with certainty until study of it was made possible at the actual concentrations

of plutonium that would exist in the large-scale chemical separation plants. In order to make this possible, weighable (actually microgram) amounts of Pu[239] were made available as the result of the irradiation of large amounts of uranium with neutrons at the cyclotrons at Berkeley and Washington University in St. Louis. Burris B. Cunningham, a young biochemist from Berkeley who joined our group in July 1942, was largely responsible for the application of the techniques of "ultramicrochemistry" to the successful isolation of such "pure" plutonium. Louis Werner and Michael Cefola also contributed to the research program on this ultramicrochemical scale, and the three of them worked in the small room 405 (Figure 5.2). Brown and Hill did experiments to test their volatility process using pure plutonium:

> *Saturday, November 14, 1942*
> It seems worthwhile to test the volatility of 94 hexafluoride using pure 94 now that this is available. Today Brown and Hill performed such an experiment. They used 0.2 microgram of 94 oxide on a copper disc furnished by Cunningham. After "weighing" the sample by counting its alpha particles, the disc was treated with anhydrous HF at 500°C and again counted. By counting the alpha particles as well as by observation under the microscope, it was found that the small sample was still completely present, although changed somewhat in appearance. The substance was then fluorinated at 250°C for half an hour and counted again. About 5% of the material, as determined from the decrease in alpha count, apparently disappeared in this operation, but the material remaining looked unchanged when viewed under the microscope. A final fluorination was made at 500°C, and this time *all of the 94*, as determined from the decrease in alpha count, *volatilized*. Less than 0.02% (limits of observation) of the original alpha counts remained behind. Likewise, all except a small fraction of the visible mass of materials, as determined by viewing under the microscope, remained after this final fluorination, which indicates that Cunningham's 94[239], while not 100% pure, had a rather high degree of purity. These experiments substantiate the conclusions that have been reached in the studies using 94 tracer, namely: (1) The lower fluoride (PuF$_4$) is nonvolatile at 500°C. (2) The higher fluoride is probably formed to a very small extent at 250°C. (3) The higher fluoride is formed and volatilizes completely at 500°C. . . .
> Allied troops have invaded Tunisia and are closing the pincers on Rommel. President Roosevelt announced that lend-lease aid will be granted to Africa.

It was important to settle the question of the relative stability and volatility of the higher fluoride of plutonium:

> *Saturday, November 28, 1942*
> Brown and Hill have conducted a number of experiments to test the

stability of the volatile higher fluoride of 94 in order to develop a method of collecting it in a fluoride volatility separation process. Some UF_4 containing 94 tracer was fluorinated at 500°C, and the 94 was collected together with the UF_6 in a trap at dry ice–acetone temperatures. The trap was then allowed to warm up to room temperature (25°C) at which temperature the vapor pressure of UF_6 is appreciable. Dry nitrogen was then slowly passed through the trap and into a water reflux condenser arrangement in which all UF_6 and 94 fluoride entering would be collected. The residue and the volatilized portions were then analyzed for the 94 present in both the oxidized (fluoride soluble) and reduced (fluoride insoluble) states.

In the first experiment *all of the uranium* was distilled off, but *only 15% of the 94* distilled with it. This was first interpreted as indicating that 94 fluoride had a considerably lower vapor pressure than UF_6, but observation soon showed that 81% of the 94 collected in the reflux condenser was in the oxidized state, while only 9% of the 94 left behind was oxidized. Since it must be assumed that the reduced 94 found in the reflux condenser was in its upper state when it volatilized with the uranium in the nitrogen stream, it is calculated that *only 23% of the total that had been completely oxidized remained in the oxidized state after the removal of the flourine.* It seems quite reasonable to conclude from this that the volatile 94 fluoride is unstable in the absence of fluorine giving as a product the very nonvolatile PuF_4.

$$PuF_6 \rightleftharpoons PuF_4 + F_2$$

Of the 94 present in the oxidized state, it will be noted that 66% of it volatilized with the uranium, thus indicating that the vapor pressure of the higher fluoride is quite appreciable.

A second experiment was performed in which the UF_6-PuF_6 mixture was kept away from contact with fluorine for a somewhat shorter period of time. This time 52% of the 94 remained in the oxidized state, of which 33% volatilized in the nitrogen stream together with 40% of the UF_6.

In the third experiment fluorine was used instead of nitrogen as a sweeping gas. Only 10% of the UF_6 was volatilized from the trap but this time 35% of the 94 *fluoride (oxidized) volatilized with it.* This we believe indicates quite strongly that: (1) The higher fluoride of element 94 is unstable in the absence of fluorine. It slowly decomposes to PuF_4 over a period of hours at room temperature. (2) The higher fluoride of element 94 has a vapor pressure at room temperature of the same order of magnitude as UF_6. . . .

Headlines today say that the full Tunisia offensive is on.

Wednesday, December 2, 1942
    During the last few days Brown and Hill have continued experiments to determine the relative volatility of UF_6 and PuF_6. They fluorinated some UF_4 containing 94^{239} tracer at 500°C for an hour and captured the volatile

fluorination products in a trap cooled by dry ice–acetone. This mixture of higher fluorides was then allowed to volatilize in a stream of fluorine by heating the trap to about 30°C. About 60% of the 94 was volatilized and only 30% of the uranium. In another experiment a temperature of 40°C was used, resulting in the volatilization of about 35% of the 94 and 9% of the uranium. Assuming a perfect solution and using the known vapor pressure of pure UF_6 at these temperatures, Brown calculates that the sublimation point of PuF_6 is in the neighborhood of 32°C, which is to be compared with the sublimation point of UF_6, namely 56°C. It will be interesting to see whether later work with pure PuF_6 confirms this determination. . . .

War news from the African front is depressing. The Axis has been on the attack and made some gains; the Allies seem to be stalled in Tunisia.

The actual boiling point of PuF_6 is 62°C, as determined by work with the pure compound. The higher temperatures required for the volatilization of PuF_6 that had been observed by Brown and Hill were apparently a result of its relative instability and the uncertainties associated with working with only tracer quantities.

Because our chemical separation processes were advancing to the stage where they needed to be tested on the pilot plant scale, a chemical engineering group, under the leadership of Charles Cooper, a Du Pont chemical engineer, had been added to the scientific personnel of the Metallurgical Laboratory. During the fall of 1942, Stanley G. Thompson, a young chemist from Standard Oil Company of California who had joined our group, conceived of a new process for the chemical separation of plutonium—the Zirconium Phosphate Process (phosphate method), based on an oxidation-reduction cycle utilizing zirconium phosphate as the carrier for plutonium. Harrison Brown joined Iz Perlman and me in sending a memorandum to Charles Cooper in which we described some combinations of methods for separating plutonium:

Monday, December 7, 1942
Today Perlman, Brown and I sent a letter to Charles Cooper, describing in some detail the status of various methods for the extraction and decontamination of 94 with emphasis on the weights of precipitates and other 94 fractions, the amounts of fission activity that are present at each step and its heating effect. We describe various combinations of wet and dry methods as follows: Process I—Extraction by simplified wet fluoride method, decontamination by dry fluoride method; Process Ia—Extraction by complete wet fluoride method, decontamination by dry fluoride method; Process II—Extraction by simplified phosphate method and decontamination by the dry fluoride method; Process IIa—Extraction by complete phosphate method, decontamination by dry fluoride method; Process III—Extraction by a dry fluoride method, decontamination by dry fluoride

method; Process IV—Decontamination by wet fluoride method after extraction by Processes I, II, III. We also mention the new zirconium phosphate method for separating 94 and describe the conditions for the precipitation of zirconium phosphate, its dissolution in HF followed by precipitation of lanthanum fluoride.

Additional experiments to test the stability of the higher fluoride of plutonium were performed.

Tuesday, December 8, 1942

Brown and Hill have carried out another experiment to determine the stability of PuF_6 using a mixture of UF_6 and PuF_6 (tracer quantities). The mixture was heated under a nitrogen atmosphere at about 100°C. Then about half of the UF_6 was volatilized in the nitrogen stream at 31°C and captured in a cold trap which was found to include essentially no 94 (approximately 1%). Thus it is clear that the higher fluoride of 94 is easily reduced by heat in the absence of fluorine. . . .

Newspapers report that a big tank battle is raging for vital hills in Tunisia.

Brown and Hill performed more experiments on the combined dry fluoride and zirconium phosphate methods:

Wednesday, December 9, 1942

During the last several days Brown and Hill have volatilized zirconium as the fluoride by hydrofluorination at 700°C of a sample of zirconium phosphate which was precipitated carrying tracer 94. They find that the 94 remains in the residue and is not volatilized along with the ZrF_4 under these conditions.

By October 1942 my group had grown to about twenty-five scientists, a secretary, and three technicians, so that our space on the fourth floor of Jones Laboratory was filled to capacity (see Figure 5.2). In addition to the fluoride volatility method being investigated by Brown and his young colleague Orville Hill, we were continuing to investigate a number of other chemical methods, with the aim of finding the best one for the separation of plutonium from the uranium and the high yield of fission product activity. The final method to be chosen would go through a pilot plant stage before its introduction in the plutonium production facility at a site yet to be chosen. The production facility would consist of plutonium piles and chemical plants for its extraction from the uranium in which it was to be produced in the piles. Among the possible chemical procedures being investigated were precipitation (wet fluoride and phosphate), solvent extraction, volatility (dry fluoride), adsorption-

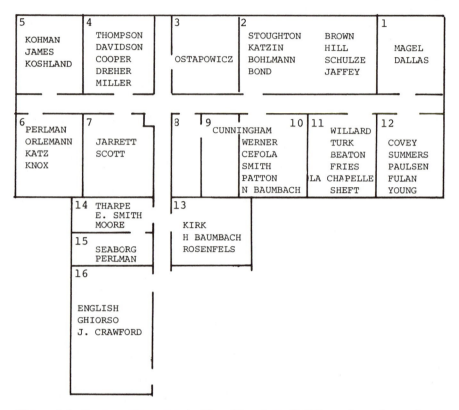

Figure 5.4. Room assignments in New Chemistry Building of members of our group as of late April 1943.

bombarded UF_6, 27.6 grams, which was exposed at the St. Louis cyclotron this month for a total of 22,000 microampere-hours (bombardment F–6–1, from December 16 to 29). The UF_6 was distilled from its container to another container but the measurements of the gamma-rays before and after the distillation didn't lead to a good material balance. . . .

The year ends with the Allies preparing for a big assault on Bizerte in Tunisia and the Soviets announcing new successes in their drive to regain Stalingrad.

Wednesday, January 13, 1943

Brown and Hill have completed their measurements on the various fractions of the neutron-bombarded UF_6 sample that they distilled on December 31. They find that the elements 93 and 94 were quantitatively separated from the uranium hexafluoride distillate and also the fission activity was separated to a remarkable extent.

Harrison continued to investigate the requirement. the expansion to production scale of his dry fluoride volatility process:

Thursday, January 14, 1943
Harrison Brown is at Niagara Falls today. He is visiting the Hooker Electrochemical Company to inspect the production facilities in connection with our interest in developing a means of producing fluorine in large enough quantities for use in our dry fluoride separation process. He plans to leave Buffalo tonight and will arrive in Chicago tomorrow. . . .
The Soviets claim a 50-mile advance in the Caucasus, and the Nazis concede their main line is broken.

The wet fluoride process continued to emerge as the favorite in fall 1942. However, this method used the very corrosive hydrofluoric acid, and it was feared that equipment failure might take place due to corrosion. It was for this reason that Stan Thompson was trying to develop the zirconium phosphate process as an alternate method; this was also based on precipitation, the most developed method of separation at that time. This process, however, had the drawback that zirconium phosphate precipitates are gelatinous and hence difficult to separate from the supernatant solution. In December 1942 Stan discovered the Bismuth Phosphate Process, which utilized the oxidation-reduction principle with bismuth phosphate, an easily separable, crystalline precipitate, as the carrier for plutonium. This is the process that, in its unmodified form, was eventually chosen for use at the pilot plant at Clinton Laboratories in Tennessee and the production plant at Hanford, Washington. This process caught the attention of Harrison Brown, who decided to investigate to see if a modification in combination with his volatility method could be developed:

Friday, January 15, 1943
Today Brown and Hill fluorinated a sample of bismuth phosphate containing 94 tracer, prepared by Turk, in order to ascertain whether the 94 can be removed. The sample was fluorinated at 600°C for one-half hour, and analysis shows that more than 99% of the 94 volatilizes from the bismuth phosphate precipitate. This indicates that the use of fluorination might be a feasible method of removing 94 from a bismuth phosphate precipitate in connection with the Bismuth Phosphate Method for separating 94.

As mentioned earlier, a pile in which the uranium fuel in the form of molten UF_6 could circulate in and out of the pile continuously might allow separations via volatile procedures. Brown and Hill investigated

Harrison and his coworkers continued some interesting experiments on the synthesis and handling of UF_6, its separation from plutonium fluoride and fission products, and the combination of the fluoride volatility method with the bismuth phosphate process:

Tuesday, February 23, 1943

Brown, Hill, and Bohlmann performed another distillation experiment with UF_6 which has been bombarded with neutrons at the St. Louis cyclotron (bombardment no. F–6–3)—this is their third experiment of this type. In this case the UF_6 was put in an oven at 72°C for a month in order to give any oxidation or reduction process that was taking place ample time to attain equilibrium. When this UF_6 sample was distilled, it was found that after essentially all of it distilled, about 5 percent of the 94 was left in the undistilled residue, in agreement with the second neutron-bombarded UF_6 experiment. . . .

Newspapers report that the Allied armies are blasting Rommel's rear guard in Kasserine Pass in Tunisia.

Thursday, March 4, 1943

Brown, Hill, and Bohlmann have devised a means for effecting fluorination reactions under pressure. Today a small sample of UF_4 was placed in a copper boat, and this was placed in a reaction vessel which was evacuated and then connected to the tank of fluorine. Fluorine was admitted at 20 pounds above atmospheric pressure and the temperature was brought to about 500°C. After a few minutes a small trap at one end of the reaction vessel was cooled with liquid nitrogen, thus condensing most of the fluorine in the system together with the UF_6. The fluorine in the trap was then allowed to boil off as dry ice was placed around the trap. The weight of the UF_6 remaining in the trap was then determined by weighing, and it was found that a yield of UF_6 of essentially 100% was produced. This procedure has general applicability to the production of fluorine compounds. . . .

Today's headlines report a Japanese naval disaster. The U.S. destroyed all the ships in the Japanese convoy headed for New Guinea; there were ten warships and twelve transports. Fifty-five planes were shot down.

Saturday, March 27, 1943

Brown, Hill, and Bohlmann have found that when a bismuth phosphate precipitate incorporating 94 and fission products is hydrofluorinated and then fluorinated that the volatile higher fluoride of plutonium goes along with the higher volatile fluoride of bismuth. They have found that the fission product gamma activity associated with the collected bismuth fluoride and plutonium fluoride is about 2% of the activity initially present in the bismuth phosphate precipitate. If it is assumed that the bismuth phosphate brings down about 10% of the fission activity in two-month-old fission-active uranium, the initial precipitation combined with one dry fluoride volatilization will achieve an overall decontamination factor of 500. It might be possible to continue a dry decontamination cycle further than one volatilization. The bismuth fluoride and plutonium fluoride might be reduced with hydrogen, then treated again with HF to remove more of the volatile fission activity. Then, if this is followed with another volatilization with fluorine, it should be possible to obtain a further decontamination factor from gamma activity. Their experiments show that this is true and that a second volatilization produces additional decontamination from gamma activity of about a factor of 50. This gives an overall decontamination factor for one bismuth phosphate precipitation and two volatilizations of 25,000.

Tuesday, April 20, 1943
Today Hill and Bohlmann, working with Brown, completed the distillation of UF_6 from UF_6 bombarded with neutrons (sample F–6–5, 53,000 microampere-hours) at the St. Louis cyclotron which was then allowed to stand for 50 days. They performed a series of four successive distillations which separated the UF_6 from 99% of the fission product gamma activity and 99% of the plutonium which were initially associated with UF_6. They find that there is apparently a volatile fission product constituent which distills with the UF_6 and is still present 50 days after the neutron bombardment.

Brown and Hill became concerned about corrosion of operating equipment that might be associated with the dry fluoride volatility process:

Monday, May 17, 1943
H. S. Brown and O. F. Hill are visiting the Du Pont Company Experimental Station in Wilmington to discuss the dry process corrosion studies being carried out there under H. L. Maxwell.

Brown and coworkers continued the investigation of the concept of a UF_6 pile and the possibility of using the volatility of PuF_6 as a means of separating it from the potential light element impurity, beryllium:

Tuesday, May 25, 1943
Brown, Hill, and Bohlmann have tested the feasibility of the distillation method for isolating the plutonium formed in a UF_6 pile using three pounds of UF_6 bombarded for 150,000 microampere-hours with neutrons from the St. Louis cyclotron (sample F–6–12). They find that, even with these larger amounts, the UF_6 can be quantitatively distilled from its brass container tank leaving the plutonium that was recovered as a residue in the tank after the distillation. . . .
Rommel received the first defeat in his Tunisian drive. There is a report that Churchill has been suffering from pneumonia.

6

BURNING THE ROCKS
FORTY YEARS LATER

ALVIN M. WEINBERG

Phil Morrison could hardly contain his excitement as he showed me his calculations: If uranium was burned in a breeder, the energy released through fission exceeded the energy required to extract the residual 4 ppm of uranium from the granitic rocks. The breeder therefore represented an essentially inexhaustible source of energy! H. G. Wells' dream of a *World Set Free* (1914) through inexhaustible nuclear energy was in principle attainable!

The time was 1943; the place the wartime Metallurgical Laboratory in Chicago. Harrison Brown was then working in the laboratory's Chemistry Division on methods for separating plutonium from irradiated fuel; he soon moved to the Clinton Laboratories in Oak Ridge to serve as assistant director of the Chemistry Division there. He, as well as the other chemists at Clinton, were aware of the ultimate potential of the breeder, and after Brown moved to Caltech, he and L. T. Silver studied the chemistry of extracting residual uranium and thorium from granite.

Brown's study of the use of low-grade uranium ores was motivated by his speculations about the shape of man's future. In *The Next Hundred Years,* which he coauthored with James Bonner and John Weir (1957), one finds an asymptotic energy budget for a world of 2060 with 7×10^9 souls. I have reproduced this budget in Table 6.1.

Brown's total of 63 terawatt years per year (TWY/Y) would now be regarded as too high; at least the International Institute for Applied Systems Analysis (IIASA) Report, *Energy in a Finite World* (1981), suggests a total energy budget (for 2030 rather than 2060) that is less than half of Brown's 63 TWY/Y. Noteworthy was Brown's notion that two-thirds of the primary energy would be provided by nuclear reactors. If each reactor produced, let us say, 2,500 megawatts of heat and 1,000

Table 6.1
Projected Energy Input Pattern for Year 2060
(World Population 7×10^9)

Source	Terawatt-years of Heat/Yr (TWY/Y)
Solar energy (for 2/3 of space heating)	14
Hydroelectricity	3.8
Wood for lumber and paper	2.4
Wood for conversion to liquid fuels and chemicals	2.1
Liquid fuels and petrochemicals produced via nuclear energy	9
Nuclear electricity	32
Total	63.3

Source: After H. Brown, J. Bonner, and J. Weir, *The Next Hundred Years* (New York: Viking Press, 1957), p. 113.

megawatts of electricity, Brown's world would require some 17,000 such reactors—about forty times as many as are now in operation or under construction. Thus for him a very large source of uranium, such as was to be found in common granite, was a key to humanity's long-term well-being.

Brown and Silver reported their results at the first International Conference on the Peaceful Uses of Atomic Energy (1955), held in Geneva. Their main finding was that, of the 4 ppm of uranium and 10 ppm of thorium in granite, about 25 percent was surprisingly easy to leach with dilute acid. Thus the energy balance for extracting uranium from granite almost surely was favorable if the uranium was burned in a breeder in which 50 percent of the ^{238}U underwent fission. Moreover, uranium from common rock, even at Brown and Silver's estimated price of $550 to $1200 per kg (1955 dollars!) might be affordable if it was burned in a breeder. To quote Brown and Silver, "There is ample uranium and thorium in the igneous rocks of the earth's crust to power a highly industrialized world economy for a very long period of time."

How inexhaustible was this source of energy? In the crust, down to a depth of 1 mile, there is 2×10^{12} tons of uranium; in the seas, another 4×10^9 tons. Brown's 17,000 breeders, each burning about 2 tons of uranium per year, could be supplied with uranium from rocks

first instance, cost was of the essence; in the second, though cost was not unimportant, it need not dominate. As a practical matter, these two goals have had to be confounded. Though the goal of inexhaustible energy is as lofty as any technological goal, one could not give a convincing reason for pursuing this goal on a short schedule, unless the breeder—or the breeder in combination with nonbreeding burner reactors—could produce competitive power. Twenty years ago the breeders appeared capable of producing economic power. At that time the Oyster Creek LWR was built for about $120 per kWe. Were a breeder to cost 50 percent more than Oyster Creek—i.e., $180 per kWe, this difference could be made up if the fuel cycle cost for the breeder were a mere 2 mills per kWh cheaper than the fuel cycle cost for the burner. The price of raw uranium used in an LWR would have to increase by $60 per kg for the fuel cost in a no-recycle LWR to rise by 2 mills per kWh: the "compensation price of uranium"—i.e., the rise in price of uranium that would compensate for the difference in capital cost between breeders and LWRs—would be $60 per kg higher than the current price of about $60 per kg. At the time, breeders at $180 per kWe seemed like an entirely plausible goal, and the U.S. response to Canada's claim that breeders are not necessary was: "But electricity from a breeder should be cheaper than from an LWR. Breeders would be introduced naturally because they were a cheap way to make electricity; that they also provided a path to inexhaustible energy was secondary. In any event, power from breeders, unlike power from LWRs, is insensitive to the cost of uranium."

The escalation in capital costs of reactors has changed this calculus. Today, a large LWR costs, on average, about $2,000 per kWe. Were an LMFBR to cost 50 percent more than a LWR, that is, $3,000 per kWe, the compensation price of uranium would come to about $1400 per kg, a price we generally consider to be much higher than the cost of uranium from Chattanooga shale. Thus unless the capital cost of the breeder can be reduced—to perhaps 1.1 times the capital cost of an LWR—energy from breeders simply would not compete with energy from nonbreeding LWRs for a very long time. The original argument for *quick* deployment of the breeder has therefore been compromised by economic realities.

These arguments were raging in 1962 when the U.S. Atomic Energy Commission published its "Civilian Nuclear Power, A Report to the President," which set forth the nuclear energy strategy of the United States. Central to the strategy was a belief that electricity demand would continue to grow into the next century at its historical rate of 7 percent per year. By the year 2000, almost forty years from the time the report was issued, 734 GWe were expected to be nuclear, according to the

1967 sequel to the 1962 report. Were this projected demand to be supplied entirely by standard LWRs, by the turn of the century the U.S. domestic demand for uranium would amount to about 100,000 tons of uranium per year. Since the U.S reserve of low-cost uranium was around 2×10^6 tons, clearly reactors that used uranium more efficiently— either advanced converters or breeders—were necessary if nuclear energy was to survive for even twenty years without a steep rise in the price of fuel. The "Report to the President" recommended that both the uranium and the thorium breeder cycles be pursued: the first by means of fast neutron breeders, the second by means of slow neutron breeders. And though a slow neutron breeder, the Light Water Breeder Reactor (LWBR), was constructed and operated by Admiral Hyman Rickover, the preponderant technical sentiment throughout the world favored the LMFBR. This reactor, cooled by sodium, represented a technological thread quite distinct from that of the mainline LWR. Thus, even by the mid-1960s, it appeared that Wigner's uncertainty as to whether breeders would develop as outgrowths of nonbreeders, or as completely different devices, seemed to be settling in favor of the latter strategy.

Within the nuclear community skeptics remain who continue to espouse breeders other than the LMFBR. The group at Oak Ridge (to some degree influenced by Harrison Brown's interest in reactors fueled with uranium in fluid form), designed and built four small reactors in which a liquid fuel was used. In the two earlier reactors, uranyl sulfate was dissolved in water; in the later ones, a molten uranium fluoride salt that could also bear the fertile thorium was used. In such fluid fuel reactors the chemical reprocessing of bred ^{233}U is relatively simple, since the bred fuel is already in the liquid state. The developers of the High Temperature Gas Reactor (HTGR) have proposed a gas-cooled fast breeder. And, as the LWBR attests, ideas for breeders based on the technology of Light Water Reactors continue to command attention.

But the main line of breeder development is the sodium-cooled LMFBR. Altogether, about a dozen such reactors have been built or are under construction. The current breeders are listed in Table 6.2. Of these the most successful, at least in the West, has been the French Phenix. It has closed its fuel cycle and has demonstrated a substantial breeding gain. Moreover, the fuel elements can sustain almost 10 percent burn-up of the uranium–plutonium oxide mixture contained in them rather than the 2 or 3 percent regarded as the limit in the earlier breeders. This means that on average a plutonium atom need be recycled only two or three times before it is fissioned. The chemical recycle can therefore be more conveniently decoupled from the breeder than was believed to be necessary in the early breeders such as EBR-I, which required ten rather than two or three recycles per fissioned plutonium. Thus the

is proliferation-resistant. Nevertheless, one must concede that any re-processing plant, whether for breeder or LWR, can be misused; prevention of such misuse would require international agreements and inspection.

Can the economic incentives to reprocess centrally be made so strong and so evident that any attempt to build one's own reprocessing plant would prima facie be regarded with suspicion? Probably not, when only a few breeders are deployed, since the economy of scale for the needed reprocessing plant is then nonexistent. On the other hand, breeders will hardly be deployed at first except in the most advanced countries—the weapons states plus West Germany and Japan; and for them, the whole issue of proliferation is clearly a political one, not a technical one. And when many breeders have been deployed, economy of scale should be so clear that a small "legitimate" reprocessing plant simply could not be justified except on grounds other than economics: for example, desire for autarky, or broad considerations of national security. And, I suppose, additional incentives to reprocess fuel centrally can be imagined. Perhaps the most powerful would be an offer to handle wastes at the reprocessing site rather than returning the wastes to their country of origin, though the difficulties of such a proposal are manifest. The Soviet Union has imposed such a quid pro quo in handling spent fuel from Soviet-built reactors in foreign countries.

OTHER INEXHAUSTIBLE ENERGY SOURCES

In contemplating the breeder's future, we must address two possible contingencies: first, a future continuing to depend on large contributions from nuclear energy; in that case, we must assure the supply of nuclear fuel, either through breeders or other means; and secondly, a world that turns away from fission and depends eventually on other inexhaustible energy sources. As for the second contingency, the only inexhaustibles other than the breeder are solar and fusion. Solar continues to be expensive, and fusion's feasibility, either technically or economically, is anything but assured. Under the circumstances, rejection of the breeder on the grounds that these other options are known to be available seems to me to be unjustified, or even foolish.

On the other hand, at least four paths to almost inexhaustible nuclear energy must be considered more seriously today than they had been at the time the breeder was first proposed. These four are improved converter reactors; exploitation of low-grade ores, particularly seawater; fission-fusion hybrids; and accelerator breeders. I shall discuss each of these briefly.

Improved Converters. A 1,000 MWe LWR operating at 70 percent capacity factor uses 4,300 tons of uranium over its 30-year nominal

Table 6.3
Lifetime Net Energy Ratio for PWR,
1,000 MWe Plant,
75 Percent Plant Factor

Ore Grade (ppm)	Pu Recycle	Net Energy Ratio
1760 (conventional ore)	No	9.6
60 (Chattanooga shale)	No	3.4
60 (Chattanooga shale)	Yes	4.9

Source: R. M. Rotty, A. M. Perry, and D. B. Reister, "Net Energy from Nuclear Power," Federal Energy Administration, FES/B-76/702, May 1976.

lifetime. Improvements in utilization of fuel in LWRs range from 15 to 30 percent with relatively small rearrangements of the lattice to factors of almost 2 with full recycle and recovery of unused fuel at end of cycle. Thus reactors that use about 100 or even 75 tons of uranium per year rather than the 150 tons per year now used may well come into commercial operation. Each such improvement lengthens the time until the supply of uranium will give out. Such improvements are inevitable regardless of whether or not breeders are developed, and improved converters will surely pose formidable economic competition to breeders at least during the next 50 years or so. On the other hand, as the conversion ratio increases in a converter, so does the frequency of recycle. Whether W. Bennett Lewis' goal of a reactor that uses 50 tons or less of thorium and uranium per year can be built at a competitive price remains rather uncertain. And, of course, the advanced converter with recycle poses the same threat of proliferation as does the breeder.

Low-grade Ores. The usefulness of very low-grade ores in converter reactors depends not only upon the cost of extracting uranium but also upon the net energy that can be derived from these sources. Both Morrison's and Brown and Silver's original calculations of the energy required to extract uranium from granites were crude; since then there have been many studies of the net energy derived from burning uranium derived from low-grade ores. Perhaps the most exhaustive study was made by R. M. Rotty, A. M. Perry, and D. B. Reister at the Institute for Energy Analysis (1976). These authors found that the ratio of energy produced to energy required to extract and enrich the uranium and to construct the reactor was comfortably greater than 1, even for a standard Pressurized Water Reactor (PWR) fueled with uranium from Chattanooga shale. A few results are quoted in Table 6.3.

energy source that we know to be technically feasible, that requires practically no mining, and that can today produce unlimited amounts of electricity at a cost that is not more than twice the cost of electricity from coal or LWRs. In the bitter arguments that now swirl over whether or not to go ahead with serious development of the breeder, this reality seems to be forgotten: The breeder eliminates *uncertainty* about the supply of uranium in relation to the demand for electricity in the future.

Thus, as many of us said years ago, the breeder can confer a large measure of energy autarky on a country that can afford to use the breeder; and it is cheaper than solar electricity and avoids the profound technical uncertainties of fusion, the other two autarkic energy sources. For the United States, with its huge coal and uranium reserves, this may seem unimportant; but for France or Japan, each of which imports most of its energy, the prospect of energy autarky will always be attractive. That autarky extracts an economic penalty is perhaps not surprising. However, there is no law of nature that requires breeders always to be very expensive. Only by continued development—tedious and expensive though it may be—shall we be able to learn whether energy can be extracted economically from fully developed breeders.

There is another aspect of the breeder that has been insufficiently considered—namely, the possibility that a breeder, once built, will *never* be decommissioned. We have little understanding of what will limit the life of an LMFBR; indeed, there is probably little in such a plant that needs replacing and nothing that is not replaceable. Breeders (or for that matter, even LWRs) may turn out to be much like dams: Their lifetime is to be measured in centuries. Should this be the case, then one must recognize the possibility that the cost of energy in Harrison Brown's reactor-dominated future could be far lower than it is today! Even to suggest such an eventuality must invite heavy criticism from skeptics; yet I cannot ignore that EBR-II has now been operating for twenty-odd years, and there is *no* sign that it is wearing out.

During my forty-two years in nuclear energy, three events (other than the bomb) have stirred the strongest emotions in me: First, the achievement of the first chain reaction on December 2, 1942; second, my realization, when I wrote "Energy as an Ultimate Raw Material, or Problems of Burning the Sea and Burning the Rocks," (1959) of how enormous was the store of energy in the low-grade ores considered by Phil Morrison and Harrison Brown; and third, in 1982 as I stood in the control room of Phenix, my realization that a practical embodiment of inexhaustible nuclear energy was no longer a dream.

That the breeder is flawed because it is costly and may be proliferation-prone must be conceded, but that these flaws cannot be overcome by human ingenuity—this I can never concede. I remain confident that these deficiencies will yield to the imagination and courage of a new generation of nuclear technologists—a generation that surely will receive inspiration from Harrison Brown's magnificent vision of an asymptotic world that draws much of its energy from common rock!

NOTES

I am very grateful to my colleagues, H. G. MacPherson, A. M. Perry, I. Spiewak, and R. Rainey, for critically reviewing my manuscript.

1. Weapons-grade plutonium is easier to milk from the breeder; however, I regard this as secondary since bombs can be made from reactor-grade plutonium also.

REFERENCES

Brown, H., J. Bonner, and J. Weir, 1957, *The Next Hundred Years,* Viking Press, New York.

Brown, H., and L. T. Silver, 1955, "The Possibilities of Securing Long Range Supplies of Uranium, Thorium and Other Substances from Igneous Rocks," in *Proceedings of the International Conference on the Peaceful Uses of Atomic Energy,* Volume 8, pp. 129–132, Geneva, Switzerland.

Cohen, B. L., January 1983, "Breeder Reactors: A Renewable Energy Source," *American Journal of Physics* 51:75–76.

Daniels, F., 1964, *Direct Use of the Sun's Energy,* Ballantine Books, New York, p. 10. Professor Daniels refers here to a symposium on solar energy held at the University of Wisconsin in 1953 and supported by the National Science Foundation.

International Institute for Applied Systems Analysis, 1981, Wolf Haefele, program leader, *Energy in a Finite World: Paths to a Sustainable Future,* Ballinger Publishing Company, Cambridge, Massachusetts.

Lewis, W. B., January 15, 1963, "Breeders are Not Necessary—A Competing Other Way for Nuclear Power," Atomic Energy of Canada, DM-69, AECL 1686.

Rotty, R. M., A. M. Perry, and D. B. Reister, May 1976, "Net Energy from Nuclear Power," Federal Energy Administration, FES/B-76/702. Available from National Technical Information Service, Springfield, Virginia 22161.

U.S. Atomic Energy Commission, 1962, "Civilian Nuclear Power, A Report to the President."

Weinberg, A. M., November 1959, "Energy as an Ultimate Raw Material, or Problems of Burning the Sea and Burning the Rocks," *Physics Today* 12(11):18–25.

Wells, H. G., 1914, *The World Set Free: A Story of Mankind,* Dutton and Company, New York.

Wigner, E. P., 1967, "A Longer Range View of Nuclear Energy," reprinted in Wigner, *Symmetries and Reflections: Scientific Essays of Eugene Paul Wigner,* Indiana University Press, Bloomington.

Table 7.1
Distribution of GNP and Energy, 1982

Country Category	1982 GNP/pers (1982 US$)	Population (millions)	GNP (billion 1982 US$)	Average GNP/pers (1982 US$)	Avg Rate of Industrial Energy Use/pers (kilowatts)	Avg Rate of Traditional Energy Use/pers (kilowatts)	Total Rate of Industrial Energy Use (terawatts)	Total Rate of Traditional Energy Use (terawatts)
Very Poor	under $500	1,286	329	256	.18	.35	.23	.45
Poor	$500–999	1,529	883	578	.55	.30	.84	.46
Low-Intermediate	$1,000–1,999	247	377	1,526	1.01	.25	.25	.06
High-Intermediate	$2,000–3,999	370	884	2,389	1.67	.20	.62	.07
Rich	$2,000–7,999	490	2,935	5,990	5.33	.15	2.61	.07
Very Rich	over $8,000	670	7,935	11,843	7.38	.15	4.94	.10
Total or Average		4,592	13,343	2,906	2.04	.27	9.49	1.22

Sources: Compiled from World Bank, *World Development Report 1984* (New York: Oxford, 1984); *BP Statistical Review of World Energy 1983* (London: British Petroleum Co., 1984); U.S. Arms Control and Disarmament Agency, *World Military Expenditures and Arms Transfers 1972–82* (Washington, D.C.: Government Printing Office, April 1984). Figures for traditional energy use are author's estimates based on a variety of sources.

person, in 1982 U.S. dollars. Population, GNP, and use of industrial and traditional energy forms are tabulated for each category. The industrial energy forms consist mainly of oil, gas, coal, hydropower, and nuclear energy. The traditional energy forms are mainly fuelwood (including charcoal), crop wastes, and dung.

Although it is well known that comparisons based on gross national product tend to overstate the gap in material well-being between rich countries and poor countries (by as much as a factor of 2 to 3 at the extremes), even allowing for this correction does not change the impression conveyed by Table 7.1: There is a tremendous disparity in average material well-being between rich countries and poor ones, and this disparity is mirrored in patterns of energy use. The poor and low-intermediate countries have two-thirds of the world's people but only 12 percent of the GNP, and they account for only 14 percent of the world's annual use of industrial energy forms. The high-intermediate and rich countries, with one-third of the world's population, account for 88 percent of the GNP and 86 percent of the industrial energy use. When the use of traditional energy forms (necessarily very roughly estimated) is included, it is seen that the poor two-thirds of the world's population accounts for less than 22 percent of total energy use, industrial plus traditional.

Although a rough relation between energy use and GNP is evident when the data are highly aggregated—the ratio ranging from 0.7 to 0.8 watts of industrial energy use per dollar of GNP for the groupings shown in Table 7.1—one should not interpret this relation as an ironclad linkage. Tabulation of the ratio of energy to GNP for all countries reveals a variation of a factor of 3 to 4—a result of differences in energy-conversion and end-use efficiencies, mixes of energy-using activities, and, in some cases, noncomparability of GNP statistics. In individual countries, moreover, the ratio can vary substantially over time. (In the United States, for example, it fell by more than 20 percent between 1973 and 1983, after correction for inflation.)

Nor can it be assumed from the loose association between energy and GNP that measures to increase the supply of energy can, by themselves, increase economic prosperity (although one might have been led to think otherwise by some of the cornucopian "technology for development" literature of twenty years and more ago, or by certain energy-company magazine advertisements of today). There is no doubt that substantially increasing the material and economic well-being of the populations of the poor countries will entail increases in energy use there, but it will also require increases in the supply of many other resources and improvements in a wide variety of capabilities and services (organization, management, education, health care, agriculture) in which energy plays

them had counted on continuing increases in their oil revenues to pay for their increasing imports of manufactured goods and for ambitious domestic development programs. Mexico (not a member of OPEC but by 1981 the world's fourth biggest oil producer—behind the Soviet Union, the United States, and Saudi Arabia) became the prime example of an overextended oil producer plunged into deep financial difficulties by the recession and oil glut at the beginning of the 1980s.

The enormous increase, throughout the 1970s and into the 1980s, in the debt burden carried by the poor countries was eventually perceived as a threat to the international banking system. (Major defaults by Brazil and Mexico, which were feared, might have toppled some of the world's largest banks.) As it turned out, major disaster in the world banking system in the early 1980s was averted, but there has been no fundamental solution for the fragile financial condition of most of the poor countries and the correspondingly precarious position of their creditors. Significantly, private lending to oil-importing LDCs plummeted from US$30.8 billion in 1981 to $22 billion in 1982 and $11.1 billion in 1983.

The conventional prescription for extricating the poor countries from their economic predicament is rapid economic growth, wherein growth of exports provides the basis for reducing foreign debt, and growth of the internal economy provides for increased consumption as well as for private investment in productive capacity and public investment in infrastructure. How this growth is to be generated in practice is problematical, however. During most of the period of rapid industrial growth in what are now the rich countries, the "engine" of growth was fueled by energy that was cheap and getting cheaper; but it is precisely the absence of this key factor of cheap energy that has made the economic problems of the poor countries in the 1970s and 1980s so much more difficult.

Growth in the rich countries in this period (itself much slower than generally desired) has been sustained in substantial part by substituting technological innovation for cheap energy, but the reliance of this approach on a highly educated and skilled workforce makes it unavailable to most of the poor countries. The handful of newly industrializing countries (NICs)—for which Japan's performance in the 1960s and 1970s provided the prototype—have been succeeding by combining labor costs much lower than those of the rich countries with production technologies of intermediate to high sophistication. Whether this model can be made to work for a much larger number of LDCs—and, if so, how quickly— is highly uncertain.

The Rural Sector and the Fuelwood Crisis

More than 1.5 billion people live in countries where the use of traditional fuels (wood, crop residues, and dung) exceeds that of fossil fuels and hydropower. And for fully half of the world's households, the most fundamental human energy needs—cooking and water heating—are met by these traditional fuels. Dependence on the traditional fuels is heaviest in the rural sector where most of the people of the Third World still reside, but the urban centers of poor countries are also major consumers of fuelwood and charcoal from the surrounding countryside. These two fuels, fuelwood and charcoal derived from it, account for 60 to 70 percent of the global use of traditional fuels.

At the same time that the worldwide petroleum squeeze was capturing the attention of decision makers and publics in the industrial world—that is, in the mid-1970s—it was becoming apparent to analysts of the problems of the world's rural poor that the well-being of this sector was imperiled by the growing scarcity of fuelwood. This problem was generated by a combination of the direct pressure on fuelwood resources by rapid population growth in the poor countries, plus the loss of forests to commercial logging (much of it for export) and land-clearing for agriculture. The best estimates of the global rate of deforestation as of 1980, based on both satellite surveys and observations on the ground, clustered around 100,000 square kilometers per year, two-thirds of it in the moist tropics.

With fuelwood use in the rural parts of many poor countries averaging a cubic meter or more of wood per person per year, consumption was outpacing the sustainable forest yield in Burundi, El Salvador, Ethiopia, Haiti, Kenya, Pakistan, Rwanda, Sierra Leone, Swaziland, Tunisia, and Uganda by 1975, with Bangladesh, Ghana, Guinea, Lebanon, Nigeria, and Upper Volta (Burkina Fasso) expected to be added to the "fuelwood deficit" list by 1990. In a much larger number of countries with theoretically adequate fuelwood supplies, moreover, heavy harvesting in the vicinity of settlements has produced chronic local scarcity. In practical terms, these localized shortages of fuelwood mean punishing expenditures of time for the villagers who must cover large distances in the search for wood to meet their basic energy needs. For urban dwellers dependent on energy from charcoal, the problem translates into rising prices, eroding this fuel's historical economic advantage over kerosene. The last inexpensive fuel to which the poor could turn is being priced out of reach.

Poor People in Rich Countries—The Problem of Energy Costs

The industrial nations, rich on the average, display distributions of wealth and income that leave the poorest members of these societies seriously disadvantaged in absolute terms. In the industrial market economies as a whole, for example, the average income per person in the poorest one-fifth of the population is less than 30 percent of the average figure for these societies as a whole; in the United States, about one-tenth of all households have incomes of less than 25 percent of the

Table 7.2
A Century of Growth in Population and Energy, 1870–1970

Year	World Population (millions)	Population Increase in Previous 20 Years (millions)	World Use Rate of Industrial Energy Forms (terawatts)	Cumulative Energy Use in Previous 20 Years (TW-yr)	Cumulative Energy Use Since 1850 (TW-yr)
1870	1,300	170	0.2	3	3
1890	1,500	200	0.5	7	10
1910	1,700	200	1.1	15	25
1930	2,000	300	2.0	30	55
1950	2,500	500	2.9	45	100
1970	3,600	1,100	7.1	100	200

Sources: Donald J. Bogue, *Principles of Demography* (New York: Wiley, 1969); W. Haefele and W. Sassin, "The Global Energy System," *Annual Review of Energy,* vol. 2 (1977), pp. 1–30.

fossil fuels, petroleum and natural gas; exploitation of economies of scale in building larger and larger facilities for energy harvesting, processing, conversion, and transport; and continuous technological advances permitting reductions in the losses of useful energy in electricity generation and transmission.

The 1970s marked the time when these favorable developments were no longer frequent enough, pervasive enough, or powerful enough to continue to offset, worldwide, the combined effect of three countervailing factors: the cumulative depletion of the most accessible, concentrated, and readily harnessed energy resources; the sheer magnitude to which the world rate of use of industrial energy forms had grown; and the growing evidence (and perception) that the environmental impacts of energy supply that had been ignored at lower levels of use would have to be reduced at great expense. The enormous effect exerted on cumulative and instantaneous energy demand by a century of unprecedented population growth, coupled with equally remarkable growth in the per-person use of industrial energy forms, is shown in Table 7.2. The environmental aspect is taken up in the next section.

It is a common mistake to attribute the turning point of the 1970s to less fundamental factors, notably the success of the OPEC cartel in "artificially" boosting the price of oil far above its production cost from Middle East wells. In reality, however, OPEC was able to set the price where it did essentially *because* most of the rest of the world could no longer produce energy adequate to its needs, either from its own oil or from other sources, at costs below the OPEC price. The world was not yet running out of energy, but enough countries were running out of (or had never possessed) the accessible and inexpensive deposits of oil and gas on which much of the prosperity of industrial society had been built, and on which all of the industrial world remained hooked, to put OPEC in firm control.

In 1973, the year of the first OPEC price boost, the world depended on petroleum liquids for over 47 percent of its total supply of industrial energy forms. (About 95 percent of world population of petroleum liquids is crude petroleum, the remaining 5 percent being natural gas liquids separated from dry natural gas at processing plants.) About 55 percent of these petroleum liquids—or 26 percent of world supply of industrial energy forms—was supplied by OPEC. OPEC, moreover, controlled about 70 percent of the world's proven petroleum reserves.

Dependence on petroleum in general and OPEC oil in particular could not be reduced drastically overnight because of the long adjustment times built into several aspects of the world energy system. The consumption habits of firms and individuals are difficult to change quickly. Much of society's oil dependence is tied to the technical characteristics of its transport systems, industrial machinery, and residential and commercial buildings, to which only modest modifications can be made in the short term and for which complete turnover takes decades. Significant expansion of the supply of existing alternatives to oil takes years, and development of new alternatives requires huge investments of money as well as decades of time.

By 1983, however, a decade after the first major OPEC price boost and four years after the second one, a significant amount of adjustment had been possible. As shown in Table 7.3, world dependence on petroleum liquids had fallen to about 40 percent of the supply of industrial energy forms, and the OPEC contribution to petroleum-liquids supply had fallen from 54 percent to less than 33 percent. Thus the percentage contribution of OPEC to the world's supply of industrial energy forms was only half as great in 1983 as it had been a decade before.

This reduction in dependence on OPEC oil came about through a combination of factors. Total demand for industrial energy forms was diminished below what it otherwise would have been by the worldwide economic recessions that followed the price increases; by a gradual reduction—through increased efficiency of energy conversion and use—in the ratio of energy use to GNP; and by a modest degree of substitution of traditional for industrial energy forms in some applications (mainly increased use of fuelwood for residential heating). Demand for oil was reduced with the help of substantial increases in the production of every

Table 7.3
World Supply of Industrial Energy Forms, 1973–1983

| | 1973 | | 1983 | | Percentage Change in Energy Supplied |
	TW-yr	Percent of Total	TW-yr	Percent of Total	
Petroleum liquids	4.09	47.2	3.92	39.5	−4.2
OPEC	(2.20)	(25.4)	(1.27)	(12.8)	−42.3
Non-OPEC	(1.89)	(21.8)	(2.65)	(26.7)	+40.2
Coal	2.41	27.8	3.02	30.4	+25.3
Natural gas	1.63	18.8	1.99	20.0	+21.5
Hydropower	0.46	5.4	0.65	6.6	+41.3
Nuclear energy	0.07	0.8	0.35	3.5	+400.0
Total	8.66	100.0	9.93	100.0	+14.7

Source: BP Statistical Review of World Energy, 1983 (London: British Petroleum, 1984), converted by the author from lower to higher heating values of fuels.

other major industrial energy form, as shown in Table 7.3. And demand for OPEC oil was reduced by increases in oil production from non-OPEC sources, most notably Mexico and the North Sea fields owned by Norway and the United Kingdom.

This combination of reduced oil demand and increased non-OPEC supplies on the world market produced a downward trend, starting in 1981, in both the official (posted) prices and the spot-market prices for OPEC oil. Having ranged from US$32 to $40 per barrel in 1981, these prices had fallen to $26 to $28 per barrel by late 1984. That price drop represents a difference of some tens of billions of dollars in world oil expenditures (and revenues) annually, but it hardly constitutes a return to cheap energy. Oil at $25 (1984) per barrel is still four times as expensive *in real terms* (that is, corrected for inflation) as oil was in 1972.

There is little reason to think, moreover, that energy prices will fall a great deal further in the late 1980s. After dropping steadily for four years, world oil demand turned upward in 1984, and, barring another major recession, a gradual upward trend is expected to continue for some years. OPEC still controls two-thirds of the world's reserves of petroleum, and the major non-OPEC exporters—Mexico, Norway, and the United Kingdom—share OPEC's interest in maintaining oil prices as high as is consistent with maintaining oil's market share against nonoil alternatives. (The upturn in oil demand in 1984 suggests that this equilibration point is currently above US$25 per barrel.) Since 1981 when the real price of oil began its fall, the real price of coal has held constant and the prices of natural gas and electricity have continued to rise.

Prospects for sharply reduced energy costs in the longer term are also poor. Ultimately recoverable resources of coal worldwide are probably five to ten times those of petroleum and conventional natural gas combined, but there is no indication that this abundant coal can be converted into synfuels that can replace oil and gas at costs of less than US$40 per barrel of oil equivalent, and coal-fired electricity generation is becoming steadily more expensive as ever more elaborate environmental controls are deemed required (see below). Unconventional types of deposits of natural gas may contain a few times more energy than the conventional gas deposits—conceivably even as much energy as coal—but no way has been found to harvest these unconventional deposits inexpensively. Oil shale may be three to ten times more abundant even than coal, but it too has no prospect of being converted to the energy forms society needs for less than $40 to $50 per barrel of oil equivalent.

For the still more inexhaustible energy sources represented by sunlight, biomass, wind, ocean thermal energy, and the two long-term nuclear sources (fissioning of uranium and thorium in breeder reactors and fusion using oceanic resources of lithium and deuterium), the superabundance of the energy in its raw forms will not mean low energy costs for society. The reason is the high costs of building and operating the facilities to convert the raw energy into the final energy forms people use (for example, electricity and fluid fuels) and to distribute them when and where they are needed. It is the perverse nature of all the superabundant energy sources that the technologies needed to make them useful tend to be technologically complex, or materials intensive, or labor intensive, or some combination of these—all of which translate into high costs.

Of course, no one can be absolutely certain that some unforeseeable breakthrough will not someday restore an era of cheap energy. (I define "cheap" to mean that less than 10 percent of GNP—or, in nonmarket economies, human productive effort—suffices to provide for energy supply, as was the case in the United States in the 1960s.) Given all the evidence available today, however, the odds are so strongly against such a development that prudent individuals, firms, and governments must now base their planning on energy that is permanently expensive.

ENERGY AND ENVIRONMENT

That the costs of providing energy to human society have risen is due in part, as argued above, to the substantial depletion of the "natural subsidies" represented by the most concentrated, accessible, and easily harnessed deposits of fossil fuels, which naturally tended to be the first to be exploited. Even for renewable energy forms, there comes a point when increases in demand produce increases in unit costs—that is, when economies based on technological improvements can no longer compensate for the consequences of having to resort to sites of lower resource quality or convenience: less attractive dam sites for hydropower, poorer soils or more remote locations for growing fuelwood, and so on.

At least as important as contributors to rising energy costs as these forms of depletion of the energy resources themselves, however, have been the environmental problems associated with energy supply. The capacity of the biogeophysical environment to absorb without intolerable consequences the effluents and other impacts of energy-supply technologies is itself a finite resource, and this finitude manifests itself in two types of environmental costs. "External" environmental costs are those imposed by environmental disruptions on various segments of society but not reflected in the monetary balance sheets of the sellers and buyers of the energy. "Internalized" environmental costs are increases in the monetary costs of supplying energy imposed by measures aimed at reducing the external costs.

Why Environmental Costs Have Been Rising

Both these kinds of environmental costs of energy supply have been rising, not merely in the aggregate but—for many energy technologies, at least—on a per-gigajoule basis. There are several reasons.

First, all else being equal, the declining quality of the remaining unexploited fossil-fuel deposits and renewable-energy sites means higher environmental impact per unit of energy delivered. The result is higher external environmental costs, or higher internalized environmental costs to avoid the external ones, or a combination of more moderate increases in both.

Second, environmental systems capable of absorbing moderate amounts of effluents or other insults without serious consequences can become saturated as the combination of growth in total energy use and resort to lower quality deposits and sites multiplies these burdens. In practical terms, such saturation means that additional insults generate disproportionate damages—the familiar "threshold" effect. (Perhaps the most prominent current example is the devastation of freshwater lakes in Europe, Canada, and the United States following the cumulative consumption of their buffering capacity by years of acid precipitation.) Again, the result is increases in some combination of external and internal costs.

Third, as higher levels of energy use, lower quality of raw resources, and greater sensitivity of an already stressed environment to increments of pollution combine to necessitate a higher degree of pollution control simply to stay even, the rising marginal costs of each additional percentage point of pollutant removal begin to force the internalized environmental costs up sharply. One sees this phenomenon reflected in the acrimonious debate between regulators and electric power companies over what degree of control over emissions of oxides of sulfur and nitrogen is to be required.

Fourth, increased scientific understanding of environmental processes, their relevance to human well-being, and their vulnerability to disruption by the technologies of energy supply has usually (although not always) led to increased concern about the magnitude of the hazards as time goes on. Coupled with industrial-society publics sensitized to environmental concerns by events of the last few decades, and the concomitant emergence of highly effective environmental lobbies, this trend has produced greatly increased pressures to internalize environmental costs. (Internalization may make society better off by reducing the external costs by more than the amount that the internal ones increase; certainly that is the idea. But since the external costs are dispersed and often unquantifiable while the internal ones are concentrated and monetized, internalization gives the appearance of making energy costlier. And, of course, if the process is carried too far, big internal costs can be generated in the attempt to reduce small external ones.)

Finally, the time needed to site and construct energy facilities has been increased substantially by the web of regulations and permitting procedures that has emerged from intensified concern with environmental impacts of energy technologies and by the associated debates about who is to bear the external and internal environmental costs. The direct result of this phenomenon is an increase in the overall costs of energy projects, due to a combination of increased interest on investment during the construction period, increased cost escalation during construction, increased administrative complexity associated with the maze of permits and regulations, and greater frequency of expensive mid-project changes in design and specifications.

It is impossible to quantify exactly the total contribution of all these environment-related factors to the increase in the monetary costs of energy supplies over the past decade and a half, in part because factors not related to environment are sometimes intertwined with the environmental ones. (Most important, the stretch-out in construction times of many kinds of energy facilities has been partly due to such factors as pursuit of economies of scale into a range of facility sizes beyond previous experience, shortages of particular types of skilled labor, and mismanagement by energy companies and construction firms.) Nevertheless, it seems likely that the environmental factors have been responsible for between 20 and 60 percent of the real increases in monetary energy costs in industrial nations since the beginning of the 1970s, with figures at the lower end of this range probably applying to gasoline and natural gas and figures at the higher end to electricity generation with coal and nuclear power.

The Nature and Magnitude of the External Environmental Damages

If internalized environmental costs of energy supply are so significant, can one at least postulate that the process of internalization has succeeded in reducing to modest levels the environmental costs that remain external? (A reasonable definition of "modest" in this connection might be that the burden on human well-being represented by the external environmental costs is less than 10 percent of that imposed by the total monetary costs—or human labor equivalent—of energy supply.) Quantification in the domain of external costs is far more difficult than for internal ones even in principle, and the uncertainties in practice range from large to enormous; nor is monetization for comparison with internal costs always possible, even when quantification in nonmonetary terms has been achieved. Nevertheless, available information—plus a willingness to suppose that the resolution of present uncertainties sometimes will reveal the hazards to be high—suggests that the answer is "no": It cannot be supposed that the external environmental costs of energy supply are modest.

Of course, the magnitude of these environmental damages is not uniform across types of energy technologies or classes of environmental harm. It is useful to distinguish, in particular, among the following categories:

A. Classes of Environmental Harm
   1. Occupational illnesses and injuries in energy-supply industries.
   2. Public illnesses and injuries directly attributable to effluents and accidents associated with energy supply.
   3. Damage to economic goods and services directly attributable to such effluents and accidents.
   4. Damage to human health, safety, and other aspects of well-being as a result of energy-associated disruption of ecological and climatological conditions and processes.
B. Types of Energy Technologies
   1. Traditional renewables (collecting and burning biomass, charcoal production, animate energy).
   2. Industrial renewables (hydropower, high-technology biomass farming and processing, solar collectors, wind turbines).

140

Table 7.4
Some Environmental Liabilities of Energy Options

Fossil Fuels

Air pollution in the form of oxides of sulfur, oxides of nitrogen, photochemical oxidants, and particulate matter can cause and/or aggravate disease.

Water pollution from coal mines, oil refineries, drilling platforms, tanker accidents, and synfuels plants can damage wildlife, recreation, and commercial fisheries and contaminate domestic water supplies.

Acid rain can damage plants, kill fish, accelerate leaching of nutrients, mobilize toxic metals, alter microbial populations and activity.

Carbon dioxide from combustion, accumulating in atmosphere, can alter climate.

Accidents can injure workers in coal mines, drilling platforms, and oil refineries; members of the public in collisions with coal trains and trucks; and public and workers in gas explosions.

Biomass

Deforestation from overharvesting fuelwood accelerates erosion, increases flooding, reduces productivity.

Soil depletion from removal of crop and forest residues reduces fertility and water-holding capacity.

Air pollution from biomass combustion is especially severe from indoor cookstoves in Third World and from heating with wood under winter inversions.

Water pollution from synfuels plants and pesticide and fertilizer runoff from biomass plantations has effects as listed under fossil fuels.

Accidents injure workers in harvesting and the public in biomass transport; woodstoves cause building fires.

Hydropower

Lake filling destroys river ecosystems and fertile bottom land; dams block anadromous fish and alter downstream ecological conditions.

Dam collapse through miscalculation, earthquake, or sabotage can kill thousands.

Nuclear Fission

Sabotage and accidents at reactors, reprocessing plants, and waste repositories and in waste transport can release large quantities of radioactivity.

Routine emissions and exposures affect uranium miners, workers at reactors, reprocessing plants, and fuel-fabrication plants, and members of the public.

Geothermal Energy

Water pollution by dissolved salts and toxic elements in geothermal water can affect streams, lakes, domestic water supplies.

Hydrogen sulfide gas is a toxic and odiferous air pollutant itself and oxidizes in the atmosphere to SO_2.

Solar Space-heating and Water Heating

Falls from roofs during collector installation/maintenance cause injuries.

Leaks of collector fluids can damage buildings and contaminate building water supply.

Wind

Accident possibilities include toppling towers, flying blades, and falls during construction and maintenance.

Aesthetic intrusion on scenic mountain ridges, passes, and coastlines is feared by some.

Photovoltaics

Toxic substances used in cell manufacture are occupational hazards, can contaminate water in manufacturing areas, and can be released from overheated or burning cells.

Ocean Thermal Energy Conversion

Marine ecosystem disruption can occur through altered temperatures and currents, leaks of working fluids, use of antifouling chemicals, entrainment of organisms.

Worker hazards on floating plants may be severe.

Nuclear Fusion

Tritium delivers radiation doses to workers and, through inevitable leaks and possible accidents, to members of the public.

Neutrons render reactor components radioactive, thus adding to routine exposures and accident hazard to public as well as requiring management of discarded components as radioactive wastes.

Increased Efficiency of Energy Use

Indoor air pollution can be caused by chemicals in insulation or aggravated by reduced ventilation rates (increasing concentrations of radon, NO_x, CO, tobacco smoke).

Decreased passenger safety results from reduced vehicle weight (all else equal).

3. Fossil fuels (coal, conventional and heavy oils, natural gas, oil shales).
4. Nuclear energy (conventional fission, fission breeder, fusion).

More complete taxonomies are provided in the references on environmental assessment in the bibliography. It becomes clear from any systematic inquiry along these lines that *no* class of energy technologies is free of potentially significant external costs—some of the possibilities are listed in Table 7.4—and that comparative assessment of the relative magnitudes of these risks and damages is difficult both conceptually and analytically. In what follows, attention is confined to a subset of particularly important and much-studied impacts.

Occupational and Public Health and Safety

Occupational injuries and illnesses in energy-supply industries in industrial nations amount to 5 to 50 deaths per exajoule of energy delivered to the final consumer (1 EJ $\cong$ 1 quadrillion Btu $\cong$ 1/30 TW-yr) and 10,000 to 150,000 additional lost workdays per exajoule, the ranges being remarkably similar across the spectrum of energy technologies. If one suppresses one's natural uneasiness about monetizing human life for long enough to multiply by figures of US$500,000 per life and $100 per lost day (loosely defensible in terms of lost economic output in industrial nations, and consistent with figures arrived at by various other approaches to this thorny question), one obtains a monetary index of $4 to $40 million per delivered exajoule for this category of harm. Since the monetary cost of a delivered exajoule of energy in industrial nations falls generally in the range of $1 to $10 billion, this index is of the order of 0.1 to 2 percent of the "internal" cost of the energy. Part of this particular environmental cost of energy supply *is* in fact internalized through wage premiums for unusually hazardous occupations, company-paid insurance and sick leave, and so on.

Direct damage to public health and safety is more difficult to quantify (not to mention monetize) convincingly. Concerning premature deaths from fossil-fuel produced air pollution, for example, the two most widely quoted assessments differ drastically. Work done in the mid-1970s at the Biomedical and Environmental Assessment Division of the Brookhaven National Laboratory yielded an estimate of 3.7 premature deaths per year per 100,000 people exposed to an average annual increment of 1 microgram of sulfate per cubic meter of air, with a 90-percent confidence interval extending from 0 to 11 and a loss of life expectancy of 5 to 15 years per death; for typical new coal plants meeting U.S. emissions standards at typical U.S. sites, these figures translate into a "best estimate" of 900 premature deaths per exajoule of electricity (90-percent confidence interval 0 to 2,800, excluding variations in sites and emissions per ton of coal), with 10 years of lost life expectancy per death. But using instead the dose-response relation put forward in a 1975 National Academy of Sciences study of this question (which reviewed and rejected the Brookhaven arguments) yields, for otherwise identical assumptions, a "best estimate" of 50 premature deaths per exajoule of coal-generated electricity (90-percent confidence interval 5 to 100), with 0.1 year of lost life expectancy per death. (Brookhaven assumed that sulfate is a contributing *cause* of cardiovascular and respiratory disease, but the academy found the data in support of this view unpersuasive and assumed that sulfate only aggravates preexisting disease, killing—in air-pollution episodes—people already near death.) Estimates of public deaths from forms of air pollution other than the sulfate-particulate complex are even cruder, but all fall well below the Brookhaven sulfate figures. Nonfatal illnesses, expressed in person-years lost to productive activity, might add between a few hundred and a few thousand person-years to these damage estimates.

Assessing the expected damage to public health from nuclear electricity generation also reveals a huge range of possibilities. Fatal cancers from routine exposures to radiation from nuclear-power facilities probably amount to 2 to 20 per exajoule of electricity if attention is confined to the generation alive when the electricity is generated. Long-lived effluents from reactors and reprocessing plants, mainly carbon-14, may produce additional cancer deaths in future generations amounting to 2 to 70 per exajoule. And if there is no low-dose-rate threshold below which no cancers occur, the ultimate burden of cancer deaths from emissions from improperly shielded uranium-mill tailings could reach 200 to 30,000 per exajoule (spread over a period of several hundred thousand years following the milling of the uranium). Use of breeder reactors instead of today's uranium-inefficient "burner" reactors could reduce the cancer burden from tailings 30- to 100-fold, but might increase other contributions to radiation doses. Because of large residual uncertainties in the probabilities of reactor accidents and the doses to be expected when they occur, moreover, a fair characterization of the uncertainty range governing expected cancer deaths from such accidents spans about five orders of magnitude, from 0.2 to 1,000 deaths per exajoule. Consideration of serious genetic illnesses produces "best estimates" about equal to those for cancer, with similarly large uncerainty ranges. Average lost life expectancy in the cases of cancer and serious genetic diseases is on the order of 10 years per death.

Both for coal-fired and nuclear electricity generation, then, lost life expectancy from direct damage to members of the public by routine emissions and accidents may amount to a figure ranging from a few tens of person-years to tens of thousands of person-years per exajoule of output. Productive activity lost to nonfatal illnesses associated with these effluents may amount to hundreds or thousands of additional person-years. At the lower ends of these ranges, rough monetization at US$25,000 to $50,000 per person-year suggests that the damages are very small compared to the internal costs of electricity (of the order of a few tenths of a percent or less). At the upper end of the ranges, however, the damages are on the order of 10 percent or more of the internal costs of the electricity.

Two important messages emerge from this exercise. First, one cannot conclude with any confidence either that the direct damages to public health from coal-fired and nuclear electricity generation are very large or that they are very small. Second, the enormous and essentially wholly overlapping uncertainty ranges governing the expectation values of the direct public-health damages from the two energy sources mean that there is little basis for preferring one over the other on these grounds.

While most analysts of energy-supply hazards have been debating the impacts of industrial energy sources like coal and nuclear energy, an extraordinary public-health menace at the "low technology" end of the energy spectrum has gone almost unnoticed: namely, indoor air pollution from wood fires used for cooking and water heating in developing countries. Recent work by Kirk Smith and others has indicated that the women cooking in Third World village huts experience an integrated exposure to respirable suspended particulate matter—the product of population, exposure time, and average pollutant concentration (measured in person-year-micrograms per cubic meter)—approximately equal to that represented by the exposure of the urban population of the entire world to respirable suspended particulates from all sources. (The figure is some 200 billion person-yr-ug/m³ in each case, distributed over 1.6 billion urban dwellers in the one instance and over 400 million Third World village cooks in the other.) Moreover, the integrated exposure of the village cooks to benzo(a)pyrene, a particularly carcinogenic component of wood smoke, and other hydrocarbon effluents appears to be two to three times that of all the world's city dwellers.

Although the public-health statistics available for rural LDCs are inadequate to sort out the consequences of this exposure (and of that of children and other family members besides the cook exposed to the indoor smoke), a figure in the range of 100,000 premature deaths per exajoule of wood energy is not implausible. Using rich-country accounting (US$500,000 per death, $5 billion per exajoule), this figure would represent an external environmental cost ten times the monetary value of the energy. If one instead compares 100,000 deaths at 20 years of lost life expectancy per death, giving 2 million person-years lost per exajoule, with the productive time invested in collecting the fuelwood (1/4 person-workday per day per household makes 5 million person-years per exajoule), the excess deaths represent an external cost 40 percent as large as the internal cost of the fuelwood. Even given that these are extremely crude estimates, it is apparent that the external public-health costs of Third World fuelwood use could be shockingly high by any measure.

Disruption of Climate and Ecosystems

Many types of energy technologies can affect climate on a local to regional scale: deforestation for fuelwood alters evapotranspiration (hence atmospheric moisture) and the energy balance at Earth's surface; atmospheric moisture is also affected locally by hydroelectric reservoirs and power-plant cooling towers; patches of airborne particulate matter from burning biomass and fossil fuels can cool or heat the underlying surface, depending on circumstances, and can seed rainfall; and large-scale energy conversion in urban regions produces local "heat islands."

The only energy-related phenomenon that seems capable of affecting climate on a global scale within a time frame of decades, however, is the accumulation of carbon dioxide in the atmosphere, apparently mostly from fossil-fuel combustion but also with some possible contribution from net deforestation. The basic facts about this syndrome can be summarized very briefly. The atmosphere's inventory of carbon dioxide has increased from about 2,200 gigatons of CO_2 (600 gigatons of C) in the middle of the last century to about 2,700 gigatons in 1985 (735 gigatons of C), an increase of about 20 percent. Fossil-fuel combustion worldwide is adding about 25 gigatons of CO_2 per year to the atmosphere, and the net increase in the atmospheric inventory is about 13 gigatons per year. Whether the biosphere is a net source or sink for atmospheric CO_2 is in dispute; dissolution of CO_2 in the ocean is the sink that accounts for the difference between the net contributions of fossil-fuel burning and the biosphere and what remains in the atmosphere.

Assuming that the net biospheric contribution is small and that the ocean continues to absorb half the CO_2 produced by burning fossil fuels, the atmospheric CO_2 burden will reach twice its preindustrial level by the year 2050 if fossil-fuel use grows at a steady 2 percent per year after 1985, by 2040 if the growth is 3 percent per year, and by 2030 if the growth is 4 percent per year. The most realistic available computer models of climate, supported by analyses of paleoclimatological data, indicate that a doubling of preindustrial CO_2 levels would produce an increase of 2°C to 3°C in the mean (space-averaged and time-averaged) global surface temperature. This increase would not be uniformly distributed: The change would be smaller near the equator and about four times larger near the poles. Such a change would alter significantly the present global and regional patterns of atmospheric circulation, precipitation, and evaporation. Some regions would become drier, others wetter. Because of the way precipitation and evaporation interact to govern runoff, river flows in some regions may change by much larger relative amounts than does precipitation itself.

The impact of such alterations on world food production could be either positive or negative in the long run; even if positive overall, however, some countries would be "losers" while others would be "winners." The short-run impact on world agriculture almost certainly will be negative—possibly drastically so—if a significant change in circulation patterns takes place more rapidly than farming practices can adapt to the new conditions. Such rapid change is possible, even though the CO_2 build-up has been gradual, because the atmosphere's response to imposed changes is known to be highly nonlinear: that is, for example, it is possible that a 30-percent increase in preindustrial CO_2 levels would produce little change in circulation patterns while a 35-percent increase would produce a drastic change. Over the longer term, rising sea level due to melting of the Greenland and Antarctic ice sheets could force expensive resettlement away from lowlands. A catastrophically rapid sea-level rise of about 5 meters is conceivable if the massive West Antarctic ice sheet is "launched" by melting at the points where it is anchored to the continent, but this mechanism is considered unlikely at present.

The uncertainties notwithstanding, it is difficult to argue that the potential consequences of a doubling of atmospheric carbon dioxide represent only a modest external cost of the use of fossil fuels. What the outcome will be no one can say for certain, but the risk is enormous. In any case, there is no simple remedy: Capturing and storing 1.5 to 3 tons of CO_2 for every ton of fossil fuel burned is out of the question, and restricting and reducing civilization's consumption of its most convenient and versatile fuels, which in the mid-1980s still supply 80 percent of the total of industrial and traditional energy forms combined, is a long-term proposition at best.

Beyond the potential for effects on climate, the most pervasive and complex ecological consequences of the use of fossil fuels almost certainly are those associated with acid precipitation. Natural rain and snow are characterized by pH in the range of 5.6, owing to the dissolution of carbon dioxide in atmospheric water to form weak carbonic acid. Over substantial areas of North America, East Asia, and Europe extending into the Soviet Union, however, typical pH figures for rain and snow are in the range of 4 to 4.5. The total land area receiving precipitation of this or greater acidity is probably several million square kilometers. Values of pH below 3 are not unusual in individual storms, and acidity records have been set by Los Angeles fogs with pH around 1.7. The primary culprits in this widespread acidification are atmospheric burdens of oxides of sulfur and nitrogen (SOx and NOx), which react in concert with an array of other atmospheric constituents to form strong sulfuric and nitric acids.

On a global basis, natural sources of SOx and NOx in the atmosphere equal or modestly exceed the human inputs of these compounds, which are dominated by the combustion of fossil fuels. Over large areas of the most industrialized parts of the planet, however, the regional anthropogenic emissions dominate the natural sources, and it is in these regions and for a thousand or so kilometers downwind from them that fossil-fuel–derived acid precipitation can be a major problem.

Three kinds of phenomena associated with acid precipitation account for much of its potential to do ecological harm. First, contact effects as the acid precipitation strikes the leaves of plants can damage their protective covering and thereby impair the plants' functioning and resistance to other agents. Second, direct effects of acidic water on organisms in the soil (including crucial nitrogen-fixing bacteria and other microorganisms) and in lakes and streams (from bacteria and algae to trout and salmon) can affect species composition and ecosystem function to the disadvantage of humans. Third, acidification of soil and surface water can accelerate the leaching of nutrients out of the root zone and increase the rates at which toxic elements (such as cadmium and aluminum) are mobilized from soil components and sediments.

For all but the effects produced by contact with the precipitation as it falls, vulnerability to acid precipitation depends strongly on the buffering capacity in the soil and water of the ecosystem receiving the precipitation. (Buffering capacity resists imposed pH changes by gobbling up the added hydrogen ions; the most important form of buffering capacity in most ecosystems is carbonate alkalinity, wherein hydrogen ions combine with carbonate ions to form bicarbonate and with bicarbonate to form CO_2 and water.) Only when the addition of hydrogen ions exceeds the available buffering capacity does the pH of soil water and of lakes and streams fall significantly. Buffering capacity is replenishable by natural processes at rates that vary widely among different types of ecosystems. In poorly buffered ecosystems, the replenishment rates are slow; these are the ecosystems that suffer drastic alterations from falling pH once the cumulative effects of years of acid precipitation have depleted the stock of buffers.

The most visible and attention-grabbing ecological consequence of acid precipitation so far has been the eradication of trout and salmon from thousands of lakes and streams in Scandinavia, Canada, and the northeastern United States. The granitic soils in these regions are very poorly buffered. Of even greater concern are the symptoms of distress now becoming apparent in forests over large areas of Europe and, to a lesser extent, in North America. In the case of the forests, effects of acid precipitation may be interacting with effects caused directly by air pollution, most probably having to do with ozone and other oxidants produced photochemically in reactions involving NOx and reactive hydrocarbon compounds. The details of what is damaging the forests remain to be completely sorted out, but the dimensions of the problem already have reached crisis proportions in Europe and may soon do so elsewhere.

As with CO_2-induced climate change, it is far from clear that the effects of acid precipitation will prove to be modest external costs when compared with the internal costs and presumed economic benefits of the energy supply generating the problems. Indeed, carbon dioxide and acid precipitation are particularly compelling examples of situations where the external costs of energy supply are not only significant compared to internal costs but also represent significant human perturbations as measured against the *absolute* yardstick of natural processes on a continental to global scale. They remind us that civilization has become a global geophysical and ecological force and that the technologies of energy supply are key contributors to this fundamental and unsettling phenomenon.

Table 7.5 provides more comprehensive evidence on the size of energy-related environmental disruptions compared to those generated by other human activities and compared to the relevant natural yardsticks on a global scale. Although many of the figures shown in this table are uncertain by as much as a factor of two up or down, it is nonetheless clear that traditional and industrial technologies of energy supply are close competitors with agriculture as the sources of the most impressive human interventions in environmental conditions and processes. Of course, such figures do not say much in themselves about the magnitude of the actual damages to human well-being that may result from such interventions, but they make plain that human activities in general and energy supply in particular are capable of affecting on a global scale the most fundamental biogeochemical variables governing the hospitability of the planet.

ENERGY AND INTERNATIONAL CONFLICT

The political, social, and environmental problem that dominates all others in its potential for damage to human well-being in the decades immediately ahead is thermonuclear war. The chances of avoiding such a war depend on progress in coping with a number of pernicious factors, including ideological conflicts, religious hatreds, territorial disputes, and destabilizing developments in armaments. Many of these factors have little or no direct connection with energy—that is, with how nations and regions choose to meet their energy needs. But there *are* links between energy and the prospects for war or peace—between energy and the roots of war, between energy and the proximate causes of war, and between energy and the tools of war. There are also ways in which the characteristics of a country's energy system (notably the degree of self-sufficiency, decentralization, redundancy, resilience of individual components, and back-up supplies) influence that country's vulnerability to military attack. The paragraphs that follow, however, focus only on the first set of linkages: the ways the energy situation affects the likelihood of international conflict and the chances that such a conflict will escalate toward thermonuclear war.

Energy and the Roots of War

The rich-poor gap in energy mirrors and helps to maintain the gulf between rich countries and poor countries in nearly every measure of human well-being. Although, as emphasized above, the supply of energy itself should not be mistaken for an index of well-being, the poor countries cannot climb up from poverty without some amelioration of their energy woes. This amelioration is not a *sufficient* condition to eradicate the poverty that plagues two-thirds of the human race, but it is a necessary one. Without it, the rich-poor gap will endure—a continuing source of frustration, despair, and, inevitably, social and political instability.

That the frustration and resentment of the disadvantaged is one of the roots of war can hardly be doubted. The most obvious connection is the historical one: Regions of social and political instability have long proven irresistible targets of military intervention both by neighboring countries and by the superpowers. Those interventions where superpower interests collide are sure to increase East-West tensions, and almost any one of them could, with bad luck, produce a miscalculation leading to confrontation and war.

Until relatively recently, the second connection—the idea that the frustrated poor could themselves make war on the rich—was not taken seriously. But terrorist acts of increasing sophistication and audacity have begun to make plain the vulnerability of industrial society to attacks against which military might is no defense at all. Readers can spin out for themselves some of the scenarios by which concerted escalation of terrorist assaults (perhaps funded by governments and perhaps employing nuclear bombs) could lead to open war.

Even direct attacks on rich-country interests by poor countries made reckless by their internal woes, and possibly seeking to distract their

Table 7.5
Indices of Global Environmental Disruption and Energy's Contributions

Index	Natural Baseline	Measure of Distruption by			
		Agriculture	Traditional Energy Supply	Industrial Energy Supply	Other Activity
Land use, in square km	135,000,000 global ice-free land	15,000,000 cultivated land (2/3 harvested each year)	5,000,000 forest land to supply 1980 fuel-wood sustainably	150,000 occupied by energy facilities (2/3 hy-dropower)	1,500,000 occupied by towns, transport systems
Water use, consumed or polluted, in cubic km	50,000 total runoff (2/3 unusable in floods)	2,000 irrigation	unquanti-fied ef-fects of deforesta-tion	800 process water, cooling, and evap-oration from hydro	500 all other in-dustrial & domestic supply
Net CO_2 added to atmosphere, in gigatons of carbon	700 atmospheric C in CO_2	0–1/year net forest clearing for agriculture	0–0.2/year net defor-estation for fuel-wood	6/year fossil-fuel combustion	0–1/year net defor-estation for lumber, ur-banization
Nitrogen fixation in NH_4, NO_x, in megatons of nitrogen	200/year biological fix-ation	60/year in-dustrial fertilizers 1/yr agric. burning	1/yr tradi-tional fuels com-bustion	30/year fossil-fuel combustion	1/yr non-energy in-dustrial processes
Sulfur emissions to atmos. as SO_x, H_2S, in megatons of sulfur	100/year from decay (60%) and sea spray (40%)	0.8/yr ag-ricultural burning	0.3/yr tra-ditional fuels com-bustion	60/yr fos-sil-fuel combustion	10/yr smelting and other processes
Hydrocar-bon emis-sions (reactive) to atmos., in mega-tons	800/yr mostly from vege-tation	30/yr agri-cultural burning	4/yr tradi-tional fuels com-bustion	30/yr, 90% fos-sil-fuel combus-tion, 10% oil refin-ing	20/yr non-energy in-dustrial processes

Particulate emissions to atmos., in megatons	500/yr, 60% sea salt, 20% volcanoes, 20% dust, 1% forest fires	30/yr agricultural burning, 10/yr wheat handling	15/yr traditional fuels combustion	40/yr fossil-fuel combustion	50/yr, 80% non-energy industrial processes, 20% other
Oil added to oceans, in megatons	0.5/yr natural seeps	negligible	negligible	3/yr from tankers, drilling platforms, coastal energy facilities	2/yr lube-oil disposal, other oil waste via rivers, etc.
Mercury mobilization, in kilotons	25/yr outgassing	0.3/yr biocides, 0.4/yr agric. burning	0.2/yr traditional fuels combustion	3/yr from oil and coal burning	13/yr of which 70% mined as Hg & 30% mobilized as byproduct
Lead emissions to atmos., in kilotons	25/yr mostly volcanic and windblown dust	0.4/yr agricultural burning	0.2/yr traditional fuels combustion	230/yr fossil-fuels combustion (90% gasoline additives)	100/yr metals production
Radiation exposure to humans, in million person-rem	800/yr natural background (300 from whole-body equivalent of radon lung dose)	unquantified extra radon release from tilling soil	negligible	1/yr 50% nuclear power, 50% from U in coal	150/yr 93% medical X rays, 7% fallout

Sources: Paul R. Ehrlich, Anne H. Ehrlich, and John P. Holdren, *Ecoscience* (San Francisco: W. H. Freeman, 1977); U.S. Council on Environmental Quality, *The Global 2000 Report* (Washington, D.C.: Government Printing Office, 1980); Committee on the Atmosphere and the Biosphere, National Research Council, *Atmosphere-Biosphere Interactions* (Washington, D.C.: National Academy Press, 1981); Wolfgang Seiler and Paul J. Crutzen, "Estimates of Gross and Net Fluxes of Carbon Between the Biosphere and the Atmosphere from Biomass Burning," *Climatic Change* 2 (1980), pp. 207–247; Committee on the Biological Effects of Ionizing Radiation, National Research Council, *The Effects on Populations of Exposure to Low Levels of Ionizing Radiation: 1980* (Washington, D.C.: National Academy Press); Study of Critical Environmental Problems (SCEP), *Man's Impact on the Global Environment* (Cambridge, Mass.: MIT Press, 1970); Committee on Lead in the Human Environment, National Research Council, *Lead in the Human Environment* (Washington, D.C.: National Academy Press, 1980); and calculations by the author.

populaces from domestic difficulties by focusing attention on an external adversary, cannot be ruled out entirely. This syndrome surely was the main force at work in stimulating the Argentinian attack on the Falklands/ Malvinas. Not only did the resulting conflict take a serious toll in casualties and frayed relations, but also it stimulated nervousness about the circumstances in which the British might have been provoked into using their nuclear weapons. It is worth pondering how the conflict could have developed if Argentina had possessed its own such weapons (an eventuality that may have been, as it turns out, only a few years away).

Energy and the Proximate Causes of War

The most obvious way in today's world in which energy itself might become the immediate cause of an international conflict is through military action to try to protect or deny access to Mideast Gulf oil. Such intervention might be stimulated by an internal upheaval in a major supplier country (Saudi Arabia being the most obvious possibility) or by a local war that interrupts oil output to an extent importers find intolerable. The Iran-Iraq war certainly could have had this latter effect if it had occurred during a period of tight international oil supplies rather than during a glut, and it could have it yet if either side becomes frustrated enough to cut off completely the tanker traffic through the Straits of Hormuz.

Given the obvious potential for direct confrontation with the Soviet Union in the event of a major U.S. military intervention in the Middle East, it may seem bizarre that this country would entertain such a venture over the less than 5 percent of its total energy supply that comes from the Gulf. It is, alas, the far greater dependence on Gulf oil of Japan, West Germany, and France that makes all too plausible U.S. intervention on behalf of the Western industrial economies as a whole. Of course, no serious analyst seems to think that military action could possibly succeed in maintaining the oil flow if any significant adversary wants to cut it off, but that probably would not stop the attempt to do the impossible. Deterrence is seen to require, after all, that the United States be prepared (and look prepared) to intervene militarily; it is part of the paradox of deterrence that such preparations, carried out in the name of preventing conflict, can under some circumstances help plunge one into it.

In the future, regional energy resources other than those in the Middle East might assume sufficient international importance to produce analogous problems. Also, there is the possibility of increased tensions and even conflict over energy resources of disputed ownership—for example, in continental-shelf areas between nations, in deeper waters subject to disputes about jurisdiction, and in Antarctica. It is even conceivable that international tensions arising from the international environmental impacts of energy technology—most notably acid rain and CO_2-induced climate change—could contribute significantly to the chance of armed conflict. This possibility seems remote now, but if rapid climate change in the next few decades drastically affects the capability of the Soviet Union or China to feed itself the situation may look very different.

Finally, Israel's 1981 attack on an Iraqi nuclear reactor underlines the possibility that energy-related facilities with significant potential military applications may become targets of preemptive attack. (That the Iraqi reactor was designed for research and training rather than for actual power production does not blunt the general point.) Such an attack, of course, could set off a larger conflict, although fortunately it did not in the Israel-Iraq episode of 1981.

Energy and the Tools of War

Some energy technologies can provide the countries that develop and use them with increased capabilities for the development, production, or use of related weapons. The most widely recognized example of such a linkage is the one between the spread of nuclear fission as an energy source and the spread of capabilities in nuclear weaponry.

It is generally conceded that the knowledge needed to design and fabricate fission bombs is by now available to almost any nation. Although the diffusion of knowledge that produced this situation was partly due to the international promotion of nuclear fission as a commercial energy source, the diffusion is already so complete that it is no longer given much weight as a liability of fission power. Lack of access to nuclear explosive materials, not lack of knowledge, has been the principal technical barrier to the spread of fission weapons capability for the past two decades or more. The continuing major threat of nuclear weapons proliferation posed by fission power is that it tends to provide this missing ingredient, either in the form of enrichment capability or in the form of plutonium extractable from spent reactor fuel by means of chemical reprocessing.

Three main arguments have been used over the years by people contending that the link between fission power and fission weapons is not so serious. The first argument—that plutonium of the sort produced by power reactors is unsuitable for the fabrication of high-quality nuclear weapons—has been discredited publicly and repeatedly by professional weapons designers and by officials of the U.S. defense establishment. There is some performance penalty associated with using reactor-grade rather than weapons-grade plutonium to construct a weapon, but the penalty can be made very small by means of clever design.

The second argument is that there are more direct and cheaper ways for a country to acquire nuclear bombs than via its commercial nuclear energy facilities. Centrifuges for uranium enrichment and special reactors dedicated to plutonium production are usually mentioned. This argument is technically correct but seriously misleading. Countries *can* get nuclear explosive material by these other means, but doing so is made much easier if the requisite technical skills and infrastructure already are in place courtesy of a nuclear power program. The existence of commercial nuclear power in a country, moreover, provides a legitimating cover for nuclear activities that, without electricity generation as their manifest purpose, would be considered unambiguously weapons oriented and thus subject both to internal dissent and external sanctions and countermeasures. Even countries that initially have no intention of acquiring nuclear weapons might later find the built-in weapons capability that comes with nuclear power too tempting to resist, particularly if their internal or external political circumstances change.

The third argument is that weapons proliferation is basically a *political* problem that must be and is being handled by such political measures as the Non-Proliferation Treaty (NPT). That the problem is partly political is true, but the NPT offers little reassurance. Many key countries have not ratified it; any of those that have can abrogate it with a few months' notice; the safeguards that have been implemented to detect violations are inadequate to the task; and the treaty is in danger of collapse in any case because of the failure of the superpowers to live up to their own NPT obligations to make serious efforts at nuclear disarmament.

It is true that additional countries inevitably will acquire nuclear weapons, whether or not commercial nuclear power is available to facilitate the process. The key issue is the *rate* of spread of nuclear weapons capability. If the proliferation problem is viewed as a race between the spread of nuclear weapons, on the one hand, and the growing (one hopes) effectiveness of political and moral barriers against the use of the weapons, on the other, then nuclear power's contribution to speeding up the spread of nuclear weaponry must be considered a serious liability of this energy source.

Some commentators offer the consolation that proliferation is not such a serious problem for most of us, inasmuch as small countries with small nuclear arsenals are likely to use them only against each other. I am neither much consoled by this possible restriction on the use of these horrible weapons, nor persuaded that small-country use of small arsenals would not provide the tinder that grows into global conflagration. It is all too easy to think of ways the latter syndrome could occur: the increased chance of superpower involvement in any conflict, once nuclear weapons are used; the increasing chance that the superpowers themselves will use nuclear weapons in conflicts into which they are drawn if the initial participants use such weapons; and the increasing probable severity of a nuclear war as the number of targets for preemptive attack represented by nuclear-armed potential adversaries proliferates.

These considerations draw attention to another set of linkages: the effects of proliferation on the status of the major powers' nuclear arms race itself. Proliferation affects this race mainly by increasing the diversity of contingencies with which the major powers think they and their nuclear forces might have to cope, thus serving as an excuse for further increases in the types and numbers of nuclear weapons the major powers possess. At best, proliferation tends to put a rising floor under the possibility of deep cuts in the nuclear arsenals of the medium-sized nuclear powers and, in turn, those of the superpowers, because these nations will wish to maintain the gaps between their own nuclear-weapons capabilities and those of lesser powers—precisely in order to preserve their major-power or superpower status. And, of course, proliferation of nuclear weapons further complicates arms control negotiations by increasing the numbers of parties who must either participate or be taken into account in these negotiations.

Unfortunately, nuclear fission is not the only energy source with links to weapons capabilities. The inertial-confinement approach to harnessing nuclear fusion as an energy source is partly classified because of the principles it shares with fusion weaponry. The spread of research on this technology is quite likely to accelerate the spread of fusion-weapons capability among nations already possessing the ability to make the fission bombs needed to trigger thermonuclear weapons. Even solar energy may not be free of a potentially important weapons connection: The development and use of orbiting solar power satellites would increase enormously the scale of human operation in Earth orbit, providing both the capability and the cover for correspondingly increased military uses of space.

Besides the links between new energy sources and new weaponry, there is a more pedestrian but perhaps equally threatening connection between contemporary energy circumstances and the means of war. It is the "recycling" of petrodollars by way of arms transfers: The oil-exporting LDCs pour substantial amounts of their oil revenues into armaments, fueling regional arms races that probably increase both the chance of armed conflict and the chance that any such conflict will expand in a way that draws in the superpowers; and the industrial-nation oil importers increase their exports of sophisticated armaments as rapidly as they can, driven in part by the need to offset the balance-of-payments deficits caused by their oil bills. Table 7.6 shows the phenomenon in quantitative terms. This situation is appalling enough in its contribution

Table 7.6
Military Expenditures and Arms Exports, 1972–1982
(In Billions of 1982 US$)

	1972	1974	1976	1978	1980	1982
MDC military expenditures	490	509	519	541	577	627
LDC military expenditures	111	135	164	168	173	191
MDC Arms Exports	20	21	25	30	30	31
LDC arms imports	15	15	19	25	26	30
OPEC share of world arms imports	10.1%	21.4%	31.5%	36.5%	27.2%	35.6%

Notes: MDC = more developed countries (1982 GNP/person > $4,000, except OPEC); LDC = less developed countries (1982 GNP/person < $4,000, plus OPEC).

Source: U.S. Arms Control and Disarmament Agency, *World Military Expenditures and Arms Transfers 1972–82* (Washington, D.C.: Government Printing Office, April 1984).

to the chance and probable severity of regional wars, but it is deplorable also for the diversion of desperately needed resources from the provision of services in support of human well-being.

ENERGY AND POPULATION

The mid-twentieth-century revival of Malthus's insight that no combination of good technology and good management can cope with unlimited population growth on a finite planet (a revival to which Harrison Brown's 1954 book, *The Challenge of Man's Future*, was the most eloquent and comprehensive contribution) is more relevant in the 1980s than ever. One sees, in the rising real costs of energy and the poor prospects for a reversal in this trend, the end of the illusion that technical fixes inevitably will outpace the effects of declining resource quality. And one sees in the accumulating evidence of environmental disruption at continental and global scale (deforestation, erosion, salination, species extinctions, carbon dioxide build-up, acid rain, groundwater depletion and contamination) the end of the companion illusion that human activities are but puny perturbations on the scale of natural processes.

Restraining to the greatest extent practical the further increase in world population will not by itself solve these problems, but it may make them solvable. The discredited notion that the opposite is true—that further population growth will be a boon because "people are the ultimate resource"—is being promoted again in the 1980s by the cornucopian fringe (myopia evidently being one resource that *is* in infinite supply); but this notion remains the dangerous nonsense it always has been. For if one takes as given that people *are* the ultimate resource, it is clear that the central resource problem in today's world is not a shortage of people but the catastrophic wastage of the human potential of people who already exist, people who are denied even a decent diet, adequate shelter, and the expectation of a reasonably long and happy life, not to mention access to educational opportunities and fulfilling jobs. Until the people now alive are being decently provided for—a task already made difficult by the large absolute numbers of people and by the continuing growth of those numbers—it is hard to imagine how concern for people can be translated into enthusiasm for more population growth.

The adverse effects of further population growth on the human prospect could hardly be plainer than they are in the energy area. Coping effectively with the energy problems of 1985's 12-terawatt world (4.8 billion people at 2.4 kilowatts per person) is manifestly beyond the technical, economic, and organizational capabilities available. Yet, for every billion people added to the world's population at that same level of energy use per person, new energy sources capable of sustaining an additional continuous drain of 2.4 terawatts must be mobilized and paid for and their environmental impacts somehow absorbed.

This figure understates the problem, of course. To narrow the rich-poor gap in prosperity at a satisfactory rate almost certainly will require some increase in energy use per person, even assuming that large gains in energy efficiency are rapidly achieved. Under a highly optimistic scenario of reductions in population growth rates, the world of 2025 might have a population of 7.5 billion consisting of 1.3 billion in what are now the rich countries and 6.2 billion in what are now the poor ones. If by then the rich-country energy use per person has fallen from the mid-1980s value of some 7 kilowatts (kW) per person to 4 kW/person and the poor-country figure has risen from 0.8 to 2 kW/person, global energy use in 2025 will total 17.6 terawatts, nearly a 50-percent increase over today's figure. The same remarkable accomplishments in increasing rich-country energy efficiency and expanding per-person energy availability in poor countries, if applied to a high-population scenario producing 1.5 billion rich and 8 billion poor by 2025, lead to a global energy use rate of 22 terawatts in that year.

Under the stated assumptions, the *difference* in the 2025 rate of energy use between the high-population and low-population scenarios is 4.4

terawatts, which is about equal to the world's total rate of energy use in 1960 and somewhat larger than the world rate of petroleum use in 1983. The difference in cumulative energy use for the period 1985–2025 between the two scenarios would be about 90 terawatt-years. Given, moreover, that the additional terawatts "on the margin" will be supplied from the most costly and probably most environmentally disruptive sources, the importance of the incremental contribution of extra population growth will be even greater than that suggested by simple addition.

The world will need all the clever technology, management skill, and good luck it can muster if 7.5 billion people are to be provided with the energy they need in 2025 (not to mention the food, water, housing, health care, education, and so on) at tolerable monetary, environmental, and sociopolitical costs. Anyone who claims that trying for 9.5 billion would do no great harm simply is not thinking clearly.

CONCLUSION

The oil crisis of the 1970s was one symptom of one part of the energy problem; it was not the whole problem. To celebrate the oil glut of the early 1980s as the end of the world's energy difficulties is, accordingly, to have failed all along to grasp the nature of the energy problem and its interaction with the rest of the human predicament.

There is in fact not one energy problem but many: the intersection of difficulties relating to declining geophysical subsidies that were largely consumed in making only part of the world rich, the inability of technological ingenuity to compensate indefinitely for declining resource quality, the magnitude of inadvertent human interventions in natural conditions and processes on which human well-being depends, the inertia built into huge technological systems and mass human behavior, and the complexities imposed on coping with all of the above by the multiple divisions of human society into competing, feuding, and often warring factions.

The world is suffering simultaneously the consequences of having too little energy (these borne mainly at present by the poor, with not enough to meet basic human needs) and the consequences of having too much of especially costly or risky kinds of energy (these borne by everyone in one form or another: excessive vulnerability to unpredictable loss of supply, increased chance of war arising from that vulnerability, increased chance that any war will be nuclear, and increasingly threatening risks to human well-being through large-scale environmental disruption).

Solutions are possible but not simple. They must include more attention to increasing the efficiency with which energy and other scarce natural resources are applied to the task of generating the goods and services people need; expansion of efforts to promote diversity in energy supplies, including increased reliance on local resources; a sustained campaign to break the linkages between energy and armaments; cooperative efforts to shrink the rich-poor gap; and humane and practical restraints on population growth. Such proposals, and many more, have been discussed at length in other forums. More proposals and more forums are needed, but it is possible to suppose that real progress still awaits the creation of consensus on the *nature* of the energy problem and its connections to other human concerns. In the spirit in which Harrison Brown wrote *The Challenge of Man's Future* some thirty years ago, this chapter has been written as a contribution to the continuing effort to help create that consensus.

BIBLIOGRAPHY

General

Brown, Harrison, *The Challenge of Man's Future* (New York: Viking, 1954).
Brown, Lester R., William U. Chandler, Christopher Flavin, Cynthia Pollock, Sandra Postel, Linda Starke, and Edward C. Wolf, *State of the World 1985* (New York: Norton, 1985).
Ehrlich, Paul R., Anne H. Ehrlich, and John P. Holdren, *Ecoscience: Population, Resources, Environment* (San Francisco: W. H. Freeman, 1977).
Yergin, Daniel, and Martin Hillenbrand, eds., *Global Insecurity: A Strategy for Energy and Economic Renewal* (New York: Houghton Mifflin, 1982).

Energy and Poverty

Bressand, Albert, *The State of the World Economy: Annual Report of the French Institute for International Relations* (Cambridge, Mass.: Ballinger, 1982).
Hughart, David, *Prospects for Traditional and Non-Conventional Energy Sources in Developing Countries* (Washington, D.C.: World Bank, 1979).
Landsberg, Hans H., and Joseph M. Dukert, *High Energy Costs* (Baltimore: Johns Hopkins, 1981).
Overseas Development Council, *U.S. Foreign Policy and the Third World Agenda* (New York: Praeger, 1982).
World Bank, *World Development Report 1984* (New York: Oxford, 1984).

Energy and Environment

Committee on the Atmosphere and the Biosphere, National Research Council, *Atmosphere-Biosphere Interactions* (Washington, D.C.: National Academy Press, 1981).
Eckholm, Erik P., *Losing Ground: Environmental Stress and World Food Prospects* (New York: Norton, 1976).

Harte, John, *Consider a Spherical Cow: A Course in Environmental Problem Solving* (Los Altos, Calif.: William Kaufmann, 1985).

Holdren, John P., "Energy and the Human Environment," in *The European Transition from Oil: Societal Impacts and Constraints on Energy Policy*, G. Goodman, L. Kristoferson, and J. Hollander, eds. (London: Academic Press, 1981).

————, "Energy Hazards: What to Measure, What to Compare," *Technology Review*, April 1982, pp. 33–38, 74–75.

Schneider, Stephen H., and Randi Londer, *Climate and Life* (San Francisco: Sierra Club Books, 1984).

Smith, Kirk R., A. L. Aggarwal, and R. M. Dave, "Air Pollution and Rural Biomass Fuels in Developing Countries," *Atmospheric Environment*, vol. 17 (1983), pp. 2343–2362.

Study of Critical Environmental Problems, *Man's Impact on the Global Environment* (Cambridge, Mass.: MIT Press, 1970).

Energy and International Conflict

Castle, Emery N., and Kent A. Price, eds., *U.S. Interests and Global Natural Resources* (Baltimore: Johns Hopkins, 1983).

Clark, Wilson, and Jake Page, *Energy, Vulnerability, and War* (New York: Norton, 1981).

Deese, David A., and Joseph S. Nye, *Energy and Security* (Cambridge, Mass.: Ballinger, 1981).

Holdren, John P., "Nuclear Power and Nuclear Weapons: The Connection Is Dangerous," *Bulletin of the Atomic Scientists* 39, no. 1 (January 1983), 40–45.

Lovins, Amory B., and Hunter L. Lovins, *Energy/War: Breaking the Nuclear Link* (New York: Harper & Row, 1980).

Sweet, William, *The Nuclear Age: Power, Proliferation, and the Arms Race* (Washington, D.C.: Congressional Quarterly, 1984).

8
SOIL DYNAMICS AND SUSTAINABLE CARRYING CAPACITY OF EARTH

ROGER REVELLE

In his classic book, *The Challenge of Man's Future,* Harrison Brown was among the first to discuss the possible consequences of the very rapid rate of increase in human populations that began after World War II. In this book and in his later writings he emphasized the huge disparities in living conditions and prospects between the rich, so-called developed countries of Europe and North America and the great majority of mankind who lived in the poor "less developed" countries. He recognized more clearly than most people that Earth's resources are limited and that the support of ever growing numbers of human beings would require human ingenuity and effort on an unprecedented scale. The world was experiencing an epidemic of births and, without extraordinary human effort, the long-term future of mankind was far from assured.

This future could be considered in two ways: first, the physical and biological constraints on the sustainable production of food and other resources; second, the constraints posed by human and social inadequacies, conflicts, and missed opportunities. Although the latter are most difficult to overcome, they must be framed in the context of the constraints established by limited resources of land, water, energy, mineral resources, and biological materials. In this chapter I shall consider only the limitations set by physical resources, recognizing, however, that human inadequacies must be remedied if future human beings are to live happy lives.

In the past, estimates of the human carrying capacity of the earth have been based on minimum human needs, for example, minimum vegetarian diets adequate to sustain human metabolism. In this chapter I shall base my computations on a much closer approach to the optimum human diet—a healthful version of the average human diet in Europe or North America. Similarly, in computing the levels of required energy, I have not considered the minimum energy needs for human life, but the levels of energy consumption presently required by developed societies similar to those of Europe.

Unlike other planets of the solar system, Earth is a benign home for living creatures. Over billions of years, the atmosphere, the oceans, and the outer layers of the solid Earth have evolved, together with bacteria, plants, and animals, to create a highly favorable environment for higher animals and especially for human beings. This environment is characterized by an abundance of sunshine, liquid water, atmospheric carbon dioxide, and nitrogen. Large quantities of free oxygen in the air provide a basis for the highly energetic chemical reactions utilized by higher animals, including man. The relatively small size of Earth is also favorable for life as we know it because the gravitational force is small enough to allow the birds of the air and land animals to move freely and rapidly over the surface. But the small size of our planet also means that its resources are limited.

Over geologic ages, living creatures, including bacteria, plants, and animals, have learned to use these resources more and more efficiently, and life has flourished more and more exuberantly. Human beings, with their ability to change rapidly through cultural evolution, have enormously increased their ability to use the resources of the earth, especially those provided by other forms of life. The result over the last 10,000 years has been a thousandfold increase in the size of the human population and a present rate of growth of that population of nearly 2 percent per year. The limitations imposed by Earth's finite resources have been pushed back beyond the imagining of our remote ancestors. The laws of chemistry and physics and the basic biological processes of photosynthesis and respiration, however, have not changed during the lifetime of man on Earth, and these still present limits to the expansion of human numbers.

For many aspects of human life, biological processes, that is, the rates of production of various kinds of organic matter, are of the greatest importance. This fact is obvious in the case of food, but it is equally valid for many materials and for the production of much primary energy. We must therefore ask ourselves: How much can the production of food, energy, and biological materials be increased to accommodate growing human populations? And to what extent can increased production be sustained for the indefinite future? It is meaningless to ask to what extent food production by itself can be increased on a sustainable basis because nonfood energy is needed at all stages of the human food system; a high level of food production can be attained only in a highly developed society in which energy is used in many forms and for many purposes and in which wood, paper, and other biological products are equally essential.

FOOD FOR FUTURE HUMAN POPULATIONS

Let us consider first the human needs for food. At the present time, according to the Food and Agricultural Organization of the United Nations (FAO) (1983a), the average diet provides 2,600 kcal/caput/day, or an annual total for the world's 4.5 billion people of 4.3×10^{15} kcal. This is the quantity of food energy contained in 1,200 million tons of wheat, rice, or maize, whereas the figure given by FAO for cereal production in 1982 is almost 1,700 million tons. Moreover, other plant products besides cereals form a large portion of human diets, and 17 percent of the caloric intake in the world average human diet comes from animals in the form of meat, eggs, milk, milk products, and fish and other seafood. Obviously, much of the total cereal production, together with large quantities of forage, is fed to domestic animals. The efficiency with which animals convert the energy of feed into food energy for humans is about 15 percent, so that the caloric value of the primary plant products consumed by farm animals is 4.8×10^{15} kcal/year, and the primary plant production for human food corresponds to 5,100 kcal/person/day, or the equivalent for the world population as a whole of 2,400 million tons of cereal equivalent per year. To this we must add perhaps 20 percent for seed and wastage, making up a total of about 6,000 kcal/person/day, or 2,800 million tons of cereal equivalent per year.

According to United Nations Population Division (1982) estimates, the world's human population will continue to grow until the latter part of the next century, reaching a total by the year 2075 of somewhere between 7,700 and 13,600 billion people, with an estimated mean of approximately 10 billion people. Less than 15 percent of this population—about 1.4 billion—will live in presently developed countries and 8.7 billion will live in presently less developed countries. The population of East and South Asia is likely to be more than 5 billion people.

The less developed countries at the present time obtain less than 200 kcal of their daily intake from animal products, in contrast to over 1,000 kcal for the developed countries. To provide a more adequate diet for the less developed countries, the world average of primary plant products should be increased to at least 7,000 kcal/person/day, including seed and wastage. The total world food supply in terms of cereal equivalents for the most probable population in 2075 should then be 7.3 billion tons of grain equivalent. A large part of this total, perhaps 50 percent, could come from permanent and temporary pasture lands and from agricultural residues.

With present and extrapolated future rates of increase in cultivated land, we can expect that about 300 million hectares will be added to the area that is presently cultivated, making a total of about 1.75 billion net cultivated hectares 100 years from now (Revelle, 1983).

Plant production is ultimately limited by atmospheric carbon dioxide and sunlight during the growing season. With the present atmospheric carbon dioxide content of close to 340 ppm and the average incoming solar radiation over the principal inhabited areas of Earth of about 0.5 kcal $cm^{-2}day^{-1}$, a modern crop plant well supplied with water and nutrients will produce over 200 kg of dry matter $ha^{-1}day^{-1}$. For a cereal crop like wheat, this growth manifests itself at first in the form of roots, leaves, and stem, but after flowering, seed formation is predominant. The seed-filling stage may have a duration of around fifty days in a disease-free environment. Under these conditions, the seed yield can be about 10,000 kg $ha^{-1}yr^{-1}$, and the total yield of organic matter including seeds can be close to 22,000 kg $ha^{-1}yr^{-1}$. Some of this total production may be used as animal feed, but a large part of it should be returned to the soil to maintain soil quality.

For our estimated 1.75 billion hectares, the total food and feed production could be more than 17.5 billion tons. This is at least two and one-half times our estimated requirement of 7.3 billion tons for the population one hundred years from now.

In the above calculations we have assumed an adequate supply of water and major and minor nutrients throughout the growing season. The supply of water depends not only on rainfall and on water supplied by irrigation but also on the water-holding capacity of the soil. Similarly, the supply of nutrients to the crop plants depends not only on the availability of fertilizers added to the soil by farmers but also on the properties of the soil, the latter determining the rate at which fertilizers are leached out of the soil or are locked up in unavailable form in soil minerals. For a yield of 10,000 kg ha^{-1} with a protein content of 10 percent, about 250 kg of fertilizer nitrogen need to be added for each crop and about an equal quantity of phosphate plus potash. Old, weathered soils may also need dressing with many minor nutrients, such as cobalt, zinc, manganese, copper, and magnesium.

Besides food, mankind also depends on agriculture for production of fibers—mainly wool, cotton, flax, hemp, jute, and sisal for use in textiles, ropes, fish nets, and many other purposes—beverages such as coffee, tea, and cocoa; waxes, tobaccos, pharmaceutical products, and some nonedible oils and natural rubber. The total arable area devoted to all these materials is only about 3 percent of presently cultivated land. Research and development have resulted in increasing yields of these products at about the same pace as for food production. We can expect that yields will continue to increase in the future and that the proportion of arable land used for these nonfood items will remain relatively constant.

The uneven world distribution of land and water resources presents a fundamental difficulty for future food production. About 45 percent of the total cultivated land at the present time exists in the developed countries, which contain only about a fourth of the world population. Inequality is particularly serious in East and Southeast Asia where the cultivated land per person is only .16 hectares compared to .57 hectares per person in the developed countries. Nearly all the potentially arable land in less developed Asia is already cultivated, in contrast to Africa and South America, where agricultural lands could be expanded by several hundred million hectares. As we have pointed out, these countries of Southeast Asia are likely to have a population of over 5 billion people in the latter part of the 21st century. Their cultivated land will then be less than .08 hectares per person. Fortunately more than one crop can be grown each year in most of this region, provided water is, or can be made available for irrigation. In almost all cases this will involve diversion and storage of river flows during the monsoon season, for use during the dry part of the year. For several reasons, including the lack of suitable reservoir sites and the inevitable rapid sedimentation of surface reservoirs, underground water storage will be essential, and this will involve the availability of adequate energy for pumping wells.

INDUSTRIAL WOOD PRODUCTS

A large land area is required for industrial wood products—lumber for construction and other purposes, wood-based panels, and paper—and the use of these materials is rapidly increasing. From 1975 to 1979 about 450 million metric tons of roundwood were harvested, corresponding to a total biomass from trees of about 750 million metric tons (Food and Agriculture Organization of the United Nations, 1983b). Nearly half of this roundwood was used in the production of pulp for paper manufacturing. By the year 2000, it is expected that the total roundwood harvest will nearly double to between 765 and 905 million metric tons. In the latter part of the twenty-first century, with an expected world population of 10 billion people, the total roundwood harvest could equal 3,700 million metric tons, the total tree harvest, counting roots, living and dead branches, leaves, and tree trunks may be about 6.1 billion metric tons.

Although the gross primary production of forests is very large, ranging from about 75 tons/ha/year in tropical rain forests to around 25 tons in southern Scandinavia, one-half to three-quarters of this production is used in the respiration of the leaves and other living tissues of the trees. The net primary production of natural forest communities varies from 13 to 28 tons/ha/year. Much of this production takes place in the leaves, which live for only a year or more, and another part is lost to microbial and insect predators. Consequently, the total yield of biomass from natural forests harvested after 50 to 60 years is only 3 to 4 tons/ha/year, and of this quantity only about 2 tons/ha/year is roundwood. Thus, to meet the expected demand for paper, sawn wood, and panel board, about 1,800 million hectares of natural forest will be required. This is two-thirds of the entire world area of "closed" forests—forests with a relatively continuous canopy of foliage (Persson, 1974).

Research in tree culture is progressing rapidly, based on tissue culture of clones from the fastest growing trees. In planted stands of eucalyptus in Brazil, about 40 bone-dry tons of biomass/ha/year are now being harvested on a seven-year cycle. The highest yielding clones so far discovered have produced nearly 75 tons/ha/year over a seven-year rotation (Kulp, 1983). In North Carolina, 14 bone-dry tons of biomass/ha/year from loblolly pine plantations is a conservative estimate for 1990. In higher latitudes with shorter growing seasons, such as southern Sweden, only about 6 tons of biomass/ha/year have so far been obtained, but the potential maximum is estimated at 17 tons.

If pulp production for paper plus lumber and other products were confined to the tropics, about half the expected biomass production from plantations of fast growing trees (or 20 tons/ha/year) could be utilized, and the total area devoted to industrial wood products could be limited to less than 200 million hectares, leaving a total of about 2,500 million hectares of closed forests to be used for other purposes, including preservation of ecosystems, watershed protection, and energy production.

MEETING ENERGY NEEDS

Human needs for energy may well represent the real limit on Earth's carrying capacity. At the present time, world demand for energy is met very largely from fossil fuels (coal, oil, and natural gas) and to a much smaller extent from hydroelectric power, wood for heating, cooking, and other purposes, geothermal and nuclear energy. The world's total commercial energy consumption (oil, gas, coal, hydropower, and nuclear power) now corresponds to about 10 billion metric tons coal equivalent—or 70×10^{15} kcal/year (Crabbe and McBride, 1978). This is slightly more than 2 tons of coal equivalent per caput per year. Most of this commercial energy is used in the developed countries, including the USSR, other parts of Europe, the United States, Canada, Japan, Australia, and New Zealand; only about 20 percent is used in the developing countries of Africa, Asia, and Latin America. But these countries consume nearly 1 billion tons of coal equivalent in the form of noncommercial energy (wood, crop residues, and animal dung) for cooking and other domestic uses.

In the future, a vast increase in energy use will be needed if populations of the developing countries are to attain adequate food supplies. In computing potential food production, we have assumed a high level of agricultural technology, which means, among other things, high commercial energy use in agriculture. Based on experience in Western Europe, North America, and Japan, an external source of energy equal to half the energy harvested in plant materials and feed is required to produce that harvest (Pimental et al., 1973). For our estimated food requirement of 7.3 billion tons for the world population one hundred years in the future, 1.8 billion tons of coal equivalent would be required for direct use in agriculture. A large part of this would be needed to produce nitrogen, phosphorus, and potassium fertilizer, and a somewhat greater quantity for manufacture and use of farm tools and farm machinery, lifting water for irrigation, manufacture of pesticides and herbicides, and crop-drying.

Only a few percent of the future world population will be engaged directly in agriculture, and energy for farm-to-market transportation, food processing, preservation, marketing, and cooking will be required to meet human dietary needs. Employment in energy-using manufacturing and service industries for the nonfarm populations will be necessary to enable them to buy their food. Space heating and cooling, lighting, and communications will also be major end uses for energy.

We may estimate that the sum of these energy requirements will correspond to about 4 tons of coal equivalent per caput one hundred years from now or a total of 40 billion tons for the expected population at that time. This is somewhat less than present per caput use in Europe and less than half that in the United States and Canada. For the next one or two centuries, energy needs could be met from available resources of coal, lignite, oil (including oil shales and tar sands), and natural gas, which are estimated at over 6,500 billion tons of coal equivalent (Revelle, 1982). Such large-scale use of fossil fuels would result in a quadrupling of atmospheric carbon dioxide, which could bring about poorly understood, but probably highly disruptive, climatic changes.

In the long run, in any case, we must depend on nuclear energy (including geothermal energy) or on the renewable energy resources provided by the sun—hydroelectric and wind power, ocean thermal energy conversion (OTEC), direct use of solar radiation for heating and cooling, photoelectric and other forms of conversion of solar radiation into electricity, and the photosynthetic conversion of solar energy into energy-rich biomass by living plants.

The world potential for hydropower is probably less than 4 billion tons of coal equivalent (Edmonds and Reilly, 1983). The sustainable geothermal electric potential may be equivalent to approximately 1 billion tons of coal; OTEC, plus windpower and solar heating and cooling, could add up to another billion tons. The remaining 34 billion tons of coal equivalent would have to be provided by nuclear fusion, fission from breeder reactors, photoelectric and other forms of direct conversion of solar energy into electricity, or from biomass produced by living plants. Because of the political, economic, and technical difficulties that have plagued the nuclear option and the probably irreducible high cost of direct conversion of solar energy to electricity, it is tempting to consider whether biomass can provide future energy needs. In making this computation for wood or other energy-containing plant material, we must take into account the energy costs of planting, cultivating, harvesting, drying, converting to usable form, and transporting such materials to the point of use. This can be done most simply by reducing the energy content of a given weight of biomass by an appropriate fraction, say by 40 percent. A metric ton of bone-dry wood with an original energy content of 4.5×10^6 kcal/metric ton would then provide 2.7×10^6 kcal/metric ton at the point of use. Consequently, our estimated 34 billion tons of coal equivalent would correspond to 88 billion tons of wood. If two-thirds of this wood, or 59 billion tons, were produced in tropical forest plantations of fast growing trees, yielding 40 tons of biomass $ha^{-1}yr^{-1}$, a total planted area of 1,475 million hectares would be required. The remaining 29 billion tons would be produced in temperate latitudes where a yield of 20 tons/ha/year would also require 1,475 hectares of forest plantations. These areas for both temperate and tropical regions are about equal to the present areas of closed forests (1,535 million hectares for temperate regions and 1,290 million hectares for the tropics [Persson, 1974]) and nearly three-fourths of the world forested area (closed and open forests) of 4,030 million hectares.

For a variety of reasons it is probably impractical and certainly undesirable to convert all of the world's forested areas to plantations of fast growing trees. Moreover, we have already assigned 200 million hectares of the tropical forested area to lumber and paper production.

It may be reasonable, however, to use a large fraction of potential agricultural land for biomass plantations.

From the earlier discussion, we have estimated that 1,750 million hectares of Earth's land area will be cultivated one hundred years from now. And we have shown that potential food production, even with one crop per year, could be two and one-half times the estimated requirement at that time. In fact, it would be possible to grow two or more crops over about a third of the cultivated areas either by rain-fed or irrigated agriculture. Thus a large fraction—perhaps 1,000 million hectares of cultivated land—could in principle be used for energy crops such as sugarcane, cassava, or trees. Moreover, the area of agricultural land could be expanded relatively easily to nearly 2,500 million hectares (Buringh et al., 1978). Another 1,000 million hectares could also be brought under cultivation, although with greater difficulty. More than half of this potentially cultivable, but presently uncultivated, land would be in Africa and Latin America. Energy plantations in these areas could make up a large fraction of the total biomass needed to meet the world's future energy requirements.

INTERACTIONS BETWEEN THE BIOTA AND THE GEOSPHERE

In the above discussion, it has been implicitly assumed that sufficient water and nutrients would be available for a high level of plant production. Although the average precipitation over Earth is more than adequate, painful experience shows that variations in precipitation and runoff from year to year and from decade to decade are so large that water is often deficient over large areas of Earth's cultivated land. These deficiencies can be at least partly remedied by storage of water in surface reservoirs and in underground aquifers, together with construction of suitable irrigation systems. For the inhabited areas of Earth as a whole, climatic *variations* from year to year result in only about a 5 percent variation in world food production.

On the other hand, the relatively permanent climatic *change* that is likely to be brought about by increasing atmospheric carbon dioxide and other greenhouse gases could seriously disrupt existing geographical patterns of seasonal temperatures, precipitation, and evapotranspiration, with disastrous consequences for some agricultural areas and beneficial results for others. Fortunately, these changes will be slow enough to allow time for human communities to adapt to them, possibly in part by large-scale migration. For worldwide agriculture and forestry two countervailing effects will appear—increased photosynthetic production because of the fertilizer action of higher atmospheric CO_2 and increased respiration because of higher temperatures. The balance between these two processes will probably be different for different plant types and geographic areas.

Equally serious from the point of view of sustainable production of food, materials, and energy are the characteristics of the soils in which crops and forests grow. In the past, soils have been utilized as a source for production of nitrogen and other plant nutrients, hence the concept of soil fertility as the availability in the soil of nutrients for plant growth. With the advent of the modern technology of use of chemical fertilizers, soil fertility in this sense has ceased to be important. But the physical properties of soils—their capacity to retain water that can be extracted by plant roots to provide calcium and other cations through base exchange in clays and to maintain fertilizer in available form for the plants—are of vital importance. Soils possessing these characteristics form a thin film over Earth's arable lands—usually less than 1 meter in thickness. These soil layers are continually renewed by weathering of rock materials at rates on the order of 1 cm per 100 years, or about 2 tons $ha^{-1}yr^{-1}$. Average soil erosion on much cultivated land in the United States is estimated at about 1 cm in 10 years (Larson et al., 1983). Because of much more violent rainfall, erosion of soil unprotected by plant cover is much more rapid in the tropics. Erosion is more rapid on sloping than on level ground; over many decades, soil loss in the United States on slopes above 6 percent will probably become intolerable. On the other hand, soil eroded from sloping areas may accumulate in flat bottom lands, and slopes less than 6 percent can apparently be farmed indefinitely.

Rates of soil erosion differ enormously for different soils, climates, and plant cover as do the rates of soil formation and accumulation in different rock types and climates. Better estimates of these rates of formation and erosion are critical if we are to be able to estimate the sustainable carrying capacity of the earth for food, energy, and materials to meet human needs.

Increased use of fertilizers may perturb the trace element balance of soils and drainage systems. For example, all natural marine phosphates (the source of superphosphate fertilizer) contain cadmium at 500 times the crustal abundance, uranium at 50 times, selenium at 40 times, and arsenic at 10 times crustal abundance. In Europe, the cadmium content of beef, fish, and cereals has reached dangerous levels (Becker, 1981).

With the very large changes in agricultural and forest technology needed to meet future human needs and the climatic changes likely to result from increases in atmospheric carbon dioxide and other greenhouse gases, much greater understanding of the processes of soil formation and erosion is needed to predict future changes in soil characteristics and to serve as a basis for protective measures. It is in the thin film of soil on the earth that the geosphere and the biota interact most intimately and dramatically from the standpoint of human welfare.

Soil characteristics depend not only on climate and biological processes but also on the nature and age of the source rocks. In general, the most productive soils occur near tectonic plate margins where recent vulcanism has provided fresh rock materials (Fyfe et al., 1983). Conversely, the least productive soils occur in continental areas where the rocks are very old and the topography has been relatively stable for long geologic periods. Highly productive soils also occur on margins of recent continental glaciation, such as the corn belt of the central United States where thick loess materials have accumulated. Soils of low productivity are characteristic of areas of relatively unweathered plateau basalt, such as the Deccan trap of India.

SUMMARY

In estimating the carrying capacity of the earth for human beings, we must consider not only potential food production on a sustainable basis but also the potential for sustainable production of paper and other wood products and the availability of renewable or essentially inexhaustible sources of energy. With modern agricultural technology, using chemical fertilizers and agricultural machinery, potential food production from presently cultivated land could be much more than adequate to meet the need of the most probable human population one hundred years from now. Plantations of fast growing trees over less than 10 percent of presently forested areas could meet needs for wood and paper. Sufficient energy could be made available from biomass, but this would require converting the entire world area of closed forests to plantations of fast growing trees. Alternatively, one-half to two-thirds of potential agricultural land could be used to produce biomass for energy purposes, plus about half of the present area of closed forests. This would not jeopardize needed food supply.

The possibility of sustained biological production over an indefinite period for food, energy, and needed materials depends on the relative rates of formation and loss of the soils that form the physical substrate for land plants. Not enough is known about these rates as a function of present and probable future environmental conditions, or about how to modify them to reach the balance needed for sustained biological production. Here is a critically important meeting ground for cooperation among earth and biological scientists.

REFERENCES

Becker, J., 1981, Environmental Cadmium—Europe to Ban? *Nature* 289, 436–437.

Buringh, P., H.D.J. Van Heemst, and G. J. Staring, 1978, *Computation of the Absolute Maximum Food Production of the World*. Wageningen: Agricultural University.

Crabbe, D., and R. McBride, 1978, *The World Energy Book*. Cambridge, Mass.: MIT Press, 247.

Edmonds, J., and J. Reilly, 1983, Global Energy Production and Use to the Year 2050. *Energy* 8, 419–432.

Food and Agriculture Organization of the United Nations, 1983a, *FAO Production Yearbook, 1982*, vol. 36.

———, 1983b, *World Forest Products, Demand and Supply, 1990 and 2000*, ix.

Fyfe, W. S., B. I. Kronberg, O. H. Leonardos, and N. Olorunfemi, 1983, Global Tectonics and Agriculture! A Geochemical Perspective. *Agriculture, Ecosystems and Environment* 9, 383–399.

Kulp, J. L., 1983, Integration of Forestry and Products Research. *Svensk Papperstidning* 11, 25–38.

Larson, W. E., F. J. Pierce, and R. H. Doudy, 1983, The Threat of Soil Erosion to Long-term Crop Production. *Science* 219, 458–468.

Persson, R., 1974, *Review of the World's Forest Resources in the Early 1970s*. Royal College of Forestry, Stockholm, no. 17.

Pimental, D., L. E. Hurd, A. C. Bellotti, M. J. Forster, I. N. Oka, O. D. Sholes, and R. J. Whitman, 1973, Food Production and the Energy Crisis. *Science* 206, 1277–1280.

Revelle, R., 1982, Resources. In *Population Growth and World Economic Development*, J. Faaland, ed. Norwegian Nobel Foundation, 50–77.

———, 1983, The Effects of Population Growth on Renewable Resources. Paper presented at UN meeting of experts on population, resources, environment, and development. Geneva, April 1983, 18 pp., tables.

United Nations Population Division, 1982, Long-range Global Population Projections as Assessed in 1980. *Population Bulletin of the United Nations* 14, 22.

9

SPECULATING ON THE GLOBAL RESOURCE FUTURE

GILBERT F. WHITE

The late 1940s and the early 1950s were years of earnest speculation as to the future condition and development of Earth's natural resources. Ambitious efforts were made to anticipate the planet's capacity for supporting people and their economic systems and to interpret the findings for the benefit of publics who might be expected to act in ways that would preserve the human family and its habitat. These tasks required analysis and projection. Thirty years later it is instructive to compare the conjectures with the actual and to ask what lessons of current relevance may be drawn from their convergence or divergence.

A rash of reviews of the global future broke out shortly after the initial reconstruction activities following World War II. These ranged from staid assessments of resource development by governmental and intergovernmental agencies to more lively appraisals by individual authors. The first substantive United Nations conference in 1949 dealt with the status of resource management and conservation (United Nations, 1950) but was cautious about venturing predictions of future conditions. Other group and agency exercises were popular. Perhaps the best known was the report of the President's Materials Policy Commission, the so-called Paley commission, which examined the world outlook for materials production and flows in the framework of assuring *Resources for Freedom* (1952). This helped generate the Mid-Century Conference on Resources for the Future (1954) and the subsequent establishment by the Ford Foundation of Resources for the Future (RFF) as a research organization devoted to resource problems (Resources for the Future, 1977). Other significant reviews and projections were in Erich Zimmerman's *World*

Resources and Industries (1951) and the Food and Agriculture Organization's *World Food Survey* (1946).

Individual analysis flourished. Early and highly influential was Fairfield Osborne's *Our Plundered Planet* (1948). In the same year, Vogt's *Road to Survival* appeared. These, too, left their organizational heritage, the Conservation Foundation, founded by Osborne, and the Populatioin Reference Bureau, founded by William Vogt, Robert Cook, and colleagues. Numerous other volumes appeared, having a somewhat similar aim of describing the condition of Earth's resources and predicting what would happen to them unless variously specified measures were to be taken. R. O. Whyte and G. V. Jacks's review of world soil erosion problems had been among the first in 1939. And these books were accompanied by volumes taking opposite views as to resource adequacy. Charles G. Darwin's *The Next Million Years* (1953) was prominent among the latter. The most comprehensive in conception and in many respects the most cautious in pondering about global resources was Harrison Brown's *The Challenge of Man's Future* (1954).

These mid-century efforts at stocktaking and prediction were not without some precedent: A number of pioneering national studies had been undertaken, as described by Marion Clawson (1981), during the period of New Deal planning. In some respects George Perkins Marsh's *The Earth as Modified by Human Action* (1974) had outlined several of the major questions of soil and forest resource adequacy. The conservation movement with its concern for North American situations had been a modest step in the same direction.

One means of gleaning experience from the mid-century exercises is to compare their conjectures with the reported situation in the early 1980s and then examine major assertions that proved accurate or inaccurate. To that end, I have not tried to examine every document of that genre and period. Rather, I take *Road to Survival* and *The Challenge of Man's Future* as examples, respectively, of highly confident and highly cautious predictions. The Vogt book may have special interest because it was an intellectual precursor of the Club of Rome volume on *The Limits to Growth* (1972) and of *The Global 2000 Report to the President* (1980). Although the latter two reports stressed the use of mathematical models with global parameters, many of their approaches, as will be suggested later, were congenial with those put forward by Vogt with regard to the likely outstripping of the carrying capacity of the globe by population growth. The United Nations Environment Programme report on *The World Environment 1972–1982* (Holdgate et al., 1982) provides a convenient record of the scientific consensus as to conditions actually prevailing in the early 1980s.

Road to Survival was clear and unequivocal in its view of the future. It concluded with this assertion:

The history of our future is already written, at least for some decades. As we are crowded together, two and a quarter billion of us, on the shrinking surface of the globe, we have set in motion historical forces that are directed by our total environment.

We might symbolize these forces by graphs. One of them is the curve of human populations that, after centuries of relative equilibrium, suddenly began to mount, and in the past fifty years have been climbing at a vertiginous rate.

The other graph is that of our resources. It represents the area and thickness of our topsoil, the abundance of our forests, available waters, life-giving grasslands, and the biophysical web that holds them together. This curve, except for local depressions, also maintained a high degree of regularity through the centuries. But it, too, has had its direction sharply diverted, especially during the past hundred and fifty years, and it is plunging downward like a rapid.

These two curves—of population and the means of survival—have long since crossed. Ever more rapidly they are growing apart. The farther they are separated the more difficult will it be to draw them together again. (p. 287)

The principal thrust of *Road to Survival* was similar in many respects to that of the summary volume of *The Global 2000 Report to the President*. Most frequently quoted, but not entirely consistent with the findings in the other chapters of that report, was its view that:

If present trends continue, the world in 2000 will be more crowded, more polluted, less stable ecologically, and more vulnerable to disruption than the world we live in now. Serious stresses involving population, resources, and environment are clearly visible ahead. Despite greater material output, the world's people will be poorer in many ways than they are today.

For hundreds of millions of the desperately poor, the outlook for food and other necessities of life will be no better. For many it will be worse. Barring revolutionary advances in technology, life for most people on earth will be more precarious in 2000 then it is now—unless the nations of the world act to alter current trends. (vol. 1, p. 1)

In contrast, Brown summed up his views in the following:

When we look into the dimness of the distant future we see the possibility of the emergence of any of three possible patterns of life. The first and by far the most likely pattern is a reversion to agrarian existence. This is the pattern which will almost certainly emerge unless man is able to abolish war, unless he is able to make the transition involving the utilization of new energy sources, and unless he is able to stabilize populations.

In spite of the difficulties that confront industrial civilization, there is a possibility that stabilization can be achieved, that war can be avoided, and that resource transition can be successfully negotiated. In that event, mankind will be confronted with a pattern which looms on the horizon of events as the second most likely possibility—the completely controlled, collectivized industrial society.

The third possibility confronting mankind is that of the worldwide free industrial society in which human beings can live in reasonable harmony with their environment. It is unlikely that such a pattern can ever exist for long. It certainly will be difficult to achieve, and it clearly will be difficult to maintain once it is established. Nevertheless, we have seen that man has it within his power to create such a society and to devise ways and means of perpetuating it on a stable basis. In view of the existence of this power, the possibility that the third pattern may eventually emerge cannot be ignored, although the probabilitiy of such an emergence, as judged from existing trends, may appear to be extremely low. (pp. 264–265)

In taking a retrospective approach to these two speculative books, I have not attempted to examine changes in the opinions of the authors as recorded in their subsequent writings. Brown, for example, made a kind of mid-course correction. Such shifts are to be hailed and encouraged, but the distinctive features of the original predictions lose clarity when intermediate adjustments are made. Neither have I attempted to compare them with regard to every assertion or step in their arguments. It has seemed rewarding to select only a few major components of their findings.

Since the mid-century predictions, the era of sophisticated regional and global models has bloomed. With somewhat larger stocks of data, with computerized calculating capacity, and with intricate mathematical expressions of environmental, economic, and social parameters, the new breed of projections of future conditions offers a battery of outputs that give an air of concreteness and specificity. The projections are accurate for the most part in reflecting the quantified inputs. Their prescience is another matter. Only another three decades can demonstrate whether or not they are more so than their predecessors. Meanwhile, it seems likely that the record of the earlier efforts warrants a few homely observations on looking into the resources future.

TWO CONJECTURES

Both Brown and Vogt saw the future as a time of possibly acute human distress unless certain governmental measures were taken. They agreed that one of those sets of measure should involve the stabilization of population growth. Beyond those points they diverged in significant ways.

Vogt emphasized the finite, dwindling stock of natural resources, saw its reduction as precipitous, and concluded that there were already more people on earth than it could support on a sustained basis at a desirable level. In almost all countries the resource base was eroding, and it was necessary to reverse that trend by conservation measures.

Brown emphasized the problem of transforming policy toward use of nonrenewable energy sources but considered resource availability more as a function of technology and social organization than of limits in materials. The remedies lay in social policy and organization.

Whereas Vogt argued that governments were obliged as a matter of survival to carry out remedial and preventative activities, Brown saw the character of the government as shaping the society's ability to conserve as well as develop resources. His extreme case would be generated by nuclear war so destructive that humans might never again manage, in the case of depleted, high-cost mineral resources, to build an industrial economy. The other two, presumably less probable, cases assumed catastrophic war might be avoided and that either authoritarian or democratic processes of governance would prevail. The fundamental difference between Vogt and Brown's views, then, grew out of appraisal of the capacity of societies to shape resource availability by social and technological means.

THE WORLD IN 1982

Three decades later, neither of the worst-case views of the mid-century had yet been realized. Cataclysmic nuclear combat had not broken out, although some observers regarded it as more nearly imminent than at any time in the post–World War II years, and the hazard of nuclear detonations had come to be labeled in some quarters as the ultimate environmental threat.

Population growth had continued at a high rate, yielding total populations higher than Brown and Vogt had anticipated. Their expectations of a reduction in rates of growth finally materialized during the period of 1975–1980, when the world annual percentage growth rate declined from 1.99 (in 1960–1965) to 1.72, somewhat contrary to forecasts at the time of the 1972 United Nations Conference on the Human Environment, held in Stockholm (Holdgate et al., 1982, p. 303).

Food production overall had barely kept pace with population growth so that by 1979 on a global scale the per capita production by comparison with 1961–1965 had increased by 30 percent for all developed countries except Japan (where it had declined 4 percent), and by 3 to 13 percent for developing countries, except African countries, which were failing to keep up (Holdgate et al., 1982, p. 259).

Statistics as to mortality and morbidity, although crude, indicated an increase in life expectancy at birth between 1950–1955 and 1975–1980, for all major regions. There was a significant reduction in communicable diseases, and among the parasitic diseases malaria, after a major decline, was becoming more hazardous (Holdgate et al., 1982, pp. 360–371).

The record of land deterioration in arid and semiarid regions as presented to the United Nations Conference on Desertification in 1977 (United Nations Environment Programme [UNEP], 1977) was one of widespread destruction, and although a plan of action had been agreed to by the principal governments there had been little evidence of substantial action in the following five years (Holdgate et al., 1982). The record of land improvement—through drainage, irrigation, tillage practices—and of land deterioration—through erosion, alkalinization— was mixed. Estimates of the rates of change in both directions for cropland and grassland suggested that for many parts of the world, physical limits of land for food and fiber production had not been reached and were not in imminent reach (Buringh, 1981). Reductions in the proportions of high-quality land were being offset by gains in medium- and low-quality land.

In the temperate zones the area of commercial forest had expanded. In the tropical zones, large areas of humid forests were being converted by expanded shifting agriculture, by selective cutting, or by clear-cutting, but the sharpest relative inroads probably were being made in savanna and deciduous forests.

On the metallic mineral front, extraction continued with greater attention given to substitutions and recycling, but no severe shortages had yet caused readjustments in industrial processes.

Fossil fuels production and consumption had mounted over the period 1950–1973, in rough association with population and manufacturing production. Per capita consumption had begun to flatten out markedly in developed market economies, and attention was beginning to turn to energy conservation and renewable resources.

Numerous other indices might be cited without altering the general picture, which was mixed and undistinguished by massive shortages and disruption. Resource deterioration was continuing rapidly in some regions, such as the Sahel and Asian mountains, but the capacity of the earth to support farming and industrial populations had not yet been thrown into grave question. Perhaps more significant, a family of problems receiving little or no attention in mid-century had come to occupy central positions on the stage of public concern.

UNRECOGNIZED PROBLEMS

It is illuminating to note the environmental topics omitted or treated only lightly in the two books. Looking at popular concerns of the mid-1980s, a few stand out.

- Acid rain was not anticipated as a national or international problem. It first came into prominence in preparation for the Stockholm Conference.
- Climate change related to build-ups in the atmosphere of carbon dioxide and other substances was not seen as an emerging issue.
- Depletion of humid tropical forests had not been identified as a major issue.
- Possible reduction in genetic diversity of plants and animals had barely been mentioned.
- Disposal of toxic substances in soil, air, or water had received only passing attention.
- Pesticide effects and management also had been treated in a relatively casual manner.
- The need of humans for open space and wild areas had been discussed only in vague terms.

All seven of these facets of resource use had come into prominence in both scientific and policy discussions after the early 1950s. They were part and parcel of what came to be considered environmental concerns. The notion of resources and the earth was broadened thereby.

It would be misleading to suggest that any of these environmental matters had been wholly unrecognized by analysts of the mid-century. All were identified in some fashion or other. None, however, was regarded by Brown or Vogt as deserving of major attention. The scientific literature on those topics from which they could draw was meager. Public debate on them was also slight.

Listing these problems encourges inquiry as to how similarly neglected problems in the contemporary scene can be lifted into a level of examination they may later deserve. Identification of such threats and opportunities is a chronic test of ingenuity and imaginative searching (Kates, 1982).

BASIC INDICATORS

A major constraint on any review of global conditions in the late 1940s and early 1950s was the lack of data on the basic indicators of resource conditions in many parts of the world. Few studies could marshall statistics with both wide coverage and reasonable validity. Indeed, by 1982 the deficiencies in collection and publication of reliable statistics on population, soils, forests, water, minerals, and energy use were still formidable (Holdgate et al., 1982, pp. 622–623).

One of the few indicators readily available was for population as a surrogate of human need and of human capacity. The estimates of total world population for 1950 placed it at about 2.4 billion. Time series for gross and net reproduction rates had been published for only a few countries. Speculation about future rates of growth for many countries therefore was crude at best. Vogt avoided estimates of global population but ventured for some countries such as China and India growth figures that proved conservative. Brown predicted a 1975 population of 3.4 billion (p. 99), which turned out to be 15 percent lower than the actual figure of 4.0 billion reported by the United Nations.

Because the global statistics were lacking for most other indicators, statements about prospective changes in those parameters had to be couched in very general terms or made by reference to examples. Where the data for the world could not be arrayed, those for a few countries could be presented and used to speculate on the conditions and trends in other areas.

Consider the ways in which Vogt and Brown treated agricultural resource productivity. *Road to Survival* examines the "carrying capacity" of a number of countries and concludes in various contexts that they were already overpopulated. Thus, after examining the United States and Great Britain, it concludes, "There are too many people in the world for its limited resources to provide a high standard of living," (p. 78) and "though few people seem to realize it, the lower standard of living is here—and it is certain to go lower" (p. 79). To support this, it recites areas where soil erosion was fierce, international aid projects had failed, and population was burgeoning.

The Challenge of Man's Future reviewed the range of possible ways of increasing food production while maintaining the soil base and assigned each a potential in proportion to then existing production as unity. These included increasing output from existing cropland (0.1), bringing in new acreage of cropland (1.0), new supplemental and complete irrigation (1.0), increases due to improved plant breeding and selection and foreseeable improvements in agricultural techniques (3.0), and production from algae farms (25.0). It concluded, "When we consider population limitation solely on the basis of potential food supply, enormous increases of numbers of human beings are possible in principle," given raw materials for plant nutrients and capital to undertake irrigation, soil-conservation algae farms, and yeast plants (p. 146). The "green revolution" thus was seen as a possible development. It was arrayed along with other changes that have not yet materialized or that may cancel each other out as in the case of new irrigation projects that are offset by deterioration of existing projects.

TRENDS AND DISCONTINUITIES

More significant than the interpolation of blank space on the statistical map from adjoining or distant areas was the use made of established trends in predictions. By comparison with some other fields, such as demography, resource analysts have limited experience in arriving at global generalizations from refined manipulation of incomplete data. A look back at the mid-century speculations and consideration of where they may have gone wrong reveals that a principal difficulty was the failure to anticipate discontinuities in trends that were projected as linear phenomena.

By the time *Limits to Growth* and *Global 2000* projections were produced there had been enough of these kinds of interpolation and extrapolation so that what appeared to be reasonably comprehensive data for the world could be presented and manipulated. Thus, *Global 2000* could conclude:

> World food production is projected to increase 90 percent over the 30 years from 1970 to 2000. This translated into a global per capita increase of less than 15 percent over the same period. The bulk of that increase goes to countries that already have relatively high per capita food consumption. Meanwhile, per capita food consumption in South Asia, the Middle East, and the LDC's of Africa will scarcely improve or will actually decline below present inadequate levels (pp. i, 1–2).

Such apparent accuracy and completeness may be more a disservice than a service to readers seeking light on the murky global future. Both accuracy and completeness were to some extent illusory and although cautions in that regard were stated in the supporting documents, and indeed *Global 2000* sought to denote this graphically with its brush marks, the summary statements did not emphasize those cautions. In that sense, Vogt and Brown, and particularly Brown, presented their readers with a quantitatively sparse but qualitatively more thoughtful view of the future than did the projections of later reports. They highlighted national situations and pointed out certain weaknesses of international aid programs as well as the potential of new technologies and social arrangements.

In the field of agricultural productivity of land resources, the most dramatic discontinuity during the three decades of 1950 to 1980 was, of course, in the unfolding of improved technology for crop production: seeds, plant breeding, fertilizers, pesticides, herbicides, fungicides, irrigation methods, and farm machinery. The reality of those improvements changed drastically the prospect for feeding growing populations in countries where rice, corn, or wheat were staples.

A second and different instance was the change in price relationships in energy consumption and production. Brown's analysis of the energy situation in the early 1950s had led him to anticipate a four-stage transformation in the world pattern of energy consumption in which, as fossil fuels disappeared, greater use would be made of solar and atomic sources until, as coal passed its peak, space heating would be provided by solar and atomic power, and liquid fuels would be obtained from wood and other vegetation. He speculated on the difficulties of disposing of nuclear waste, the practicability of breeder reactors, and the comparative capital costs of atomic and solar energy.

In the final stage, solar might become the dominant source. This conjecture was, of course, for a time horizon far beyond thirty years, and it envisaged the technical capacity to supply the energy needs of 7 billion people after fossil fuels were no longer available at competitive prices. Unlike the agricultural productivity analysis, it did not examine the whole range of alternatives in the middle term and thus failed to anticipate the cost barriers to nuclear power and the major effects of managing demand instead of supply. Where the emphasis was on projection of trends there was less attention to the radical departures in technology or social policy that in the short run would strongly influence the course of development.

One other instance of unanticipated events deserves mention. Brown and Vogt, like most of their contemporaries, stressed in one fashion or another the cultivation of public awareness of the global resource situation and of the responsibility of the United States in giving leadership to worldwide action. They did not observe that most such programs, like the early conservation and New Deal efforts in the United States, had come in waves. The tendency was to think of education and public policy as a slow, gradual process. Although earnest pleas were made for heightened public awareness of problems of resource adequacy and although educational programs were seen as essential to lasting improvements, the great environmental movements culminating in celebration of Earth Day and in the Stockholm conference were not expected by Brown and Vogt, nor did they discuss the conditions in which such advances might be generated or strengthened.

EITHER/OR PROJECTIONS

With only a few exceptions, the predictions of the mid-century were directed at policy choices, and many of those were presented in either/ or terms. Vogt's concluding statement, quoted above, was typical. Unless a specified course of action were to be taken, certain consequences would ensue. Similarly, Osborne, speaking of the world of the future, remarked: "The question remains. Are we to continue on the same dusty perilous road once traveled to its dead end by other mighty and splendid nations, or, in our wisdom, are we going to choose the only route that does not lead to the disaster that has already befallen so many peoples of the earth?" (p. 156). This kind of choice sharpens the issue of whether or not a particular action program should be supported. Its rhetoric is strong, and endorsement of policy issues is not hampered by the appraisal of other options.

There also is logic in that mode of presentation. The analyst presumably has reviewed the evidence, canvassed the options for future action, and selected a course that appears most likely to remedy the anticipated ills. There may be no highly persuasive grounds for selecting one option over another, however, and an appropriate stance may be to outline a range of options. Brown was one of the few who followed this practice. Although he did conclude that three, in contrast to the conventional two, futures might be envisaged, in some instances he examined a variety of options, pointing out strengths and weaknesses of each.

An example is the treatment in *The Challenge of Man's Future* of the future of materials from nonrenewable resources. After reviewing the numerous means employed by societies to cope with resource scarcity, the text outlines a course of events in which refinements will occur in industrial processes, regional specialization will flourish, and industries "will pass through several stages; at the end of which mineral resources will cease to be important factors in world economy" (p. 217). The basic materials then will be sea water, air, ordinary rock, sedimentary deposits of limestone and phosphate, and sunlight. Complexity and integration will be the order of the day. In pursuing this argument, however, *The Challenge* finds that only that combination of circumstances would seem plausible and from that position moves on to conclude, "With increasing necessity and demand for efficiency, integration, and minimizing of waste in the economic world there will be increasing demand for efficiency, integration, and minimization of waste in the social world" (p. 218). Much of the weight of thoughtful appraisal of options is weakened by the final judgment that only one sequence of events may be the alternate to disaster.

RESOURCES IN THE SOCIAL AND POLITICAL CONTEXT

More than any other analyst at the time, Brown tried to place his appraisal of resource availability in a social and political context. The underlying recognition was of the crucial role of culture and social organization in shaping the uses of technology and conditions of resource use. In that framework the natural resource was not a fixed quantity or a physical-biological complex having a finite carrying capacity for the human race; these qualities were mediated by society. The society and its political structure were themselves continually evolving.

Vogt saw the mode of preserving or managing the resource as governed by the political process. The resource was a quantity that would be used widely or destroyed according to political guidance, but not augmented. According to this view, environmentalists could be dismayed or pleased by political action or its lack; they were not inclined to expect a changing definition of a resource in response to scientific, economic, or political action. The future good lay in preserving the resource base.

The view expressed by Vogt was dominant in many environmental circles until after the Stockholm conference of 1972. Then attention began to shift toward the social and political guides and constraints. Ten years later the UNEP review of the preceding decade concluded that:

> Finally, the 1970s emphasized that the great problems of the world environment have political roots. Stable administrations, supported by popular consensus, are needed if long-term environmental developments are to proceed, and resources are not to be dissipated in strife and preparations for war. This review shows that despite serious local disruption, the world environment is not in imminent danger of disintegration. But it needs thoughtful, committed management which can only be achieved in an atmosphere of peace, security and stability. (Holdgate et al., 1982, p. 630).

Changes in the social and political realm are difficult enough for political seers to foresee, let alone students of environmental matters. One response to the difficulty is to assume relatively stable, unchanging political organization and social values. Another is to expect a variety of possible changes and either to seek to specify a number of them or to refrain from forecasting them.

SUMMARY

All things considered, in my opinion Brown came closer than anyone else during that whole mid-century period to recognizing the forces likely to be at work in the three decades to follow. He achieved this by recognizing the lack of resources data and by being cautious in extrapolating from what was available. He favored examination of factors possibly making for discontinuities rather than projection of linear trends, and he canvassed a wide range of options but was inclined to cap the analysis with an either/or kind of prediction. He directed attention to the broad social and political context within which resource use takes place. In all this he, like most others of his time, gave little or no weight to a number of issues subsequently regarded as highly important. The final outcome was recognition of large opportunities to meet demands of an increasing population. He did not predict early disaster, but neither was he sanguine that the opportunities could be realized.

Brown was dramatic without being shrill or condescending in his observations of his contemporaries and their proclivities. He was concerned without being committed irrevocably to one course of action. He was candid in stating the deficiencies of analysis and data. For those problems he did identify, the analysis has not proven distressingly far from the mark in subsequent events.

As we enter a new generation of conjectures advancing beyond the crude global modeling of 1972 to 1982, those involved may derive a few useful homilies from the texts of the mid-century meditations on things to come.

REFERENCES

Brown, H., 1954. *The Challenge of Man's Future: An Inquiry Concerning the Condition of Man During the Years That Lie Ahead.* New York: Viking Press. (Reprinted in 1984 by Westview Press, Boulder, Colo.)

Buringh, P., 1981. *An Assessment of Losses and Degradation of Productive Agricultural Land in the World.* Wageningen: Agricultural University.

Clawson, M., 1981. *New Deal Planning: The National Resources Planning Board.* Baltimore: Johns Hopkins University Press.

Darwin, C. G., 1953. *The Next Million Years.* New York: Doubleday and Co.

Food and Agriculture Organization, 1946. *World Food Survey.* Rome: FAO.

Global 2000 Report to the President, The: Entering the Twenty-First Century (1980). A Report prepared by the Council on Environmental Quality and the Department of State. n.d. Washington, D.C.: Government Printing Office. 3 volumes.

Holdgate, M. W., M. Kassas, and G. F. White (eds.), 1982. *The World Environment 1972–1982: A Report to the United Nations Environment Programme.* Dublin: Tycooly International Publishing Ltd.

Kates, R. W., 1982. *The Human Environment: Penultimate Problems of Survival.* Boulder: Institute of Behavioral Science.

Meadows, D. H., D. L. Meadows, J. Randers, and W. W. Behrens, III, 1972. *The Limits to Growth*, New York: Universe Books.

Marsh, C. P., 1974. *The Earth as Modified by Human Action: A New Edition.* New York: Scribner, Armstrong & Co.

Mid-Century Conference on Resources for the Future, 1954. *The Nation Looks at its Resources.* Washington, D.C.: Resources for the Future.

Osborne, F., 1948. *Our Plundered Planet.* Boston: Little, Brown & Co.

President's Materials Policy Commission, 1952. *Resources for Freedom.* Washington, D.C.: Government Printing Office. 5 volumes.

Resources for the Future, 1977. *The First 25 Years: 1952–1977.* Washington, D.C.: Resources for the Future.

United Nations, 1950. *Proceedings of the United Nations Scientific Conference on the Conservation and Utilization of Resources,* 1949. Lake Success: United Nations. 8 volumes.

United Nations Environment Programme, 1977. *United Nations Conference on Desertification: Desertification, an Overview.* Nairobi: UNEP.

U.S. Department of Agriculture, 1980. *World Food Production.* Washington, D.C.: Department of Agriculture.

Whyte, R. O., and G. V. Jacks, 1939. *Vanishing Lands.* New York: Doubleday, Doran and Co.

Zimmerman, E. W., 1951. *World Resources and Industries.* New York: Harper and Brothers.

PART THREE
INTERNATIONAL COOPERATION AND THE HUMAN FUTURE

INTRODUCTION

FEREIDUN FESHARAKI

Harrison Brown is a man of vision. He is a man of science who has devoted a major portion of his life to studying issues that affect the future of humanity. As his career began to blossom in the 1940s, he was already concerned with the effect of science on the future of humanity. He realized early on that the issues that shape human destiny are so complex and multifaceted that only an interdisciplinary approach could highlight the problems. Thirty years after the publication of his remarkable book, *The Challenge of Man's Future,* many of the issues he raised remain topical, though the scale and the foci of some of the issues may have changed somewhat.

Harrison Brown is a great believer in international cooperation as a means of pooling efforts to avoid the dangers faced by humanity. He has participated in initiatives that resulted in the establishment of organizations that have become important forces for international cooperation. In Harrison's view, international cooperation among scientists was the most useful type of dialogue. As a man of science himself, he felt scientists could rise above self-interest and political rivalries and could engage in discussions on issues well beyond their own national boundaries.

In their chapter in honor of Harrison, Victor Rabinowitch and John Hurley have selected four examples of international scientific cooperation in which Harrison Brown played a major role: the International Council of Scientific Unions; Science and Technology for International Development; the Pugwash Conference on Science and World Affairs; and the International Institute for Applied Systems Analysis. These examples range from an organization of scientists concerned with peace and security to improving communications among scientists and helping to improve human conditions in the Third World through international cooperation as well as a highly regarded, internationally funded research institute where scientists from the Soviet Union and the United States (among those of many other nations) could be involved in joint research activities.

Chapter 11, by Victor Urquidi, is a discussion of the concept and validity of endogenous development. This chapter does not deal with Harrison Brown's influence on thinking but is written in the spirit of Harrison Brown's challenges of conventional wisdoms. Dr. Urquidi questions the validity of the rhetoric that has become a central concept in the transfer of technology from the industrialized nations to the Third World. Such concepts as "appropriate technology" and "endogenous development" rose out of attempts by intellectuals and international organizations to resist wholesale transfer of advanced technologies that transplant the way of life of the industrial world onto the developing nations with totally different cultural, ethnic, and social priorities. Although he agrees in many instances about the importance of fully considering the internal dynamics of any society before importing technology from outside, he questions the validity of arguments that every piece of the technology and each strategy of development should be recreated in that society to match the societal needs. Such an approach, he argues, would deprive the inhabitants of that society of the value of accumulated knowledge and technical advances made by scientists all over the world.

Chapter 12, by Rector Soedjatmoko, is a discussion of the need for institutions of unity for protecting the global commons. He argues that the global commons—Earth's crust and atmosphere, climate, tropical rain forests, seas, soils, and other essential components of planetary life—can be efficiently managed only on a regional and international basis. Soedjatmoko advocates a multidisciplinary approach for managing the problems—much in the same way as Harrison Brown has always advocated. He sees single-issue politics as an important barrier to a multidisciplinary approach; such politics lead policymakers to abdicate broader responsibilities. He notes that both governments and intergovernmental systems must learn to cope with new conflicts of interest, such as those in the field of communication. He also argues for the adoption of international legal instruments to help regulate and enforce sounder environmental practice on an international scale. The progress in international agreements on the law of the sea is a step in the right direction, but much more needs to be done. Because national governments are often so reluctant to establish legal measures for enforcing environmental practices, there may well be no choice but to start at the global level and hope that national laws will follow one day. Soedjatmoko doubts whether the existing international institutions are inherently capable of dealing with the massive problems that lie ahead. He argues that there may well be need for new types of institutions that represent not only governments but also scientists and other constituencies concerned with global commons.

Chapter 13, by Robert H. Randolph and Kirk R. Smith, relates to Harrison Brown's work at the East-West Center and its impact on the Asia-Pacific region. Kirk Smith, a doctoral student of John Holdren, is a coeditor of this book. Smith, whose own work and thinking were influenced by Harrison Brown's writings, joined the East-West Center in 1977, soon after Harrison assumed the directorship of the Resource Systems Institute (RSI) at the center. Thus Smith was able to work with Harrison Brown for six years while Brown pursued research activities to strengthen international cooperation in the Asia-Pacific region. Robert Randolph, a historian with advanced training in computer applications, teleconferencing, and technology assessment, came to the center from IIASA and joined Harrison as his assistant director. Like Smith, Randolph also had the opportunity to work closely with Harrison Brown. In their chapter, Randolph and Smith provide a detailed explanation of how Harrison Brown started the research programs at RSI and list the research projects that eventually developed under the three program areas of energy, food, and raw materials. The authors then turn their attention to the lessons that can be learned from multidisciplinary research by drawing on their combined experience at RSI. Their advice on the approaches to the multidisciplinary research and pitfalls in achieving international cooperation is perceptive. Finally, the authors turn their attention to the changing conditions and prospects for policy research cooperation, noting with grave concern the U.S. pullback from the past vigorous involvement in international science.

These four chapters, which form Part 3 of this book, are in themselves a tribute to a man whom the authors wish to honor; a tribute to a vision for a better world created not only out of internal efficiency and reform but also through international cooperation and understanding.

10

THE COOPERATIVE IMPERATIVE IN SCIENCE AND TECHNOLOGY

VICTOR RABINOWITCH
AND JOHN HURLEY

It is quite gratifying to us as "students" of Harrison Brown in the practice of international scientific affairs to be invited to honor him through a contribution to this volume. On accepting the invitation from the organizers, we thought it might be particularly instructive to review international scientific cooperation from its earliest expression through the period of the so-called scientific revolution to the present. This review would give a better sense of the evolution of the process.

A search of the literature brought a surprise, however, for it failed to turn up any substantial efforts to systematically study international cooperation in science. Though there exist many isolated examples of scientific cooperation, and more recently, many conferences on the subject, it appears that sociologists, historians of science, students of science policy, and scientists themselves have neglected the subject as an area of serious academic concern. Our brief review suggests that there is a fertile area of study here, and we hope that this recognition will stimulate more analysis in the future, for it is clear that international cooperation has been and will continue to be one of the basic characteristics of the scientific enterprise.

In this contribution we have selected four examples of international scientific cooperation that demonstrate both the wide range of experience and varied nature of the cooperative process and the significant involvement in it of the man we honor, Harrison Brown. The four examples we have chosen to describe briefly are (1) the International Council of Scientific Unions (ICSU)—an organization concerned with communication and cooperation among scientists worldwide and with the health of the scientific enterprise; (2) Science and Technology for International Development—an approach to finding ways to improve the human condition in the poorer countries of the world through international cooperation; (3) the Pugwash Conference on Science and World Affairs— an organization of scientists concerned with finding ways to resolve world problems and insure peace and security; and (4) the International Institute for Applied Systems Analysis (IIASA)—an organization concerned with finding solutions to critical societal problems through the use of modern methods of analysis.

THE INTERNATIONAL COUNCIL OF SCIENTIFIC UNIONS

Students of science are impressed in their most elementary classes that scientific discovery and accomplishment are the product of hundreds, indeed, thousands, of individual efforts building one on the other to provide ever greater understanding of the laws of nature and the processes they govern. This being the case, it is not surprising that scientists everywhere feel the need to communicate their experiences, test their hypotheses, organize and systematize their results, and ensure that scientific research will continue in a free and open way. The International Council of Scientific Unions exists precisely for these purposes.

Created in Brussels in 1931, ICSU traces its origins back to the International Association of Academies (1898) and the International Research Council (IRC), which was formed in 1919 to coordinate international efforts in the different branches of science through the formation of international associations or unions. Building on the experiences, objectives, and goals of the past, ICSU provides for membership of scientific communities from throughout the world, not just the post–World War I allies, as was the case with the IRC. It continues also the unique dual-membership character of the organization: National Members are represented by national academies of science or research councils, Scientific Members are represented by the individual disciplinary unions.

As a federation of unions, one of ICSU's prime objectives is to foster the efforts of its autonomous member unions to facilitate global scientific interchange. To this end the unions convene regular international conferences and engage in a variety of other activities. In addition, ICSU's special contribution is to mobilize and organize interdisciplinary research programs, like the International Geophysical Year and the International Biological Program, which combine the talents and resources of the national academies and the scientific unions. The ICSU expresses its concern for the health and welfare of science and scientists through special committees devoted to a range of global issues such as problems of the environment; science and technology for development; oceanic, space, and water research; and genetic engineering.

During the fifteen-year period that Harrison Brown was actively involved in ICSU affairs (1963–1978), he encouraged global collaboration on several multidisciplinary projects. Drawing on his service as chairman of a major National Research Council (NRC) effort to evaluate the world food situation, he urged scientists in ICSU to utilize the basic biological skills represented in the member unions to address problems of agricultural productivity. He believed that progress in enhancing food production could be significantly aided by closer collaboration among basic and applied scientists, a marriage, if you will, of biological and agricultural sciences.

During his presidency of ICSU (1974–1976), a group was formed to discuss the global implications of recombinant DNA research at a time when many national science communities were wrestling with problems associated with the potential hazards of research and were searching for appropriate safety guidelines. He believed that within an international nongovernmental forum, important contributions could be made to assure the safe conduct of research. Another multidisciplinary activity organized by ICSU was the Global Atmospheric Research Program, carried out jointly with the World Meteorological Organization. Harrison played an important role in this activity by drawing attention to the need for a coordinated program to gain better understanding of climatic change.

Harrison also devoted considerable energy to the stimulation and encouragement of international cooperation in scientific and technical information. As a vice president of ICSU, he was instrumental in the establishment of CODATA, the ICSU Committee on Data for Science and Technology, to promote the worldwide evaluation, compilation, and dissemination of data, particularly of interdisciplinary significance. In 1966–1970, he was convener of the ICSU-UNESCO (United Nations Economic, Scientific, and Cultural Organization) effort to consider the establishment of a World Science Information System (UNISIST). As a result of this study, a major intergovernmental program that set the stage for further international cooperative activities in science information that continue today was launched within UNESCO.

It is to his credit that Harrison appreciated perhaps more than many of his scientific colleagues the importance of involvement by the scientific community in matters relating to scientific information. He was acutely aware that information and communication problems are not susceptible to facile technological solutions, that underlying the problems are economic, organizational, and legal complications, both within individual countries and among intergovernmental and nongovernmental organizations through which countries conduct their international scientific relations.

Throughout his association with ICSU, and especially during his presidency of that organization, Harrison Brown concentrated his efforts on defending and developing further three basic principles that have guided ICSU operations: (1) the nonpolitical nature of ICSU and its unions, (2) universality of membership and participation, and (3) free circulation of scientists. He displayed a deep concern about scientists' freedom to pursue their research with colleagues, wherever they might be, and worked assiduously to meet the challenges that arose over the years to the principle of free circulation.

The ICSU Committee on the Free Circulation of Scientists benefited substantially from Brown's active leadership and spirit. In pursuit of the ICSU principle of universality, he negotiated with colleagues in Beijing and Taipei to achieve national membership in ICSU of the scientific community of the People's Republic of China without losing the membership of the Taiwan community. Eventually he became convinced that an overall political solution would have to precede a resolution within ICSU, and in this he was correct. It was not until 1982 that a solution was found within ICSU to this vexing problem. Harrison Brown's efforts to nurture this dialogue were significant, however, and the leadership and commitment he demonstrated towards ICSU's basic principles strengthened ICSU as a major organization of international science cooperation. He was an effective spokesman on these issues and consistently pushed ICSU to pursue a leadership role in the world science community.

SCIENCE AND TECHNOLOGY
FOR INTERNATIONAL DEVELOPMENT

One of Harrison Brown's most significant contributions has been to point out that the imperative for scientific cooperation extends to the developing countries as well as the industrialized countries and that it looms large in the equation for economic well-being and social progress. Harrison is deeply committed to the belief that global problems of population growth, the scarcity and maldistribution of food, the destruction of vital natural resources, and the human effects of poverty can be alleviated only through active cooperation between the industrialized and the developing countries. During his tenure as foreign secretary of the National Academy of Sciences from 1962 to 1974, much of his energy was devoted to finding ways to increase the contacts between U.S. scientists and their Third World counterparts and to build support within the development assistance agencies for expanding the use of science and technology in their programs.

The assumptions underlying these efforts were outlined by Harrison and Theresa Tellez as follows (1973): "(1) Scientific and technological growth is an essential element of national development; (2) Indigenous scientific capability or local problem-solving competence is requisite for a country to lessen its dependence on others; and (3) Science can be applied to human betterment in general, and specifically to the problems of poor nations suffering from hunger, disease, and inadequate resources" (p. 2).

The interest of the United States in developing countries, as Harrison frequently has pointed out, is more than an academic or altruistic concern. The developing countries increasingly have come to play a vital role in U.S. political, trade, and security concerns; and therefore, it is worthwhile to review the salient features of the worldwide development scene.

The progress achieved in the 1970s by the Third World as a whole was in some respects very striking. Annual GNP growth rate for all developing countries was 5.3 percent (compared with 3.2 percent in the industrial market economies.) Aggregate manufactured exports, as a share of world exports, increased from 18.4 percent in 1970 to 21.4 percent in 1980. This occurred despite the fact that oil import bills skyrocketed in the 1970s.

Some of the so-called advanced or newly industrializing developing countries such as Singapore, Korea, and Brazil did extremely well in the last decade, achieving annual growth in per capita GNP greater than that of the United States, even though their populations grew twice as fast. A rung below the newly industrializing countries on the development ladder comes a middle tier of developing countries including about eighty nations with per capita GNPs of $400 or more, averaging around $1,200, but with wide differences in their development progress. At the lower end of the ladder come the thirty-nine poorest developing countries, concentrated in South Asia and sub-Saharan Africa, whose situation did not change much in the past decade. These countries, with per capita GNPs below $400, had real growth rates in GNP per capita of only 0.7 percent in the 1970s (World Bank, 1982; Hansen et al., 1982).

Considerable progress has been made in the developing countries in terms of certain aspects of human well-being. Life expectancy in the Third World increased in two decades by as much as it increased in the industrialized nations in a century, and a number of major diseases, including smallpox, were virtually eradicated. Improved grain varieties helped to ease the pressure on world food supplies.

But problems still abound. Average life expectancy in the low-income developing countries is still seventeen years lower than in the industrialized countries, and infant mortality is more than five times as high. It has been estimated that nearly 1 billion people in developing countries live in absolute poverty, and some 460 million people (over half of them children) are malnourished. About 850 million people still have no access to schools. Only one-quarter of the people in developing countries have safe water, and only half of all urban households have minimally adequate housing.

Despite the rapid industrialization and urbanization that is taking place in many developing countries, rural populations are still vast and are closely tied to agricultural pursuits. For people in rural areas, the effects of poverty frequently include high levels of morbidity and mortality, inability to sustain hard work on a regular basis, and lack of access to education and vital services.

National development, therefore, must involve strategies to increase production and raise productivity as a means of improving the conditions of life for large numbers of people. At the same time, these improvements also will enable the citizens of developing countries to contribute to the wider process of national economic and social development.

This task of national development, however, is complex and difficult. Rapid population growth puts increasing pressure on available resources and especially increases the food supplies needed. Since good farmland is limited, the production of food per hectare will need to be increased further. There is also a great need to increase the level of nonfarm employment.

Because the growth rate of energy consumption in developing countries is greater than in industrialized countries, development is affected by the severe problems faced by countries that rely heavily on imported petroleum. When prices rise, governments in the developing countries face the necessity of using increasingly large sums of foreign exchange for imported oil, thus diverting resources that might be used for other development activities. Although energy prices have fallen in recent years, the worldwide recession created conditions in which energy costs still represent an enormous burden for many developing countries.

It is becoming ever more apparent that the ecosystem of a planet with strained natural resources and increasing population presents problems that truly are global. Like it or not, we are all interdependent and must act in concert to address common problems such as the need for greater food production; the need for diversified and renewable energy sources; the destruction of forests and depletion of soil; and increasing atmospheric, terrestrial, and aquatic contamination.

Besides the critical problems of agriculture, health, energy, and resources, the development equation includes important issues of a different dimension. For example, the behavioral, cultural, and social implications of technological achievements and of economic change are profound and must be better understood.

Many of the middle-income countries now are grappling with the second generation problems of more intensive development. Industrialization, for example, has created unacceptable environmental problems in some places. The rapid and unplanned use of natural resources has created an urgent need for sound management and renewal of the resources where that is possible or for planning the best economic stewardship and equitable use of nonrenewable resources.

In many developing countries, economic achievements are not based on the participation of the entire labor force. Rapid growth at the national level does not automatically reduce poverty and inequality or provide sufficient productive employment. The present outlook is that the problems of unemployment and underemployment will not disappear; they are, in fact, likely to deepen.

Another challenge of development is the need to chart a course that recognizes changes in the appropriate emphasis on labor and capital. As economic development occurs, labor costs often rise, giving an advantage in certain types of industry to less developed countries with lower labor costs. Industrial planning and scientific and technological planning must involve farsighted strategies that anticipate these possibilities.

Most of these critical development problems involve the physical, natural, and social sciences and cannot be effectively addressed by one country alone. Both greater understanding of the problems and the consequent development of practical applications will require collaboration among many countries and institutions.

Global interdependence is a fact of modern life that demands serious international effort in working together toward solutions to the problems that face every nation. We live in a constantly changing environment. Development is a continuing journey, not a destination, and the journey requires continuing adjustments to an ever-changing scene.

It has become clear that there are no technological fixes that will quickly reverse the large, complex problems facing the developing countries and the entire global community. Instead, careful attention will have to be given to making as many small advances as possible, reaching good decisions about priorities among many needs, and taking care to cause the least possible disruption to the resources that are the mortar binding together our societies and our lives.

With the clarity that has characterized his vision in examining global issues, Harrison Brown realized early in his study of development problems that science and technology must play a key role in alleviating them. In a paper written in 1958, Harrison said, "In the decades ahead, we are going to be faced by a sequence of problems of great complexity, all of which will demand solution and which must be anticipated if they are to be solved." Further on, he noted, "Solution of the problems will necessitate the concerted and intensive application of science and technology on an unprecedented scale" (Brown, 1963).

Time has proved the correctness of this view of the role of science and technology in development, as they have already made important contributions. The development of improved, higher-yielding grain varieties has been perhaps the classic example. The combination of greater biomedical knowledge and improved epidemiological techniques led to the eradication of smallpox as a disease that afflicts mankind. Other examples could be cited in telecommunications, materials, computers, and especially the techniques that have emerged from biotechnology research that are applied to agriculture, energy, health, and industrial processes.

Harrison Brown's valuable and catalytic contribution to the vital issues of scientific cooperation for development has been to create mechanisms that would focus attention on needs, address them in innovative ways, and possess the flexibility to change with changing circumstances. Three of the most important mechanisms nurtured by Brown while he was foreign secretary of the National Academy of Sciences involved scientific cooperation with developing countries, a major examination of the research required to meet world food needs, and scholarly exchange with the People's Republic of China.

At the academy, cooperation with developing countries had been carried out in the 1960s through several small committees with a geographic focus. Harrison, however, felt that greater impact could be achieved if efforts were concentrated in a single organization, and this realization led him to the creation in 1969 of the Board on Science and Technology for International Development (BOSTID).

BOSTID organizes activities aimed at applying science and technology to development-related problems. Its activities are based on close collaboration with counterpart institutions and individuals in the developing countries, and BOSTID, therefore, tries to be responsive rather than prescriptive in the projects that it organizes. With financial support from the U.S. Agency for International Development, other government agencies, and private foundations, BOSTID provides research grants to developing country institutions; has an active program of publications that examines problems of general concern to developing countries and also focuses on innovative uses of technologies, plants, and animals; carries out projects with specific developing countries that range from seminars and workshops on specific topics to ongoing programs that aim at strengthening local capabilities for science planning and research; and advises development agencies on new work in science and technology that may have important future implications.

The work of BOSTID is carried out by volunteers from the U.S. scientific and technological communities. Thousands of participants from universities, private industry, and government agencies have served on expert committees to produce publications for free distribution in developing countries, have made trips abroad as members of advisory groups, or have reviewed research grant proposals and provided help to grant recipients. As a committee of the National Research Council, BOSTID has the support of the National Academy of Sciences, National Academy of Engineering, and Institute of Medicine.

The development interests of Harrison Brown were focused on a particularly crucial problem in connection with the World Food Conference held in Rome in 1974. The conference gave attention to the problem of world hunger and malnutrition and shortly thereafter the National Academy of Sciences was requested by the president of the United States to "make an assessment of this problem and develop specific recommendations on how our research and development capabilities can best be applied to meeting this challenge" (National Research Council, 1977, p. iii). Harrison Brown was asked to chair the steering committee that was responsible for the study.

The problems of food and nutrition throughout the world are extremely complex. The supply of food is a critical element of the problem, of course, but widespread poverty in developing countries, the stability of supplies and prices, the rate of population growth, and access by farmers to credit and agricultural inputs are other important elements that are not always well understood. Brown and his colleagues set up fourteen different study teams that looked at aspects of the problem, ranging from crop productivity to food availability for consumers. The result was a report entitled *World Food and Nutrition Study: The Potential Contributions of Research* (1977), which is summarized in one main volume along with five volumes of supporting papers. This study stands as one of the most comprehensive examinations in recent times of the ways in which science and technology can be applied to the ever-present and ever-pressing problem of world hunger and malnutrition.

At a different level of scientific cooperation, Harrison Brown saw an opportunity to use scientific and technical cooperation as a vehicle for increasing the level of contact and understanding between China and the United States. As the first openings began to appear in the Bamboo Curtain in the mid-1960s, Brown began to mobilize the U.S. scientific and social science communities for a program of interaction with their counterparts in China.

The Committee on Scholarly Communication with the People's Republic of China (CSCPRC) was created in 1966 by the American Council of Learned Societies (ACLS), the Social Science Research Council (SSRC), and the National Academy of Sciences (NAS) to explore opportunities for scholarly communication with China. Designated by both the United States and Chinese governments to manage the "facilitated" exchanges called for in the Shanghai Communique (resulting from Richard Nixon's 1972 visit to China), during the 1970s the CSCPRC sponsored more than eighty exchange programs, laying the foundation for the scientific bilateral agreements and university programs that flourish today. Since normalization of political relations in 1979, the CSCPRC has designed an integrated academic program of bilateral conferences and short- and long-term visits by individual scholars. Emphasis is placed on developing research access for U.S. scholars in China and encouraging dialogue on topics of significant interest to the U.S. academic community.

Through the three efforts so briefly described here, Harrison Brown's contribution to establishing better communication between the scientists in the United States and in the developing world has been prodigious. His personal participation in a variety of programs has been impressive, but his most significant contribution is the creation of mechanisms that contribute to finding solutions to the development problems critical to all of us.

PUGWASH CONFERENCE ON SCIENCE AND WORLD AFFAIRS

The image of the scientist as an intellectual in an ivory tower, concerned only with a single-minded search for knowledge, has often been invoked when frustrations with technological advance have caused society and government to raise basic questions about scientists and how they work. This, we believe, is an unfortunate and distorted image that does a disservice to a community of people whose contributions have led to significant improvements in the human condition. It is not assumed that the fruits of scientific research are always for the social good, for there are numerous examples of threats to society directly related to the use of science and technology—as, for example, the effects of various technologies on the environment or the potential for disaster from ever more powerful nuclear weapons. But to suggest that scientists lack a concern for these societal impacts is to deny their many important contributions to the amelioration or avoidance of the problems resulting from scientific advance.

Nowhere is this concern more clearly demonstrated than with the discovery of the processes of nuclear fission and fusion. Scientists were the first to recognize that the world could be fundamentally altered by the new knowledge and that it was critical that governments and the public be educated about the potential for completely changing the relations among nations if atomic energy were turned to military objectives. Many of the very scientists responsible for the basic discoveries were at the forefront of efforts to make their potential effect understood, for they realized that once the genie was released from the bottle there was no way to get it back in again.

Once governments possessed and had used nuclear weapons, it was again the scientific community that attempted to meet the challenge to world peace through the traditional mechanism that had served science so well—international cooperation.

Stimulated by Bertrand Russell's appeal to scientists from East and West to join together to educate world leaders and the general public about the dangers arising from the development of weapons of mass destruction, nine Nobel laureates signed a manifesto that contained the following resolution:

> In view of the fact that in any future world war nuclear weapons will certainly be employed, and that such weapons threaten the continued existence of mankind, we urge the governments of the world to realize, and to acknowledge publicly, that their purposes cannot be furthered by a world war, and we urge them, consequently, to find peaceful means for the settlement of all matters of dispute between them.

Because Albert Einstein signed this manifesto just days before his death, it has come to be known as the Russell-Einstein manifesto.

The eloquent words of the statement and the appeal itself have been the inspiration for many groups concerned with peace, but to one group particularly it represents the rationale for existence—the Pugwash movement. Responding to the Russell-Einstein manifesto, scientists in the United Kingdom and the United States initiated efforts to convene the meeting called for in the manifesto. Through the hospitality and financial support of Cyrus Eaton, a wealthy Cleveland industrialist, a meeting of scientists from East and West was called in 1957 in a small fishing village, Pugwash, Nova Scotia, Eaton's childhood home.

The first meeting brought together twenty-two distinguished scientists from ten countries as individuals and not as representatives of any government or organization to discuss privately the issues raised by the Russell-Einstein manifesto: hazards arising from the use of atomic energy in peace and war; control of nuclear weapons; and the social responsibility of scientists. The principles of independence from conference sponsors, privacy, and participation on the basis of individual invitation that characterized the first meeting in Pugwash have been retained to the present day.

The initial meeting was historic in that it was perhaps the first in which scientists met to discuss critical issues arising from scientific discoveries and not science itself. As such, it represented a unique step towards the involvement of the international scientific community in controversial political issues.

As successive meetings of scientists were convened in various countries of the world under the Pugwash banner, the basic characteristics have remained constant. Though discussions have often been difficult, sometimes seemingly close to collapse, the spirit of Pugwash that brought the first group together has prevailed. Increased numbers of participants, broadened scope of the discussions, and heightened world tensions and other pressures have failed to undermine this spirit. What started out in 1957 as a small group of scientists has now become a movement of thousands of scientists striving together to understand better "man's peril" and ways to avoid it. Pugwash has become synonymous with the search for peace and though it has employed various mechanisms for its search, it remains a forum for frank discussion among scientists of the world.

As a scientist involved in the development of the atomic bomb, Harrison Brown felt then and continues to feel strongly the need for nuclear control and for creating an environment that provides security for all the peoples of the world.

Harrison recognized, moreover, that true peace is possible only if the world's resources can be managed properly and if the fruits of scientific and technological advances are made available to all the world's people. He saw also that education and population control are critical to these efforts. His contribution to the Pugwash movement both as a member of the Continuing Committee and as a participant in many conferences has been to give proper balance to these many influences on peace and security and to stimulate others to do the same.

The thirty-third Pugwash conference was held in Venice in 1983, coming at a time when cold war rhetoric was higher than at any time since the early 1950s. Nonetheless, serious discussions on sensitive political issues were held without acrimony and with a minimum of propaganda, demonstrating once again the unique value of the Pugwash forum.

World leaders have, as Lord Russell hoped, often listened to the scientists' voices. Though it is difficult to attribute specific policy decisions to Pugwash efforts, it is clear that contributions have been made to the lessening of world tensions. Since the most important decision—that of abolishing nuclear weapons from the earth—still eludes us, however, the cooperation among scientists in the Pugwash spirit must continue.

INTERNATIONAL INSTITUTE FOR APPLIED SYSTEMS ANALYSIS

The reasons for creating international institutions are usually complex, involving the convergence of need, opportunity, and political, economic, and other conditions. International scientific institutions are no exception. A good example of this has been the establishment of IIASA, the International Institute for Applied Systems Analysis.

This institute was established as a result of the recognition that there are enormously complex global problems that must be addressed in a systematic way; that certain techniques and methods, especially systems analysis and operations research, offer unique perspectives to address these problems; and that international cooperation is essential to the effective use of these techniques.

As the scientific support for developing an institutional mechanism to implement this recognition reached a peak, political conditions and events converged to make possible a bold new initiative. In the 1960s, relations between the United States and the Soviet Union had been essentially static, with very little communication going on between the two countries. Leaders in both countries were in search of exciting initiatives that might serve the purpose of improving relations and of moving the world closer to peace.

In 1966, President Lyndon Johnson, recognizing the growing need for international cooperation on problems common to industrialized societies, proposed a new initiative in the area. Through McGeorge Bundy, special assistant to the president, discussion began in Moscow with Soviet officials, who received the idea with enthusiasm. Together with Jerman M. Gvishiani, then deputy chairman of the State Committee for Science and Technology of the USSR and member of the USSR Council of Ministers, Bundy began negotiations for the establishment of a new international institution. These negotiations, surviving changes of administration in the United States and the peak of U.S. involvement in Vietnam, eventually bore fruit in 1972, with the establishment of the International Institute for Applied Systems Analysis, located in Schloss Laxenburg, just south of Vienna, in neutral Austria.

Harrison Brown, then foreign secretary of the NAS, which became the U.S. adhering body to IIASA, was matched in his own enthusiasm and dedication to the IIASA concept by NAS President Philip Handler, President Johnson's choice to lead the substantive negotiations for creation of the institute. Largely through their efforts, within a few years of its establishment IIASA had the active participation of the scientific communities of seventeen countries, East and West, and links with many more. Harrison served as the first U.S. representative to IIASA's Governing Council and chairman of the finance committee, an important group.

As the concept evolved, IIASA's central emphasis was on honing and applying the methodology of systems analysis so that it could provide a basis for formulation of alternative solutions to critical world problems. This could only be done through truly cooperative efforts in international problem solving. Involvement of researchers from a wide range of natural and social science disciplines was essential, as was the participation of individuals from diverse social, political, and economic systems.

Over the past thirteen years, the Institute has made valuable scientific contributions and met the range of frustrations, disappointments, and joys inherent in being a center for exchange and learning for scientists of many nations. IIASA's most prominent accomplishments have been in energy studies and applied mathematics. The Institute's energy project, in which Harrison took a great interest, helped define the national and international terms of debate on long-range energy issues and led to impressive publications of lasting value. More generally, the Institute helped develop tools of mathematical modeling and applications in such areas as environment, water resources, food, and demography. Exchange between East and West has been especially lively and satisfying in applied mathematics.

Nonetheless, many political and institutional problems have troubled IIASA and threaten its continuing existence. The charter members of IIASA were all scientific bodies rather than governments (to insulate as far as possible the Institute from ideology and the transient pressures that might come from direct government involvement). But these national scientific institutions have had difficulty in protecting and supporting IIASA in times of financial stress, a decline in interest in U.S.-USSR cooperation, concern about security issues and transfer of technology, and continuing questions regarding the significance and power of systems analysis in problem solving.

IIASA has been highly successful in promoting exchange and cooperation among scientists of different countries and disciplines—its alumni are devoted and loyal to an extent quite uncharacteristic for international organizations. Yet the hope that solutions to the fundamental problems would emerge from the work of IIASA has been replaced by a recognition that often the best contribution of the scientific community is to engage in timely reconsideration of issues and to pose better questions rather than to offer answers or technological fixes. IIASA was founded in an era of optimism about the usefulness of new intellectual tools for opening up the human future; its continuing existence must be based on that vision but grounded by a better sense of the political, economic, and social milieu in which they must be used.

SUMMARY

As one surveys Harrison Brown's lifetime in science, one sees that his most striking achievement has been his outreach. He has been recognized and honored for his distinguished contribution to the body of knowledge. Yet perhaps a more fundamental accomplishment has been his role as a catalyst to initiate scientific interaction throughout the world.

Whereas most scientists are specialists within well-bounded areas of work, Harrison has been an inspired and creative generalist. He has perceived and called attention to the global nature of vital issues such as population growth, food supply, and the precarious balance of the planet's ecosystem and resources. He has seen that science and technology can flourish only through constant nurturing of free and independent discourse among their practitioners. He has communicated the possibilities of science and technology to national leaders and administrators and has helped the scientific community become more aware of the needs and aspirations of society.

Oliver Wendell Holmes said, "I think that, as life is action and passion, it is required of a man that he should share the passion and action of his time at peril of being judged not to have lived." Harrison Brown has fully shared and continues to share the passion and action that seek to make science a vehicle for international understanding and for improving the life of mankind.

REFERENCES

Brown, H., 1963. Science, Technology, and World Development, in M. Grodzins and E. Rabinowitch (eds.). *The Atomic Age,* New York: Basic Books.

Brown, H., and T. Tellez, 1973. International Development Programs of the Office of the Foreign Secretary. Washington, D.C.: National Academy of Sciences.

Hansen, R., et al., 1982. *U.S. Foreign Policy and the Third World.* New York: Praeger for the Overseas Development Council.

National Research Council, 1977. *World Food and Nutrition Study: The Potential Contributors of Research.* Washington, D.C.: National Academy of Sciences.

World Bank, 1982. *World Development Report.* Washington, D.C.

11

SCIENCE, TECHNOLOGY, AND ENDOGENOUS DEVELOPMENT: SOME NOTES ON THE OBJECTIVES AND THE POSSIBILITIES

VICTOR L. URQUIDI

The early development of science and technology, including that in non-Western societies, resulted from the pursuit of knowledge about Nature and the Universe and from the need to raise productivity and improve quality in the production of goods and services. The goods and services required before the second half of the eighteenth century were relatively simple—basic food, clothing, housing, transportation, tools and weapons. Monuments, mainly religious, were also built, but were an expression of the state of knowledge and of aesthetic qualities. The first technological revolution of the seventeenth and eighteenth centuries meant a breakthrough in transportation and in industrial manufacturing, as well as in agriculture. Science was later to develop considerably and to have an impact on health and medicine, eliminating, at least in the more developed nations of the Western world, the scourge of epidemics, as well as reducing mortality generally. Farming also benefited from science and technology.

All this occurred in a particular socioeconomic context, mainly that of the development of production and distribution through privately

---

This essay was written in April 1982.

owned means of production and, consequently, capitalist accumulation, with free enterprise at the fore and the feudal structures in retreat. In world trade, also, mercantilism and control of ocean routes gave way to free trade and freedom of the seas. There was little regard in each nation—and some could hardly be called nations—for what we would now call the overall situation, macroeconomic or macrosocial. There was even less consideration for the possible negative consequences of technology, either directly, through some specific damage to the environment or to humans, or indirectly, through the whole system of production and distribution in the sense that some technologies might lead to undesirable social results or have serious backlashes. There was on the whole great faith in the possibilities that technology could open up, in innovation as such, and in industrial development. Such minor problems as the displacement of labor by machines remained as mere incidents to be recorded in textbooks on economic history and were soon overcome. The "global" approach was understandably absent—after all, systems analysis had not arisen as a scientific endeavor.

Industrial capitalism in the nineteenth and early twentieth centuries fed on technological development and spread out from the early industrializers in search of raw materials, including food, and markets. Technology became in turn the servant of economic expansion of the industrial countries throughout most parts of the world economy, then only partially integrated. There were few cases of transfer of technology, limited mostly to starting up metallurgy, textiles production, and production of some foods. Local or native technologies did not prosper; they were limited to handicrafts, agriculture, some types of housing, and other "primitive" pursuits.

The introduction of new industrial technologies, although it raised productivity, also gave rise to social and economic inequities in the Western countries. Social reforms to redress such inequities, to improve conditions of work in mines and factories, to improve health, to raise educational levels, and finally to establish and implement welfare standards took a long time and were part of a political process involving enlarged participation. There began to be awareness by the early twentieth century that not all technology was beneficial, or at least that it could have both good and evil effects on humans and on the environment. Many decades were to pass, however, before environmental and health considerations were to become nationally, and universally, important, and before science and technology were to be applied deliberately to ecological and environmental purposes.

The expansion of the Western industrial world under those conditions, with the technologies involved, reproduced in the "backward" countries and in the colonial empires much the same set of social and economic inequities and the various consequences of technological development that characterized the industrial leaders. Social reforms, however, were much later in coming to the developing world, and they did not come without much political upheaval, including independence movements, civil wars, and limited international warfare.

In the industrial countries, technology also became an important contributor to warfare during the last quarter of the nineteenth century and the period leading up to and including World War I. Although by today's standards World War I was quite primitive, it nevertheless epitomized the technological progress of the times, including the beginning of chemical warfare.

INDUSTRIALIZATION IN DEVELOPING COUNTRIES

From the point of view of the developing economies, mainly exporters of minerals, food, and spices, their early stages of industrialization—limited to not more than a dozen or so countries—relied mostly on venture capital with existing European or North American technology. Such technology for the most part was borrowed or adopted with the whole package of capital and entrepreneurship; it occasionally was bought by local interests, sometimes with the help of the state. Metallurgy, textiles, food production, and manufacture of some intermediate goods— construction materials, chemicals, metal products—were the main features of such incipient industrialization in the nineteenth century and the first quarter of the twentieth. There was little scientific development in the backward countries, even the larger ones, and research in the field of technology was practically nonexistent. In most cases, furthermore, educational development was poor, and local universities were not geared to training much more than lawyers and medical doctors. Higher education in fact was obtained generally from universities and colleges in the industrial countries. Neither cultural conditions nor the socioeconomic structures were conducive to the growth of local technology. There was simply no interest in doing so. Economic development, both industrial and agricultural, and development of the services, was to be imitative of that of the countries at the industrial centers—quite the opposite of endogenous development.

The pattern continued after World War I, with more emphasis on industrial growth. The impact of the world depression of the 1930s on a great many countries in the Southern Hemisphere was to stimulate industrialization further as a result of depreciation in their currencies' exchange value and tariff barriers. World War II accentuated these trends as did the economic and balance of payments difficulties of the postwar period. In the major countries of Latin America, as a substitute for imports, industrialization with support from the state became the standard policy.

The weakening or slow growth of world markets for basic products (many of them subject to competition from synthetic substitutes resulting from technological development in the industrial economies) led to a "development doctrine," arising mainly out of the secretariat of the UN Economic Commission for Latin America (ECLA). According to the ECLA approach, the loss of dynamism of exports of basic products made it necessary to replace imports deliberately and by every means. Among such means were high tariff protection, import controls, fiscal incentives, financial inducements, subsidies, establishment of state-owned enterprises, and many others. Foreign borrowing was to be encouraged and—although not very explicitly stated—direct foreign investment in manufacturing for the domestic market was also admissible. Curiously, at no time in the 1950s and 1960s did science and technology enter the picture as a matter of policy nor was local research and development encouraged, not even the formulation of science and technology assessments, at least in Latin America. The transfer of technology in industry and services was left essentially to direct foreign investment and to the licensing of know-how through subsidiaries and affiliates, or locally organized licensees, from the expanding transnational enterprises of the industrial countries.

During the 1960s and early 1970s, as science and technology became an issue among the industrialized nations, at the OECD, and in the UN agencies, and as a result of research in the social sciences in many quarters including field research in Latin America, the onerous nature of most technology-licensing agreements was made explicit and led to restrictive legislation in many countries in the region. In addition, science and technology policy began to be formulated, and more resources were put into research and into the training of scientists and engineers. In other areas of the Third World, similar events occurred, and on a local level in some countries, together with spectacular assimilations of modern technology for export-oriented industries, substantial research efforts were made.

Nevertheless, it can hardly be said that the industrialization patterns and the socioeconomic structures giving them context have been essentially modified in the developing countries. Furthermore, a good deal of the industrial development has been costly and inefficient. In some cases it has introduced through licensing agreements high technology in order to exploit a captive domestic market at great profit. In others it has amounted to nothing more than the production of consumer durables and household appliances more sophisticated than the general standard of living demanded, directed rather at the growing middle-

and high-income classes, with appropriate advertising inducements. Consumerism now characterizes a major part of the direct and indirect demand (through intermediate products necessary to make the final products) of households in the developing countries, and it feeds on continuous technological developments in the industrialized nations of the West and Japan. A more irrational way to develop, in the belief that somehow it will trickle down to benefit the low-income majority, could hardly have been devised.

With few exceptions, the essential needs of the growing population (the median age of which is declining) have been neglected not only by the science and technology culture of the industrialized nations but also by the developing societies themselves. Despite thirty years of postwar development and much international ado about it, inroads have scarcely been made into low agricultural productivity, malnutrition, illiteracy, ill health, or poor housing. And in addition, negative environmental and ecological influences that arise from whatever industrialization has taken place in Third World countries are now present.

POPULATION GROWTH AND TECHNOLOGY

As this point it seems necessary to discuss the population issue as a possible contributing factor. The decline in mortality of the last forty years—a proof that there have been some gains at least in medicine and health, many of the gains originating in the science and technology of the developed countries—has, in the absence of sufficiently strong social factors inducing lower fertility, especially in rural areas, actually raised the rate of growth of population in the Third World or large parts of it or maintained past high rates of increase. And although there has been considerable change in fertility trends and in attitudes to family size in the past fifteen years, supported in many major cases by public and private family planning programs and projects, the fact remains that the population of Third World countries as a whole is still rising at about 2 percent per year. In some countries, the rate of increase is 3 percent or more. In many developing countries, the ratio of people to arable land and to urban services is very high and continues to rise.

Aside from whatever social, cultural, and political effects rapid population growth has in the developing countries, this growth's main connection with technology is through employment. Most industrial and much of the agricultural technology that has been and continues to be transferred to the developing countries is—in some respects even more at present—labor saving. Industrial development in the developing countries, unless it occurs at very high rates of growth, has been unable to absorb the growing labor force (reinforced by rural-urban migration and by the higher participation rate of women) into productive employment. The excess supply of labor finds occupation and scanty income in the so-called informal activities, i.e., underemployment. In addition, official unemployment rates are quite high in many developing countries. Very little of the capital-intensive and labor-saving high technology of the industrialized countries—including the industrialized countries with centrally planned economies—has contributed to solving the imbalance between the population growth–induced, fast-rising supply of mostly unskilled labor and the urban demand for industrial labor, increasingly for semiskilled and skilled personnel. As has been repeatedly pointed out in the literature of the past fifteen years, the research and development carried out in the industrialized countries, either by the transnational corporations or by independent research institutes, occurs basically in response to highly competitive markets in which labor costs have to be maintained at a minimum or practically eliminated. Such research and development is biased against employment, especially of unskilled labor. The inventive engineering minds put to work on such research and development are not trained to think in terms of the employment needs of the developing countries with high population growth or large reservoirs of unskilled underemployed or unemployed labor. Nor does the educational system of an industrialized country prepare a scientist or an engineer to consider those circumstances.

Attempting a synthesis, one can say that trends in technological development, combined with high population growth at natural rates never experienced by Western countries (except through immigration), have largely contributed to the failure of developing countries to solve the problems or reduce the manifestations of extreme poverty, malnutrition, ill health, poor housing, and so forth. Of course there have been other factors determining the social and economic structures and also contributing to that failure, including inadequate international cooperation. I am also aware of the frequently stated position, based apparently on Marxist economics, that growth in population is itself a source of income and wealth (somehow regardless of capital accumulation, i.e., high rates of investment), and that none of the ills of the Third World should be attributed to population growth but rather to the economic and social system, both domestic and international. Curiously, socialist countries also export highly capital-intensive technology (i.e., labor saving) to the developing countries, and it is not clear how they expect large increases in employment to take place. And it can also be said of that line of thinking about population growth that they fail to distinguish between the impact of 2.5 or 3 percent growth and that of 1 percent. A mere neglect of elementary mathematics!

PRODUCTION: SCALE AND SCOPE

Another linkage of technology to the economy of developing countries, especially those with vast rural populations, is through the scale and nature of production. Again, most industrial technology is developed for its application to large-scale output in increasingly sophisticated settings and involving highly complex administration. In the market-oriented developing countries, all this leads, among other things, to industrial concentration and to the neglect, if not the destruction, of small-scale production, particularly outside the large urban centers. Small enterprises and workshops are not able to compete nor do they get much help from the large enterprises except in specific cases of sub-contracting; the small enterprises get even less aid from government services, technology or productivity centers, financial institutions, or training schemes. Opportunities for employment and for development of local innovative talent are thus passed up, and the development strategy loses its potential for production in small towns. In the rural areas the prospect for any kind of technology inspired in the industrial world is even worse. Either technology cannot be grafted upon the particular set of rural conditions, or when it is introduced it disrupts the rural society or uproots a substantial fraction of its young labor force.

At this stage in the argument, it also seems necessary to say something of the socialist countries' use of technology for development. Most countries of socialist organization (centrally planned economies, in UN jargon) have low population growth rates, some in fact below replacement. In addition, from the start they have given extremely high priority to the development of a defense industrial economy and to production of high-technology weapons. Their economic predicament has led them to neglect the satisfaction of civilian demand beyond basic health and education measures, housing, and standard foodstuffs (not always satisfied in the latter case because of poor agricultural conditions or inadequate policies). Malnutrition, high mortality, illiteracy, poor housing, and unemployment, however, no longer exist in the socialist economies by and large, even in the poorest or in the tropical countries.

In every case, advanced education and science and technology have developed to high levels or are in the process of doing so and in some instances are geared toward the solving of basic economic problems (by developing new crops and agroindustry and by increasing industrial productivity) of underdeveloped societies. Science and technology policies in the socialist economies are oriented (aside from military needs) to strengthen economic autonomy, industrial development and, in some cases, self-sufficiency. Technology is not only developed within the system but also imported from the Western capitalist industrialized economies, in line with the long-term strategies adopted. China, in particular, has been successful in the so-called "two-leg approach" and has combined high technology where appropriate with intermediate or appropriate technology where applicable, the latter based on the traditional fund of knowledge available to the Chinese people. Interesting experiments have also been done in countries such as Tanzania that pursue a policy of self-reliance in a noncapitalist or socialistic setting. The lessons of these experiences and the many departures from the historical development of technology in the West and Japan should not be lost in the current discussions on science and technology for development.

NEW DEVELOPMENT THINKING

Even the most cursory analysis and evaluation of the situation in the developing countries, mainly the market-oriented ones, in the recent three decades and even the most superficial view of the so-called international economic order lead to the conclusion that the patterns of development and the science and technology that go with them are far from satisfactory. In effect, as so many reports have argued and documented, the international gaps are widening and in most developing nations the internal inequalities have not been lessened or have actually increased. In the 1960s and 1970s the conventional wisdom about development began to be questioned even outside the pale of Marxist thinking. Economists, sociologists, anthropologists, philosophers, and others raised well-founded doubts and produced serious critiques of the development patterns and styles recommended to the Third World or arising from cultural inertia. Some of these new lines of thought found expression in resolutions made under UN auspices, although mostly at the level of rhetoric and politics. The call for a New International Economic Order (NIEO) probably represents succinctly the dissatisfaction of the Third World, but it is far from clear whether there are truly common interests among the Third World countries—especially after the OPEC-induced increase in oil prices and the emergence of the Newly Industrialized Country (NIC) concept—or whether there is consistency between NIEO demands by the Third World and domestic development needs and objectives.

The main thrust in the evolution of new ideas about development has come from intellectuals, frequently supported by certain UN agencies. Remarkably, most of the new formulations have been made by intellectuals of the developed countries, and relatively little has come from the developing countries themselves, especially those least developed and perhaps more in need of a reassessment of development goals and means. (Could this be an extension of the developed countries' culture and the "we know best what is good for you" attitude?) The "other developers" are concerned not only with the Third World, but with the First World itself, and secondarily with the Second World of socialist countries. Perhaps the 1972 UN Conference on the Human Environment held at Stockholm served to bring out the strongest and most articulate dissatisfactions and protests concerning the established economic order, particularly those regarding as the consequences of technology on environment and quality of life and the dangers of atomic power for humanity. But it is important not to forget that some developing countries, albeit alienated by the historical correlation between industrialization and higher standards of living, actually stated that they welcomed pollution if it meant the development of industry. (Harrison Brown was a U.S. delegate at the Stockholm conference, as he was at the succession of UN conferences, including the 1979 meeting on Science and Technology for Development.) At the conference, the "developmentalist" approach overshadowed other considerations such as environment, land reform, population policy, science and technology, food policy, and educational reform. Although there are many contradictions in the stand taken by the developing countries (or the so-called group of 77), and the position of the industrialized countries is defensive, nevertheless the noneconomic and costly additions to the development effort, however conceived, are regarded as an imposition of the rich countries on the poor. This should be taken as a warning about international efforts to promote "other developments" and the like, including the concept of endogenous development.

These new concepts need to be carefully considered and analyzed. The "small is beautiful" approach has gained much support in spite of its origin and its exaggerations. "Appropriate technology" has been the subject of serious research both from the social and economic viewpoint and from the purely technical standpoint. The International Labour Organization's (ILO) series of studies on technology and employment and the work of many universities and institutes have left an impressive groundwork of evidence and shown many possibilities. The United Nations, through its earlier Industrial Development Division, through its Advisory Committee on the Application of Science and Technology to Development (ACAST), and finally and mainly through the United Nations Industrial Development Organization (UNIDO), recommended not only the application of employment-creating technologies where feasible (on the basis of already existing knowledge), but also that research be directed towards this objective, and, under the aegis of UNIDO, drew attention to actual experiences in the industrial field in many less developed countries.

The concept of appropriate technology has been broadened to include not only the employment objective, but also energy-saving and capital-saving criteria, the ability to meet small-scale industrial and agricultural needs, protection of the environment, and so on. Sometimes appropriate technology has meant, especially for economists in the developed countries and for semanticists, any technology that responds to the needs of a particular society in given social and economic conditions. Thus, every technology ends up by being appropriate at a given moment. This, of course, is to make nonsense of the term. Unfortunately, this line of thinking has its supporters among Third World economists trained in the conventional wisdom of the First World or in the standard Marxist approach to development.

It has been made clear in UN discussions—but the word has not always reached the practitioners and the ideologues—that no one espousing the use of appropriate technology has claimed that it is the answer to the problems of the Third World but only that it may and should be applicable to certain activities, whether urban or rural, agricultural or industrial, where it can be shown to be economically effective, directly or indirectly, and socially recommendable (partly a value judgment). Thus appropriate technology can coexist with high technology (the Chinese "two-leg" approach). The trouble is that in most LDCs, governments are unconcerned with appropriate technology. Indeed, in many they are not concerned with any policy on technology. Appropriate technology is therefore mostly the brainchild of and applied by private groups. Much experience has been garnered by these groups in all major developing regions and even in some developed countries. UNIDO has a long catalog of such experiences; extensive bibliographies have been compiled, and there is abundant documentation available. From the *Tinkabi* tractor in Swaziland and the small-scale cement plants in India, to the biogas digestors in China and elsewhere in Asia, to the rural housing technique in Guatemala, and so forth, there is a vast array of examples, pilot projects, and research projects.

But, again, appropriate technology—and the scientific effort behind it—runs counter to the strong trends in technological development in the industrialized countries and finds little support even among the governments of Third World countries. To this is now added the concept of "endogenous development," apparently very much supported by the Third World countries, or certain ones in the world of UNESCO, and among certain groups of thinkers.

In a recent UNESCO document (21 C/4, 1981), "endogenous development" is defined, somewhat obliquely, as "technological systems . . . evolving in an endogenous manner, i.e. by developing in line with needs, through *fairly radical changes* . . . the initiative for those changes [being taken] in the country itself." The document goes on to say that "in many fields . . . the present phase is one of re-establishing [*sic*], through judicious technological choices, the conditions under which the growth of the national economy will come about, while taking account of social objectives such as the improvement of employment, *and will irreversibly rid itself of the effects of technological domination.*" (References are to paragraph 183, author's emphasis added.)

In later paragraphs, the UNESCO document explains that

> an endogenous form of development . . . takes account of the resources, values and aspirations of each community, the inexpedience of blindly adopting foreign models, the need to respect the social equilibrium [*sic*], and progress toward greater justice, to subordinate growth requirements to respect for the individual and the advancement of man [and presumably woman], and to secure the active participation of the people at large [*sic*] in the making and implementing of decisions concerning them. . . ." (The reference is to paragraph 205.)

A case is made not only for endogenous science and technology, but also for the "endogeneity" of the social sciences (paragraph 216). In fact, "development must be seen as a process in which a community *rejects the slavish imitation of outside models* which in most cases are poorly suited to its needs, potentials and aspirations, determining independently the objectives it will pursue and the means it will employ, which *to a considerable extent have to be invented in the light of its own internal imperatives.*" (The reference is to paragraph 226, both emphases added, syntax and style as is.) And the social sciences should continue to "explore . . . the endogenous development concept, [which] implies respect for cultural identity and spiritual values, as well as concern for responsiveness to people's aspirations, readiness to appeal to their motivations and reliance on their capacity for initiative in the context of collective participation in decision-making" (paragraph 228).

Leaving aside the sometimes hyperbolic and inappropriate language of these statements, and with due respect for the work of UNESCO in the field and the positions of many intellectuals and many governments, it seems to me that endogenous development boils down to the idea that things should start from the bottom up, in accordance with community or national desires and aims, however defined and formulated. Of course, if UNESCO or some other body is to tell countries what to do in this direction, then the principle of endogeneity is probably being violated. And this raises the question of where the starting point is and what is the sequence to follow. The UNESCO document referred to is vague on this point, although mention is made of the sequence issue in connection with science and technology (paragraph 184), with the argument running in favor of an eclectic approach, in which emphasis is given at the same time to the rejection of "slavish imitation" of outside models and the "irreversible riddance" of the effects of technological domination. One may well repeat: where is the starting point for endogenous development?

I would argue that it is not clear. Should a developing nation actually start from scratch, that is, erase whatever undesirable conventional development has taken place and start anew from the bottom up, in accordance with these new principles? Should a "middle stage" under-developed country with many aspects of modernization/alienation accept what it has achieved, but reorient its efforts in accordance with the endogenous development doctrine? What happens to a semi-industrialized developing country, specifically an NIC? Should steel technology, oil-drilling techniques, chemical or pharmaceutical production technology, packaged food technology, and others be scrapped in favor of endogenous technology? Is it likely to happen? How should a developing country that is already involved in industrialization efforts treat its backward rural areas, namely, should it apply to them the endogenous development concept or bring in "judicious technological choices"?

The relationship of science and technology to endogenous development presupposes that in a low-productivity situation there is a fostering of scientific effort, research and development, and evaluation and adaptation of technology, and that the right choices are made. It should also presuppose—but this point is not clear either—that some imported technology may be not only necessary but also beneficial, in its present form, e.g., medical technology or polyester textiles (with all due respect to herbal medicine and to the hand-loomed cotton fabrics). Nothing is said, at least in the UNESCO document, about imports of technology from other developing countries—would this be a violation of endogenous development?

If one assumes that a developing country is able not only to establish an indigenous science and technology infrastructure as recommended by the 1979 United Nations Plan of Action on Science and Technology, but also to make the right choices and take the right steps in terms of endogenous development, one should ask at what stage is there to be a transition to a more advanced stage of development in fuller interaction with the world economy, be it market-oriented or centrally planned, with high technology used wherever most needed (e.g., for industrial, internationally competitive exports). Should a developing country refuse to use a technology, be it food conservation techniques or ore-smelting, for the export market if there is no equivalent domestic market? This has actually been advocated by some experts.

Once the complexity of the Third World is admitted, together with the diverse cultural conditions, it becomes less and less clear how endogenous development, at least in its narrower sense, can be carried out. Can a small community, or a small African country, pull itself up by its bootstraps? Is any rural community in a developing country, except for some tribal areas in Africa or North Borneo, immune from the information provided by the transistor radio? Are there any airtight cultures?

As I see it, endogenous development can best be started, in low-productivity economies, with the aid of an exogenous factor. Perhaps this brings to the discussion among the sociologists and others something that appears to have been absent: economics. Assume a backward rural community in the Andes, or in southern Mexico, or for that matter anywhere else. There is some ancestral indigenous technology to raise corn, chickens, or pigs, for bare subsistence (with occasional periods of hunger). The community demands improvement in living standards, including better health facilities, water supply, education, and housing, plus some consumer goods, the tidings of which are borne by an occasional transistor radio. It is unlikely that the community will be able to generate sufficient savings (an "old-fashioned" economic concept), even in the form of longer workdays, to divert enough effort into building a school or tapping water from a nearby source of captured rainwater, in time to create some sort of infrastructure. There is no science base nor is there likely to be one, and capacity to create new technology is practically nil.

Would it not be rational to bring in an exogenous factor in the form of, let us say, advice on how to plant and grow onions or asparagus for "export" to consumers in another, larger and urban, community. If, as is usually the case, resources are underutilized in such a backward community, the allocation of some land for the new crop for export will not impoverish the community by substituting for staple food. On the other hand, it will bring in some cash income and add to the community savings that can be used both to increase basic consumption above subsistence, by means of "imports," and to divert resources toward the building of some infrastructure intended to improve education, health, and productivity. "Other developers" might argue that this pattern will immediately set up distortions, power grabs, and inequalities (except under socialistic or noncapitalistic styles of development) and that there is the further danger that outside forces dominating the exogenous factor will exploit the community and pay it less than it is due for its onions or its asparagus. But none of this need necessarily happen, provided government, both local and provincial or national, can intervene to ensure that the purposes of the project are carried out fairly, honestly, and with proper advice. There is in any event an opportunity cost. Here we have old-fashioned economics—rarely mentioned by the "other developers" and the proponents of endogenous development—coming to the aid of the quite valid social aspiration of the community.

The above example is used to argue that endogenous development, however defined, cannot take place in isolation. The world is as it is, for good or for evil, and, barring nuclear holocaust, is likely to develop in multiple fashion. This is neither to argue for the *status quo* nor to be fatalistic about present trends. It is merely to affirm the need to base alternatives to the present patterns of development on reality and to recognize that the promotion of endogenous develoment must take account of the existing situation—and to utilize what good there may be in exogenous science and technology. This implies (unfortunately for some thinkers) the introduction of the transfer of knowledge, a heavily paternalistic approach in the social dimension. Better that local participation should exist and be expressed in connection with science, technology, and development. But refusal to consider the exogenous factors and possible advantages to be derived from them might only lead to no development at all, in effect to antidevelopment.

SELF-RELIANCE

Self-reliance, a close cousin of endogenous development, is a broader concept and one that is capable of adapting better to different circumstances. It may also be carried to extremes, when the slightest whiff of dependency is considered inimical to self-reliance. I would not wish to quibble, but since in the social and economic scene, especially on a worldwide scale, nothing is absolute, and in essence practically everything is interdependent—all the more in this age of instant communication— a self-reliant economy can still indulge in some dependence if that is in its own interests. I understand self-reliance to mean that a society is capable of making its own decisions in the major strategic matters concerning development, including the use and conditions of international cooperation and even the use of private foreign loans or investments, provided it judges these forms of assistance of benefit for its own long-term objectives. Thus the idea of self-reliance could imply anything from nondevelopment at one end to full integration into the world economy at the other, either through the market system or through the socialist system, as long as the path followed is consciously adopted and is subject to (relatively) autonomous decision-making. And in between there may be the different strategies and styles of development, the "other developments" and the like.

To require that self-reliance be based on a full participatory process from the grassroots up is probably unrealistic. This may be possible in a Scandinavian society, perhaps even in Switzerland; it is doubtful that it could occur in any Third World nation, much less in those involved with tribal disputes or having as a base an Andean type of social stratification. To require that decisions on the export of bananas should be made with the direct producers deciding what to produce and how, is almost grotesque, to say the least; a certain amount of technocracy is necessary in any society: Some people have technical knowledge, and there has to be a minimum of hierarchical organization to get anything done. I agree, however, that a process of democratization is essential, as opposed to authoritarianism, be it by private groups or by government.

If technological choices have to be made—and this is a reasonable assumption—they must be made with the fullest information possible, including that available from international sources, so that such choices will be meaningful in terms of the self-reliant development strategy to be followed. Science and technology are not mere ingredients analogous to seeds that upon being planted will produce stalks of corn. They are part of a system of wheels within wheels that turn at different speeds and relate to other parts of the system that react in turn. This is true even in a primitive, undeveloped society, for some technology is bound to exist in it, resulting in a kind of activity or output.

If self-reliance/endogenous development are to be encouraged—accepting for a moment that there is no inherent contradiction in their encouragement from the top, i.e., by governments themselves or by UN agencies—the starting point is perforce the real world as we know it or think we know it. The developing countries are in various stages of evolution, and among them several stages of preindustrial societies are to be found. Rural societies are subject to different cultural conditions; some rural societies are quite primitive (admittedly, an ethnocentric term); some have related to other parts of the world for centuries but are strongly culture-bound; some have a capacity for evolution or transformation; some are in danger of being too readily absorbed into the alienating urban industrial civilization. In a great many, a form of modern communication and technology has made an inroad or is available. The first thing to do to encourage development is to evaluate the local situation and reach a consensus on objectives and means, including an appropriate mix of small-scale and traditional technologies and exogenous technologies, if only to improve agricultural productivity, water supply and drainage, health, and housing. Appropriate education and training will also be necessary.

SCIENCE AND TECHNOLOGY IN DEVELOPING COUNTRIES

A number of developing nations are in the early stages of industrialization and others have reached the category of NICs, which implies some heavy industry and the ability to apply science and technology, whether domestic or imported, to industrial development and to sophisticated services. Such countries, both the starters in industrialization and the fairly advanced ones, are in a better position to evaluate fully their science and technology position and its relationship to their development objectives and strategies, with a view to achieving eventually a high degree of self-reliance. The preparation of national documents for the UN Conference on Science and Technology for Development was supposed to help in that direction. It seems, however, that the results were on the whole poor; in fact very few countries were able to assess their science and technology situation and to formulate medium- and long-term policies in the direction of self-reliance and relative autonomy.

Most developing countries have so far been slow and inefficient in defining their development objectives or have been unable to cover the wide spectrum of social, economic, and cultural objectives in an interrelated manner. There are many examples of fairly successful economic growth, but with sore neglect of improvement in social conditions and scarce attention paid to achieving a more equitable distribution of income and wealth. Technology has been introduced in response to what may be termed "micro" interests—that is, the raising of productivity at the level of the firm or at most of a branch of industry—with little regard for "macro" economic and social considerations. Some technology has led to deterioration of the environment or to serious ecological damage. The aggregate technological input into those economies and the manner in which it is obtained and transferred have created distortions and rigidities, as well as dependencies that will not be easy to correct or modify.

Nevertheless, some countries have adopted science and technology policies involving evaluation of imported technologies, assessment and development of domestic infrastructure, and research and development in terms of nationally perceived needs. Such efforts often include information and other support services. Higher education has been improved and oriented toward science and technology. Large numbers of fellowships for study abroad have become available. Special training programs have been adopted. Subject to proper evaluation, these efforts, albeit confined to a dozen or so developing countries, may be considered to be moves in the direction of self-reliance or autonomic decision-making. They all involve a certain measure of state intervention, sometimes against the wishes of the elite scientific communities (an admittedly difficult question to settle where scientific freedom might be threatened). Within a market structure where mixed economies prevail, the state-enterprise sector should be able to make decisions regarding technology consistent with the national science and technology policy, but this is not always the case. Where noncapitalist or socialistic economies prevail or in centrally planned economies, it can be presumed that decisions in matters of science and technology are part of the macrostrategy or are in effect integrated into the overall planning process.

There is no way to simplify the attainment of autonomy in science and technology. For most developing countries, especially those that participate in world trade of basic products and manufactures, many outside pressures determine technological choices. Part of the pressures result from the growing operations of transnational corporations; others are found in the particular workings of specific technology markets, including lack of information and of decision-making capacity on the part of users or buyers of technology at the level of the firm; yet others arise from the tied loans obtained through bilateral cooperation programs, or even from semitied loans available through multilateral financial institutions. Domestic inertia, lack of information, and even political factors often slow down the process of formulating an adequate national science and technology policy, of setting up suitable coordinating bodies, and of allocating financial and human resources to research and development and related activities.

The appropriate technology sector is usually the weakest client for resource and development support and must rely on voluntary organizations. Technology assessment has rarely gone beyond the stage of reading the UN reports on the subject. There are definite time lags that have to be planned for, even under the best circumstances. Attention also has to be given to the brain drain and to means to counter it and even reverse it. In a developing country, finally, development of science and technology has to compete with other needs—some of more immediate practical and political importance, such as primary schooling, introduction of water supply and drainage—for the necessary financial resources from budget offices and parliamentary budget committees. Science and technology are not necessarily a high priority in the minds of legislators, or of cabinet members. Economists involved in the development-planning process are rarely trained to understand the intricacies of a science and technology policy, their limited ability deriving largely from their being steeped in neoclassical economics, in which technical change is taken as a totally exogenous factor and is viewed essentially as subject to market forces in a general equilibrium system.

In most developing countries, moreover, there is insufficient knowledge of existing and potential natural resources, and the necessary surveys are expensive and time-consuming and require sophisticated technologies. This is often forgotten in the discussions on endogenous development and the like. Precise knowledge of the quality and trends in human resources is frequently absent—in some cases basic population data are lacking. Institutions and leadership are not always appropriate. Cultural factors also condition the nature and speed of the process of developing self-reliant science and technology policies for development. This may be perhaps more serious in certain African nations and in South and Southeast Asia, but some argue also for an "Islamic science and technology."

What should be the role of the UN system in science and technology for endogenous or self-reliant development? A broader question is how can science and technology best serve humankind and the planet. This philosophical question has been answered by many. We can assume, however, that science and technology are useful both for the pursuit of knowledge and to increase output to meet at least the essential needs of the world's population, particularly to make it possible to eliminate poverty and to guarantee good health and an acceptable quality of life. Ecological and environmental considerations are equally important, locally, regionally, and on a global scale: The "outer limits" must not be reached.

At present, some 40 percent of the world's research and development is devoted to military preparedness and weapons development, and an undetermined part of outer space exploration (and the research and development behind it) must surely be for defense purposes. It is frequently stated that defense and space research and development have important spin-offs for civilian purposes. How important are these spin-offs, and could such results not be obtained by directly-oriented research and not through defense research? If there is a cost, what is the cost? How much of the defense research and development, in terms of real resources, including human resources, could be reoriented toward development needs and made available gradually to the developing countries? This is something that should concern the United Nations, and studies should be undertaken to find out what the capacity for "reconversion" is.

The orientation of even civilian research and development toward the requirements of the developing countries has not been possible in more than a rather secondary way. When the 1971 UN World Plan of Action for the Application of Science and Technology to Development was written between 1968 and 1971, a number of regional plans were also produced. It was estimated that not more than 5 percent of the research and development carried out in the developed countries was in response to the needs of the developing world. It is not likely that this percentage has risen very much, nor that the UN Plan of Action arising from the Vienna conference in 1979 has had much effect so far in that particular direction. The 1971 UN World Plan of Action still has validity, as was readily recognized by the United Nations Development Programme (UNDP) in its main documents for the Vienna meeting. On the basis of it, plus knowledge gathered since 1971, including the results of new research and development, and taking into account the various national documents submitted to Vienna and the myriad other proposals and suggestions, the UN Interim Fund for Science and Technology is now in a position to place more emphasis, within the United Nations system, on priority needs and requests. The Vienna conference was unable to set up any adequate coordination or harmonization machinery among the different agencies of the United Nations system in the matter of science and technology, and it is doubtful that the Inter-Governmental Committee will deal adequately with the problem or that the "reincarnation" of ACAST set up in 1981 will be able to make a meaningful contribution. In addition, the whole subject of science and technology as part of the NIEO dialogue has become quite politicized.

The developing countries as a whole have conflicting objectives. Obviously, they see technology as power, which it has always meant—up to now power mostly for the benefit of the industrialized nations. Technology gives its holder economic power and, under appropriate circumstances, the ability to bring about development. The developing countries, by and large, want to attain a better kind of development, with desirable social implications. The scientific communities—not frequently or adequately heard in these debates—call for the use of science and technology not only for development, but also for safeguarding the planet from deterioration and possible destruction. These objectives are shared throughout the world, but short-term, security considerations have more influence on policy. And the fact remains that many important developing countries make an indiscriminate use of technology, without due regard for employment trends or for its application to small-scale rural and urban activities as a means to benefit the disadvantaged groups of society.

A major role of UN agencies can be assumed to be one of creating greater awareness of the problems of development and of organizing and coordinating international cooperation to help member states solve them. UNESCO has an especially important role in this matter because of its vast range, encompassing science and technology in the traditional sense, the social sciences, and the humanities, in addition to its functions in education and culture. Given the lack of clarity in some of the concepts that have crept into the resolutions and programs of UNESCO and other UN agencies, and the extensive commentary and critique of sociologists and other intellectuals on the question of endogenous development, self-reliance, and "other developments," perhaps UNESCO could attempt to help enlighten those who are grappling with the issues at levels of national governments, specific action-oriented programs, universities and research institutes. A case could be made specifically to incorporate economists into the effort of clarification, not because of any possible superiority of economists in dealing with development, but because they seem to be absent from the debate and from the prescriptive follow-up.

As to science and technology, quite enough seems to have been said and recommended in UN conferences and presumably in UNESCO documents. What is lacking, essentially, is the will or the ability, as the case may be, of national governments to engage themselves in a fuller process of development planning and, in this context, of science and technology planning for the particular development objectives in mind, of which self-reliance or, if the term in vogue is preferred, endogenous development, could advisedly be in the center. UNESCO's role in helping to increase communication and bringing about greater awareness should be a large one, adequately coordinated with the activities of other UN agencies. UNESCO could do more than that and press increasingly in favor of endogenous development. But would UNESCO's participation be endogenous, or the exogenous factor that, it is argued, may be necessary in many cases? Only national governments, with support and participation of the scientific communities, the development planners, and sectors of opinion below them, can give the answer.

12

TOWARD INSTITUTIONS
OF UNITY FOR THE
GLOBAL COMMONS

RECTOR SOEDJATMOKO

I am grateful to have the opportunity of adding my voice to those of the many distinguished contributors who pay tribute in this volume to the life and vision of Harrison Brown. My modest contribution is the dedication of this chapter about the need for new international institutions to help ensure the survival of what I call "the global commons"—our shared heritage of sea and forest space. Its relevance to Harrison Brown's work is that it attempts to follow the example he has set of always looking forward to see how we might anticipate the opportunities and difficulties that lie ahead of us.

This consistent emphasis in his work was first seen in his 1954 book, *The Challenge of Man's Future* (Viking; reprinted in 1984 by Westview), with its disarmingly simple subtitle, *An Inquiry Concerning the Condition of Man During the Years That Lie Ahead.* In chapter after chapter, with such headings as "Food," "Energy," and "Things," Harrison started our journey on a road along which, even today, we recognize for the first time landscapes and points of interest that he mapped thirty years ago.

Today, some people might describe Harrison as a futurologist. But somehow the term seems remote and wrong for him because his writings are imbued with such direct personal insight and common sense. In the preface to *The Challenge of Man's Future* he said, "This book represents an attempt to examine man's past and present and, on the basis of the clues derived from such a study, to examine his future. I have not attempted to predict that future, for the course of events ahead of us depends on the actions of man himself, which are, in the main, unpredictable." Then, significantly, he added later in the preface, "I believe that man has the power, the intelligence, and the imagination to extricate himself from the serious predicament that now confronts him." (Incidentally, the preface is, in itself, a small jewel of lucid wisdom as translucent as the Caribbean that was in his view from his porch in Jamaica as he wrote it.)

I suppose that some would suspend judgment on whether Harrison's optimism about man's capacity to handle his future has been justified; on balance, I think it has—and, in no small measure, precisely because of the foresight and wisdom that he has shown, and continues to show and share, in his writings. Certainly, for me, *The Challenge of Man's Future* and *The Human Future Revisited* (Norton, 1978) were books of enormous importance and influence. I think in time they may come to be ranked with the seminal works of Malthus and Ricardo.

MAN AND THE GLOBAL COMMONS

As this century comes to a close, we are becoming more aware that we are the trustees of the global commons—those regions of the earth's crust and atmosphere in whose protection and preservation all living creatures have a stake. Such physical resources as climate, tropical rain forests, seas, soils, and other essential components of planetary life-support can be efficiently monitored and managed only on a regional and international basis. The concept of a global commons can be broadened to embrace also such nonphysical and unseen resources as knowledge, communication, space, and radio frequency spectra. Here, too, some form of international cooperation and management seems essential.

Our experience with the commons of English country towns in the eighteenth and nineteenth centuries illustrates this need for human solidarity to ensure the survival of common resources. Such commons suffered destruction by individual farmers who enlarged their herds without regard for the grazing needs of neighboring farmers. Ultimately, the resources of these commons were exhausted by a few, to the detriment of all. And so it will be with the global commons. If nations continue to overload the atmosphere with carbon dioxide, to overfish the seas, or to destroy tropical rain forests, while ignoring larger, international interests, these commons will inevitably suffer irreversible damage.

How are we fulfilling our collective role as trustees of the global commons? The present state of the world environment would suggest, in all likelihood, that the plan generated in the years since the United Nations Conference on the Human Environment (Stockholm conference) still has major gaps, evidence of the degree to which we have become prisoners of our academic inclination to approach a problem as immensely complicated as the environment primarily along single disciplinary lines. Such narrow approaches—however much they deepen understanding of particular facets of the problem—will avail us little in trying to unravel the tightly knit web of social, political, economic, technological, and ecological forces ensnaring most environmental issues.

At the national level, the difficulties that hinder effective implementation of environmental action plans have proven to be much greater than expected. Among these are the inadequate data base and the lack of analytical tools with which to clarify the different trade-offs between economic and environmental imperatives, to reconcile the differential impacts of environmental intervention on regions and populations, and to develop the technological and other solutions that might accommodate such conflicting interests. The most crucial and difficult problem has been dealing with the profound and complex linkages between environmental deterioration at the national and global levels and the special needs posed by the persistent, deep poverty in the poor countries of the world. Environmental policies that have not taken into account the food and energy needs of the poor (and their general economic and social interests) have failed. Similarly, those ministries or agencies established solely for the environment have proved incapable of dealing with indifference and hostility or of reconciling conflicting policies and bureaucratic interests and equally powerful commercial and vested interests.

These national problems testify to our failure to formulate policies that address critical management issues adequately and to develop effective tools for managing and monitoring the environment. They also highlight the inability of educational systems to develop the necessary manpower and management expertise for this task. As a result, our collective capacity to monitor and manage environmental change has not kept pace with the rate of environmental deterioration in many areas. Many Third World countries can make only the crudest guesses about the extent of exploitation, depletion, and deterioration of their natural resources. Without an improvement in this capacity, their ability to develop a sustainable and appropriate resource base and sound environmental management policies is sharply limited.

Nor have we been able to arrest environmental deterioration on a global scale. Millions of hectares of the world's forests are disappearing each year. Six million hectares are lost annually to deserts and another million or more are paved over or otherwise lost to urban sprawl. Moreover, in the process, species that might have been priceless weapons against human hunger and disease are disappearing at a frightening rate.

Environmental crises are not new. The desolate wastelands in various river basins in the world, once the locations of great ancient civilizations, are mute testimony to this fact. What is unique about the current crisis, however, is its rate and scale. Deterioration that might have taken centuries in the past is now compressed into a few decades and occurs worldwide. For example, the carbon dioxide content of the atmosphere has increased by one-tenth, mostly in the last twenty years, and the greenhouse effect is awaited with fear and uncertainty. The present crisis illustrates the folly in seeing environmental problems only in national terms. Building taller smokestacks to ameliorate pollution in one country feeds acid rains in another.

Another factor is equally disturbing. We are witnessing once again the emergence of the view that developers and preservers of the environment are rival players—one is seen as champion of human advance, the other as guardian of virgin wilderness. Sadly, this view is gaining popularity (not so much in the Third World, where it was once widespread, as in the First) among policymakers who hold that environmental concern and control are desirable only until they interfere with the progress of business and industry and with efforts to overcome economic recession. This view ignores evidence that production patterns that pay little heed to environmental degradation or resource depletion may create irreversible environmental havoc and are themselves ultimately doomed to failure.

In addition to this change in viewpoint, interest in international cooperation has declined over the last decade. Ironically, this waning interest occurs at a time when we face the most serious environmental problems of this or any age. These problems exist in a world where many human activities have potential international repercussions. For example, the international fluidity of the economic system has grown; inflation, interest rates, and unemployment are not confined by national boundaries. A similar dynamic applies in the fields of aviation, meteorology, and public health.

In the use of outer space, international law has kept pace with humankind's progress, particularly through the Outer Space Treaty of 1967, but the notion of space as a global commons is threatened. Indeed, there is a dangerous trend toward the use of outer space for military purposes. Moreover, many technicalities have made the distinction between military and nonmilitary uses of space difficult to establish. Military satellites, for instance, have been useful for monitoring and implementing disarmament policies, whereas civilian satellites are capable of serving military purposes.

As for the biosphere, we are only beginning to grapple with the implications of present-day human activity on such components as the ozone layer and the global climate. The same can be said for the protection of our natural heritage because species conservation has not yet been considered in its full ecological context.

In the oceans, deterioration of the marine environment continues despite the adoption of a UN convention concerning the definition of a global commons zone for the oceans and their resources. In both the Pacific and Atlantic oceans, for example, coral reefs are dead or dying for causes not yet known. The implications for marine ecology and, by extension, for human life are serious, and it is imperative that these life-sustaining reefs be considered another part of the global commons.

In many ways, then, the pace of destruction of the global commons is tragically outstripping man's knowledge of these very same commons. This holds particularly true for those global commons that are nonphysical in nature. For example, knowledge developed within specific cultural contexts is fast disappearing from the earth in the wake of advances in modern technology and ways of life. Each year, another human culture disappears, and too often its last living exponent dies without putting key knowledge of traditions and practices on record. Yet, traditional knowledge about medicinal plants, energy-conserving architecture, food crops, and many other kinds of technical, social, or organizational experience still offers valuable help for present-day living.

Information and communication could also be considered new forms of the unseen global commons. In these areas, the major problems involve equality in distribution and access. The developed world controls 75 percent of the television programs, 50 percent of the film industry, 60 percent of the record and cassette industries, and 89 percent of computerized commercial information. These figures raise concerns not only about the balanced production of a common resource but also about its equal consumption.

CHALLENGES TO THE ENVIRONMENT AND INTERNATIONAL RESPONSES

The most fundamental and important environmental challenge in this second decade after the 1972 Stockholm conference is the development of improved ways of managing the global commons. In some ways, the most important breakthrough on the environmental front would be the creation of innovative and imaginative management tools. A management toolkit for the national and international policy planner of the 1980s should contain ways to respond more flexibly, to adapt to the unexpected and the uncertain, and to break down bureaucratic rigidities. The 1959 Antarctica treaty offers one model of the management of a global commons, with its board of directors and its provision for present and future international cooperation in station and expedition activities. This kind of management, beneficial for the countries directly involved, has also been a means of territorial demilitarization and environmental protection (species conservation). The treaty expires in 1989, and some member states have suggested to the UN General Assembly that Antarctica be opened to a "wider international concert."

Management strategies must particularly recognize the intimate links between environmental problems and the problems of the poor. The future shape of the global environment will be determined by, among other factors, millions of decisions made by poor farmers and villagers. Our ability to manage this environment will hinge on our capacity to incorporate those decisions into our scientific and technological planning.

Three particularly important dimensions to the development of appropriate environmental management policies at the global and regional levels have emerged. First, we must prepare planners and decision makers to manage complex interactive systems. Environmental issues cannot be solved one at a time. Such attempts in the past have too often triggered other, more stubborn problems. A multiple approach is necessary for dealing with many different aspects and levels of the problem simultaneously.

One barrier to the multidisciplinary approach is single-issue politics, which can divert valuable human and material resources away from broader and more complicated issues. Whatever their other merits, we must recognize that at times single-issue politics can be essentially a "cop-out," an abdication of broader, interrelated responsibilities that entail responses at different levels of power and sophistication. As individual nations, we will have to develop political constituencies for a multidisciplinary approach to environmental management. Another important element of global environmental planning will be the development of new forms of public education—of global learning.

Second, both government and intergovernmental systems must learn to cope with new conflicts of interest. For example, in the communications field, extreme difficulties and much inconclusive debate have ensued over criteria for assigning priorities for the use of limited resources. Regarding satellite use, for example, who should determine the relative importance, based on what standard, of the various needs of meteorology? Of navigation? Of broadcasting? Of remote sensing? Obviously, we need new management systems to cope equitably with competing demands.

Third, consideration should be given to adopting international legal instruments to help regulate and enforce sounder environmental practice on a global basis. International law must be extended to cover a variety of human uses of the biosphere. Perhaps the effort to codify the law of the sea marks a valuable beginning in this direction, but it is significant that this effort really has very little to do with some of the broader, more long-term environmental considerations of marine resource use.

Given the reluctance of so many governments to establish legal measures for enforcing environmental practices, we may well have no choice but to start at the international level in establishing standards and agreements and hope that national governments eventually follow suit.

International decision-making is proposed in the recognition that certain pressing environmental problems are too global in their implications and may impinge too disastrously on the lives of all humanity to be left untended. Therefore, we must begin to design global and regional management mechanisms to address problems that threaten irreversible change and damage. By their very nature, these problems are the toughest and most complex. But if ignored in favor of the more immediate or the more solvable, they would only become bigger, more cancerous, and less solvable during the lives of our children.

To accept such responsibilities, however, and to cope with their complexities, we may need an institutional response that far exceeds the capabilities of present international bodies. We must question whether our present intergovernmental bodies have proved sufficient for the task. Regardless of increased future cooperation between the United Nations and other international agencies, we may need the kinds of institutions and mechanisms that would represent not only the interests of governments but also those of concerned publics, scientists, and other experts—institutions, in other words, capable of representing and managing the affairs of the many constituencies of the global commons.

Such institutions must encourage thinking that seeks neither the ideal nor the merely possible solution but, rather, the most desirable one. Finding desirable solutions to our environmental and resource needs will be challenging and could entail balancing a country's sovereign rights regarding its own natural resources with responsibility and accountability for the transnational and global impact of each country's resource use. For example, certain pollution-abating policies and massive interventions in riverflows for irrigation purposes that have affected the regional or global climate or access to shared resources will force us to face these problems.

Barbara Ward, with her usual unforgettable eloquence and perspicacity, left us this invaluable message in the foreword that she wrote just before her death for the book *Down to Earth,* by Erik Eckholm (Eckholm, Norton, 1982).

> No matter how much we try to think of ourselves as separate sovereign entities, nature itself reminds us of humanity's basic unity. The vision of unity shared by so many of the great philosophers and so central to all

the great religions is recognized now as an inescapable scientific fact. Could it be a vocation of this generation to give the planet the institutions of unity and cooperation that can express this insight?

Barbara Ward's words define the institutions we seek for the closing years of this century and set the resolve of all who wish to save both the environment and humanity's share in its benefits.

13

INTERNATIONAL COLLABORATIVE RESEARCH: THE EXPERIENCE OF THE RESOURCE SYSTEMS INSTITUTE

ROBERT H. RANDOLPH
AND KIRK R. SMITH

Among the several themes that wind through Harrison Brown's career is a strong belief in the value and necessity of international scientific cooperation. The serious, international, and long-term problems surrounding the interaction of resources and population that he was among the first to articulate were natural targets for such cooperation. Thus it was perhaps inevitable that his last institutional job, taken six years before his 1983 retirement, was as director of an institute dedicated to international cooperative research on the troubling resource issues facing the most dynamic part of the world, the Asia-Pacific region.

THE SETTING OF THE MID-1970s

In the mid-1970s, the need for international scientific cooperation was widely considered to be of increasing importance (Forman, 1973; Salomon, 1971; Salomon, 1973).[1] Such cooperation, it was argued, had become especially crucial since the advent of "big science" during and after World War II. Because of limitations on scientific resources, all but the richest countries found themselves obliged to approach many complex scientific problems either cooperatively or not at all. Moreover, as noted at the 1967 Pugwash conference in its Declaration of Vienna, it was recognized that "the ability of scientists all over the world to understand one another and work together is an excellent instrument for bridging the gap between nations and uniting them around common aims" (Rotblatt, 1967). In the tense international environment of the postwar world, such bridge building had great appeal—as indeed it does today.

For these reasons, among others, international scientific cooperation was in the 1970s an official tenet of state policy for many countries, including the United States (Pollack, 1971; U.S. Department of State, 1974). Cooperative activities in science in the 1970s continued the dramatic upsurge that had begun in the previous two decades, as illustrated by the large number of major international scientific bodies (discipline-oriented scientific unions and interdisciplinary committees, commissions, and services) that came into being during these decades (see Figure 13.1).

Harrison Brown's concern for international science began early and remained strong. It is no accident that today, in 1985, the title of his most recent book (*Science, Technology, and Economic Development*) echoes that of an article he wrote twenty-seven years earlier ("Science, Technology, and World Development"). As foreign secretary of the U.S. National Academy of Sciences from 1962 to 1974, and as president of the International Council of Scientific Unions from 1974 to 1976, Harrison was himself a major actor in many international scientific activities during these years.

During this increase in scientific cooperation in the 1960s and 1970s an important change took place in the atmosphere, and hence the agenda, of international scientific cooperation. As Harrison noted at the time (1978a), the technological optimism prevalent in the 1950s had given way to a profound concern for the unintended consequences of technology and the limits to growth caused by resource depletion and other effects of economic development. Such concerns had been expressed before (for example, by Hubbert, 1949), as Harrison noted, and indeed he himself earlier had flagged such basic problems as the catastrophic potential of nuclear weapons technology and the ever-expanding need for physical resources implied by rapid population growth (1959).

But now the voices expressing alarm were no longer an easily disregarded minority. To compound matters, Harrison—like many others—was no longer confident that existing economic and political mechanisms could automatically solve emerging problems. He argued, for example, that energy systems in industrial countries must be diversified in order to reduce their vulnerability to disruption and that, because the capital costs and time needed for developing and converting to alternative energy sources would be large, energy prices would have to rise sharply before

Figure 13.1. Founding of major international scientific bodies, by decade, 1910–1984. The following is a compilation of the major scientific bodies, listed by the decade in which they were founded: **1910–1920** IAU, IUGG, IUPAC, URSI; **1920–1930** IGU, IUBS, IUPAP; **1930–1940** ICSU; **1940–1950** IUCr, IUHS, IUTAM; **1950–1960** COSPAR, FAGS, ICSU-AB, IMU, IUB, IUCRM, IUHPS, IUPS, SCAR, SCOR; **1960–1970** CODATA, COSTED, COWAR, CTS, IUCAF, IUCS, IUGS, IUNS, IUPAB, SCOPE, SCOSTEP, WDC; **1970–1980** CASAFA, CCMP, COGENE, IBN, IUIS, IUPHAR; **1980–1984** ICL, IUMS, IUPsyS.

SOURCE: Compiled from data in ICSU Yearbook, 1983/1984 (Paris: ICSU Secretariat, [1984]).

necessary steps would be likely to occur on economic grounds alone. Harrison concluded that government intervention was essential (Brown, 1978a; Tong, 1978), and yet he warned that present political institutions might not be able to cope with the pressures involved (1978b).

In face of increasingly powerful global forces and complex patterns of interdependence and vulnerability, Harrison argued that problem-oriented research was urgently needed to reduce uncertainties and facilitate wise choices among policy alternatives having far-reaching implications. Conventional academic institutions, in his view, were inadequate for the purpose, due to the incompatibility between their disciplinary structure and the inherently interdisciplinary nature of the problems being confronted. Furthermore, he maintained that "none of these problems—energy, food, global environment, weaponry—can really be examined effectively from a purely national point of view. The problems themselves, as well as the solutions, are too strongly interlocked across national boundaries." He concluded that much of the needed research must be international. Unfortunately, he continued, "the world suffers from the lack of an adequate international mechanism for undertaking analytic studies of global problems." Existing institutions such as the UN agencies, OECD, and World Bank too often face "political constraints [that] make difficult the goal of reaching meaningful conclusions" (1979b).

One possible remedy to this situation that Harrison considered was for the ICSU—the world's premier scientific body—to take up the challenge. He acknowledged, however, that this would require considerable "broadening and strengthening" of the ICSU (1979b). Another possibility, he suggested, would be to create "something new."

During the 1970s, a small number of new international institutions were indeed established to attack global problems through policy-oriented research. One of the most important—and one in whose founding Harrison was deeply involved—was the International Institute for Applied Systems Analysis (IIASA), which Victor Rabinowitch and John Hurley have so capably described elsewhere in this volume. IIASA's concern, at least initially, was mainly with problems of developed countries; indeed, in the planning stages there was some thought of naming it the International Institute for the Study of the Problems of Advanced Societies. Founded on the basis of U.S.-Soviet collaboration at a time of great hopes for détente, IIASA has since been hurt by the current chill in East-West relations (Schmandt, 1982; Walsh, 1982). Yet the fact that it is still functioning and providing opportunities for multinational, interdisciplinary research related to global problems is a tribute to the vision of its founders, including Harrison Brown. IIASA remains the only major international scientific institution devoted to policy analysis as such.

Another important—though very different—institution concerned with a wide range of global problems is the United Nations University (UNU). Proposed in 1969 by UN Secretary General U Thant, the UNU was formally established in 1973 by a resolution of the UN General Assembly and, thanks largely to an endowment grant from the Japanese government, began operations in 1975–1976. Although the UNU does have a small central staff of about eighty people at its Tokyo headquarters, one of its unique characteristics is its principal reliance on international networks of associated institutions and scholars to carry out its programs. Moreover, the UNU does not have students in the conventional sense; instead it accomplishes its educational objectives by supporting UNU fellows, young professionals who receive advanced training at the associated institutions.

Besides practical objectives related to the strengthening of research and advanced training in Third World countries and the promotion of international collaboration generally, the UNU is expressly concerned with increasing human understanding of the causes and potential solutions of major global problems. UNU programs to date have dealt with such major problem areas as world hunger, human and social development, and the use and management of natural resources.

While the IIASA and the UNU tend to emphasize the problems of the industrialized North and the less developed South respectively, Harrison Brown saw a need for other institutions that could bridge the North-South gap, defining their scope of interest in a way that could embrace at least part of both North and South. One such institution that attracted Harrison's attention and to which he eventually devoted six years of his life is the East-West Center (EWC) in Honolulu.

Harrison's interest in the East-West Center arose at least partly from his recognition that the Asia-Pacific region (the East-West Center's geographical purview) constitutes an increasingly important arena of world affairs. Asia-Pacific countries, as Harrison later noted in congressional testimony on the Pacific Community concept (1979a), possess a wide range of shared problems related in many cases to a colonial heritage, and more generally to economic disparities, competition for markets and resources, wars and internal upheavals, and racial, cultural, and national antagonisms. At the same time, they are experiencing ever greater interdependence brought about by international flows of raw materials, food, manufactured goods, people, technologies, and ideas. Harrison's vision was that if these countries can work together on the management of their interdependence, they may be able to reduce tensions; if not, he feared that "new explosive situations" could result.

In the mid-1970s, when Harrison first turned his attention fully toward Asia and the Pacific, numerous regional cooperative programs in science and technology already existed (UNESCO, 1981). But there was no regional institution, other than the East-West Center, specifically dedicated to policy-level research on the problems that Harrison had identified.

This, then, would appear to have been his principal motivation in accepting the invitation to head a new institute to be created at the EWC—the East-West Resource Systems Institute.

THE RESOURCE SYSTEMS INSTITUTE

Founded in October 1977 with Harrison Brown as its first director, the Resource Systems Institute (RSI) took as its main objective "to analyze, in collaboration with sister institutions, policy alternatives of the Asia-Pacific region, to examine the consequences of possible policies, and to elucidate, and to lessen, the uncertainties associated with policy formulation." More specifically, the new institute's research would be aimed at "understanding how nations can maintain adequate, equitable, and reliable access to resources." Reflecting Harrison's deep concern for problems of instability (short-term fluctuations) and irreversibility (permanent consequences of crucial events and decisions), RSI research was intended to "explore the feasibility, advantages, and costs of moving the resource systems of the East-West area toward greater stability and resilience" (Brown, 1980). Later, RSI's stated objectives were expanded somewhat to address more explicitly the situation of countries that have resources to exploit by examining the question of "how nations can efficiently manage the development and utilization of natural resources to achieve national development goals."

The institute's initial staff was obtained primarily through the merger of two previous EWC institutes (the Food Institute and the Technology and Development Institute), and additional staff members were drawn in as the new institute's programs developed. As part of the East-West Center complex of institutes,[2] RSI received major financial support from the EWC's federally appropriated budget, as well as the use of EWC facilities (conference center, residence halls, etc.). By the same token, of course, RSI was obliged to operate within the structure of EWC policies and procedures based on an explicit standard of "federal comparability"— i.e., functionally equivalent to those followed in agencies of the U.S. federal government.

In its substantive activities, RSI under Harrison Brown was organized into three main programs, each concerned with a particular class of resources—food, energy, and raw materials (minerals). Each program was to be headed by a program leader and was subdivided into a number of projects, typically multiyear in duration and directed by an individual member of the research staff.

The *Food Systems Program* took as its overarching objective "to clarify how nations can meet the food needs of the most people in a manner that is consistent with socio-economic goals, ecological sustainability, and international stability" (Brown, 1980). Specific projects undertaken in pursuit of this goal included:

- Food security—an investigation of sources and consequences of variations in food supplies and prices based on empirical studies of markets for selected commodities, development of a multicommodity global food trade model, and examination of the effects of government policy (in particular, intervention in domestic markets and foreign trade) on food production and consumption.
- Famine warning systems—a project to develop methods based on cartographic and other data for identifying geographical areas at risk of famine.
- Food and the city—an examination of food supply systems for large Asian cities, including field studies of food marketing patterns in selected case cities.
- Technology assessment of biological nitrogen fixation—a study of future prospects and potential implications of energy-conserving biological nitrogen fixation technologies applied to the production of major cereal grains.
- Botanical pest control—a worldwide survey of plants reputed to have pest-control properties and development of a network of cooperating institutions to conduct coordinated field trials of promising botanical pest control strategies.
- Research policy—an examination of the international roles and capabilities of the U.S. land-grant agricultural research system.

Due primarily to shifts in RSI's substantive emphases following Harrison Brown's retirement as its director in 1983, the Food Systems Program was phased out in late 1984, although some on-going projects were continued under other organizational rubrics.

RSI's *Energy Systems Program* took as its overall purpose "to help human well-being in the Asia-Pacific Region through development of the knowledge necessary to beneficially alter energy supply, delivery, and consumption systems" (Brown, 1980). Among its specific projects have been:

- The Asia-Pacific Energy Studies Consultative Group (APESC)—an informal organization of cooperating institutions throughout the

Asia-Pacific region designed to facilitate examination of common energy problems. (APESC is described more fully later in this chapter.)

- China's energy supply system—a detailed study and modeling exercise on China's domestic energy economy and external energy relations.
- Electric future of the Asia-Pacific region—an integrated multicountry study exploring past, present, and future development of electric power networks in participating countries.
- Energy for rural development—an investigation of key policy and technology development issues affecting rural energy systems in Asia, conducted mainly through a network of cooperating institutions in the region.
- Biomass fuels and air pollution—an international experimental and policy-oriented study of air pollution emissions from the use of traditional biomass fuels, their effects on health, and possible ways to reduce such pollution.
- OPEC Downstream—a detailed study of hydrocarbon processing (refining and petrochemical production) and tanker transportation in OPEC countries, effects on world oil markets, and implications for both developed and developing countries.
- Energy and industrialization in the Asia-Pacific region—an investigation of the effects of oil price increases and changing international market structures on Asia-Pacific developing countries.
- Pacific island energy studies—a study of energy problems and prospects in ten South Pacific countries, emphasizing the evaluation of renewable energy alternatives.
- Academic energy program—a joint program with the University of Hawaii to develop a graduate-level curriculum in energy policy, planning, and economics and to provide for a visiting professorship of energy policy studies.

The RSI *Raw Materials Program* is concerned with providing "policymakers and implementors with a more informed basis for the management of a nation's mineral resources to meet regional and national development goals," including information on mineral policy options and on the physical distribution of mineral resources. Specific projects have included:

- Mineral policies to achieve development objectives—a review of mineral policies and related research needs in the Asia-Pacific region.
- Alternative taxation methods for mineral resources—a study of the economic implications of various terms of agreement between governments and international mining firms.

- Resource assessment for national development planning—a project to develop and apply methods for quantitative assessment of undiscovered minerals potential.
- Mining project case study—a detailed analysis of Papua New Guinea's experience in developing the billion-dollar Ok Tedi gold-copper project.
- Cobalt-rich manganese crust potential of the Pacific—an analysis of the potential for these deposits within the 200–nautical-mile exclusive economic zones of all Pacific nations.
- South Pacific chromite study—an assessment of chromite potential in five Southwest Pacific island countries and related possibilities for diversification of U.S. chromite sources.
- Fertilizer flows—a multicountry study regarding fertilizer marketing, fertilizer raw materials resources, and alternative approaches to efficient fertilizer use.
- Phosphate resources of Asia and the Pacific—an international study involving field work and policy evaluation of phosphate resources in the EWC region.

As is evident from these brief descriptions, RSI programs and projects have been carried out by means of diverse modes and methods of operation. The one consistent feature of nearly all projects is that they have been conducted by international teams of researchers working with one or more RSI staff members. Such teams have varied in size and composition from an individual researcher working with one or two graduate students to complex intercountry networks of institutions complete with such mechanisms as steering committees and secretariats.

Specific types of project activities have included the following:

- Policy dialogue—high-level international conferences and workshops with participation by public and private decision makers as well as academic specialists.
- Other types of meetings and workshops—for purposes such as research planning and coordination, brainstorming-group responses to research questions requiring expert judgment, sharing and disseminating research results, and training.
- Development of research methods—for example, to estimate currently unproven resource potentials, to compute resource-related statistical indicators and indexes, to assess particular types of technologies for their resource requirements or economic effects, and to evaluate alternative resource-development projects and strategies.
- Survey research and other forms of primary data collection.

- Compilation of computerized databases (bibliographic, statistical, and other types).
- Creation of quantitative models—usually computerized, ranging from simple models of farm-level production economics to global food trade models, and from oil refinery simulation models to energy-economic models of entire nations.
- In rare cases, experimental research—for example, the use of a simulated village hut instrumented to permit measurement of air pollution effects from alternative cookstove designs and fuels.

Results of RSI projects are typically of three kinds: (1) development of interpersonal and interinstitutional networks linking Asia-Pacific scholars and policymakers concerned with a particular problem area; (2) publication or other dissemination of research products (e.g., methods, data, models, analyses, forecasts, recommendations); and (3) in some cases, a demonstrable effect on public or private decision-making. Certainly this last type of result is the most dramatic and is generally considered desirable as the ultimate proof of the value of the research (provided of course that the effect is beneficial). Often, however, such "real-world" effects are difficult to trace, partly because research results from any source constitute only one input to a decision-making process and also because new knowledge commonly affects action only after a certain period of time (even as much as a generation, in cases where policy change is possible only through turnover of policy-making personnel).

An example of an RSI-initiated program that produced all three of these types of results is the Asia-Pacific Energy Studies Consultative Group (APESC). APESC is Harrison's brainchild, born soon after the creation of the institute. He recognized that communication among energy policymakers and research workers in the Asia-Pacific region had been poor. In view of this, RSI in July 1978 held a major conference that brought together government officials and energy experts from the greater part of the region. Approximately forty-five persons from nine countries took part. The participants were divided about equally between persons who were at or close to the policy-making levels of government and industry and specialists in technical and other fields pertinent to the formulation of national energy policies.

The group discussed the energy problems that confront the respective nations and reached several important conclusions:

- All nations of the region face energy problems that differ in degree but not in kind.

- All nations of the region must of necessity formulate energy policies despite considerable uncertainty.
- Communication among Asian and Pacific nations concerning our respective energy problems has been inadequate.
- An important approach to the alleviation of these problems would be to develop mechanisms that would strengthen ties between energy-oriented research institutions, foster collaborative research efforts, and enhance communication and exchange of information.

A specific mechanism for accomplishing these goals was proposed; namely, the establishment of a network of cooperating institutions, perhaps with a leading institution in each country. Representatives would meet periodically to discuss problems of mutual concern. The meetings would be kept small and informal so that all participants would have the opportunity to get to know one another. The intention was to provide opportunities for senior policymakers, administrators, and scholars to interact and exchange views, something like the meetings held at the Royal Institute of International Affairs in London.

The second meeting of the group, held in 1979, was used to explore the possibility of creating a more formal organization; the group agreed upon the name Asia-Pacific Energy Studies Consultative Group (APESC). Subsequent meetings have concentrated on problem areas. APESC III (1980) considered individual national energy policies; APESC IV (1981) considered the rational and efficient use of energy (conservation); APESC V (1982) considered the role of the energy economies while oil is phased out and before we can rely totally on the direct and indirect use of solar energy. APESC VI (1983) examined the future of electric power in the Asia-Pacific region, and APESC VII in 1984 focused on the changing world market for oil. Decisions concerning conference topics are made by an informal executive committee consisting of representatives from each participating country and RSI. The East-West Center provides a modest secretariat to organize the meetings, arrange for the editing and publication of the proceedings, and provide continuity.

LESSONS ABOUT INTERNATIONAL MULTIDISCIPLINARY RESEARCH

Like any research institution, RSI has found some of its efforts to be more successful than others, largely because of varying circumstances. Experience accumulated in RSI's wide range of projects over the past seven years suggests a number of practical lessons for the conduct of international policy research, particularly with regard to the conditions for success.

Ensuring that policy-oriented research will in fact be useful from the standpoint of intended audiences (policymakers and their advisers) is difficult unless representatives of such audiences are involved in shaping the research from the outset. Perfunctory and nonrepresentative governing bodies or advisory panels can provide little substantive guidance, and ad hoc institutional evaluation panels having no connection with the institute's particular areas of research can do more harm than good.

To obtain maximum research productivity, it is essential to provide a supportive research environment, including suitable physical surroundings, as little bureaucratic red tape and busywork as possible, and convenient access to all needed support services and facilities (e.g., secretarial and administrative assistance, computer equipment and programming support, libraries with competent reference staff, editorial and other publication-related services, conference facilities). To skimp on such support services is a false economy, since it can greatly impair the effectiveness of expensive research staff and, even worse, deter first-class researchers from joining an institute in the first place. To let administrative convenience dictate policies and procedures at the expense of the research environment is understandable only if one assumes that producing high-quality research is not the institution's actual objective.

Under conditions of budgetary constraint, it is important not to spread financial resources too thin. It is far better to support a few projects properly than many poorly. New visions and goals for an institution need to be developed jointly with both old and new staff as well as representatives of potential audiences. Not all researchers, however competent they may be in their individual fields, are appropriate for dealing with large-scale national and international problems of the sort that Harrison Brown intended RSI to tackle. The ideal combination is proven competence in a pertinent discipline plus a genuine interest in attacking problems that cannot be handled fully by that discipline alone (implying a willingness to learn from and adapt to the contributions of others).

To ensure adequate flexibility in the face of changing research priorities and budgetary uncertainties, most research personnel should be recruited on a limited-term, task-specific basis. Permanent (tenured) positions should be used mainly for administrative and support staff or other personnel whose contributions are likely to be needed even when research foci shift, as they inevitably will.

Personal links with researchers in other institutions are essential and should be fostered through such activities as travel and conferences. Where such relations exist, joint research ideas and projects can follow easily. If ideas and tasks are predetermined and collaborators are sought afterward, however, success is less likely. Links with practitioners (government and private-sector decision makers) are also important but even more difficult to achieve. Obtaining their participation in a conference, for instance, may require having other distinguished participants already confirmed to attend, or scheduling the conference to precede or follow another event of interest to the desired participants.

Political factors can sometimes block seemingly worthy avenues of research. For instance, any government that opposes the research can prevent its nationals from participating by denying them exit visas. "Scientific politics" can have an equally stifling effect if persons whose participation is needed decide not to take part.

True collaborative research is difficult to achieve among scholars who come from different disciplinary backgrounds. Good results are easier to achieve among collaborators in a single discipline, for instance through design and conduct of parallel studies for each of which the responsible researcher can take personal credit, thus satisfying the reward systems of his or her discipline.

Modern microcomputer technology provides powerful new capabilities for data compilation and analysis, freed at last from dependence on centralized and often administratively constrained mainframe computer facilities. In a sense, development of the affordable personal computer may prove analogous to the invention of printing, in that it makes available to a broad user community an intellectual resource that had formerly been controlled by a self-serving elite. In the context of international cooperative policy research, such tools permit models, databases, and other information tools and resources to be shared among participating institutions and individuals far more easily than in the past.

Formal methods for analysis of large-scale interdisciplinary problems (e.g., economic modeling) have considerable power but have in some cases been oversold and therefore may encounter skepticism. They should be used with circumspection; their limitations should be frankly acknowledged, and wherever possible they should be developed or at least adapted to match the specific problem being investigated.

CHANGING CONDITIONS AND PROSPECTS FOR POLICY-RESEARCH COOPERATION

In the early 1980s, conditions for international scientific cooperation have become significantly less propitious than before, at least as far as U.S. participation is concerned. Under present federal policies, the United States has pulled back from its earlier vigorous involvement in international science. Funding for the National Science Foundation's international programs has been cut, official U.S. support for IIASA has been terminated, U.S.-Soviet scientific cooperation agreements have been allowed to lapse, and the United States has carried out its plan to withdraw from UNESCO.

Distinguished scientists such as Philip Abelson (1982) of the American Association for the Advancement of Science and Lewis Thomas (1984) of the Memorial Sloan-Kettering Cancer Center have expressed alarm at the rising barriers to international science, arguing that such cooperation continues to be a major avenue for promoting international understanding and goodwill, and that the global problems that cooperative research can and should address are becoming more dangerous, not less—so much so in fact that humanity should now be seen as a seriously endangered species. To note that political constraints on scientific cooperation are nothing new is small consolation (de Beer, 1965; Hagstrom, 1965; King, 1964; Salomon, 1973).

As U.S. official participation in international science has declined, the importance of other actors and institutional arrangements has increased. The minimal case is that of individual scientists who share a concern about pressing human problems and find ways to continue working together in spite of intergovernmental difficulties; the ongoing interchange among U.S. and Soviet scientists investigating the environmental consequences of nuclear war is a good example (Aleksandrov, 1984; White and London, 1984). On a more formal level, a number of national governments have become increasingly prominent in international scientific affairs, to some extent supplanting the United States; these include Japan, some OPEC countries, and mid-level powers such as China, India, and various countries of both eastern and western Europe. France, for instance, was the prime mover in the 1982 establishment of international working groups on key areas of high-technology research (Dickson, 1984). Also, nongovernmental mechanisms for promoting needed research have assumed increasing significance. As an example, private foundations have provided major support for the new Center for European Policy Studies in Brussels (Walsh, 1983) and for the Washington-based World Resources Institute (Holden, 1982). Many other cooperative activities continue to be carried out under the aegis of worldwide bodies such as ICSU, the Commonwealth Science Council, and the various UN agencies; but there appears to be increasing interest in regional cooperation through organizations such as the Organization of American States (OAS), the European Economic Community (EEC), the Association for Science Cooperation in Asia (ASCA), and the Association of Southeast Asian Nations (ASEAN). There is perhaps still greater interest in bilateral arrangements between specific pairs of countries, due perhaps to the comparative ease of managing bilateral programs and also a heightened concern for maximizing the comparative advantage of one's own country vis-à-vis others in a particular regional or economic grouping.

This last point relates closely to another important change under way, a major shift in the agenda of issues and hence research priorities addressed by policy-level researchers in many countries. Whereas the 1970s were a decade of concern about physical limits to growth, such as absolute resource shortages and environmental degradation, the 1980s have seen a reaction to the often-overstated predictions of imminent scarcity. This point of view is supported by OPEC's present disarray and the soft oil market that prevailed for the first half of the 1980s. In the research agenda, much greater importance is attached now to practical questions of economic and technological progress—identification of potential areas of national competitive advantage and their development through suitable policies regarding investment, trade, technology transfer, and other elements of export-led growth in an economically interdependent world.

Each of the three international policy-oriented research institutions described earlier (IIASA, UNU, and RSI) has adapted to these changing circumstances. IIASA, for instance, has found in the American Academy of Arts and Sciences a new conduit for U.S. participation, with private-sector funds substituting for the earlier U.S. government contributions. IIASA also has taken steps to intensify its collaborative links with key audiences and has greatly increased its explicit attention to economic mechanisms (investment, trade, markets, economic structure, industrial adjustment) in its research programs. Since its reorganization in 1982, the UNU has also begun to emphasize increasingly economic development. In 1983, for example, it announced the first of the UNU Research and Training Centres would be in Helsinki and be named the World Institute for Development Economics Research (WIDER). And RSI, under its new director, economist Seiji Naya, has initiated a broad-gauged development-policy research program intended to address directly some of the complex economic issues that have now joined resource availability as major foci of concern.

While a swing away from the excess zeal that characterized some resource analysis in the 1970s is understandable, it should not be at the cost of forgetting the problems identified by Harrison Brown in the early 1950s. Those problems have not gone away, and, indeed, are in general unsolvable by increased economic growth alone. Thermonuclear war resulting from competition over resources, damage to long-term ecosystem stability from land clearing and pollution, and the vicious cycle of poverty and overpopulation of the world's poorest populations are crucial problems confronting humanity that must be addressed directly.

They cannot be left to be solved eventually by some form of trickle down from economic growth centers in a few countries.

Important as economic growth is, it is not enough. In addition, it is well to remember that understanding and promoting economic growth are directly or indirectly the goals of a broad range of national and international organizations, both public and private. Where, however, will the issues brought to focus by Harrison's career be addressed if not in the few international research centers? There is no other place except as might sporadically occur in geographically widespread and uncoordinated university settings. In his article in this volume, Rector Soedjatmoto makes an eloquent plea for promoting and maintaining institutions to mind the global commons.

Hidden also by an agenda focusing primarily on economic growth is one of the major unresolved questions of the last decade. Will it be possible to achieve an equitable and peaceful world society by economic growth alone, albeit at different rates in different places? Or will it be necessary for economic stability or even retreat to occur in the many parts of the developed world where the marginal utility of additional growth is low? If this is to be so, how can humanity achieve this without widespread disruption? This dilemma casts a shadow across any but the most short-term views of the benefits of economic growth.

And what of the future? Current trends point toward increasing diversity in the institutional arrangements, methods, and issue foci of international policy-oriented research. Levels of U.S. participation will depend chiefly on political developments in Washington, D.C., and are virtually certain to rebound eventually, but probably with increased circumspection about the topics, methods, and arrangements to be pursued. Other countries will continue taking on increasingly independent roles, one important advantage of which will be a broadening of the intellectual base for dealing with global problems; indeed it seems likely that the countries that have dominated debates over such problems in the past may have much to gain by a willingness to listen and learn from ideas originating in other cultures. By evolving toward a multi-dimensional and open-minded sharing of such ideas, perhaps humanity can achieve a greater degree of that "stability" and "resilience" for which Harrison Brown has so fervently and effectively wished and worked.

NOTES

1. For earlier views, see King (1964) and Salomon (1965).

2. Other EWC institutes in existence when RSI was formed included the Population Institute (PI), the Communication Institute (CI), and the Culture Learning Institute (CLI). Another new institute, the Environment and Policy

252 Robert H. Randolph and Kirk R. Smith

Institute (EAPI) was created at the same time as RSI. In 1983, CI and CLI were merged to form a new Institute of Culture and Communication (ICC).

REFERENCES

Abelson, Philip H. 1982. "International Science." *Science* 218 (4574):745. November 19.

Aleksandrov, Vladimir. 1984. "'Nuclear Winter' Studies." *Science* 225 (4666):978. September 7.

Brown, Harrison. 1958. "Science, Technology, and World Development." *Bulletin of the Atomic Scientists* 14 (10):409–412. December.

———. 1959. "Natural Resources and the Future of Mankind." *Challenge* 8 (2):33–34. November.

———. 1978a. "Resources and Environment in the Next Quarter Century," in Charles J. Hitch, ed. *Resources for an Uncertain Future.* Baltimore and London: Johns Hopkins University Press. 25–42.

———. 1978b. *The Human Future Revisited: The World Predicament and Possible Solutions.* New York: Norton.

———. 1979a. "The Pacific Community," in U.S. Congress, House Committee on Foreign Affairs, Subcommittee on Asian and Pacific Affairs. *The Pacific Community Idea: Hearings.* Washington, D.C.: Government Printing Office.

———. 1979b. "Some Notes Concerning the Importance of International Collaborative Efforts in the 1980s," remarks at a meeting of the Commission on International Relations, National Academy of Sciences. Washington, D.C. October 29.

———. 1980. "Resource Systems Institute," in *East-West Center Twentieth Annual Report.* Honolulu: East-West Center. 45–82.

———. 1985. *Science, Technology, and Economic Development.* Washington, D.C.: Federation of American Scientists.

de Beer, Sir Gavin. 1965. "The Sciences Were Never at War," in Norman Kaplan, ed. *Science and Society.* Chicago: Rand McNally. 14–18.

Dickson, David. 1984. "A European Academy of Science?" *Science* 225 (4669):1455. September 28.

Forman, Paul. 1973. "Scientific Internationalism and the Weimar Physicists: The Ideology and Its Manipulation in Germany After World War I." *Isis* 64 (222):151–180.

Hagstrom, Warren O. 1965. *The Scientific Community.* New York: Basic Books.

Holden, Constance. 1982. "$15-Million Gift Launches New Global Think Tank." *Science* 216 (4552):1298–1299. June 18.

Hubbert, M. King. 1949. "Energy From Fossil Fuels." *Science* 109 (2823):103–109. February 14.

King, Alexander. 1964. "Science International," in Maurice Goldsmith and Alan Mackay, eds. *The Science of Science.* London: Souvenir. 114–126.

Pollack, Herman. 1971. "Objectives of International Cooperation in Science and Technology." *U.S. Department of State Bulletin.* 837–841. June 28.

Rotblatt, Joseph. 1967. *Pugwash—The First Ten Years; History of the Conferences of Science and World Affairs.* London: Heinemann.
Salomon, Jean Jacques. 1965. *International Scientific Organizations.* Paris: OECD.
_____. 1971. "The *Internationale* of Science." *Science Studies* 1 (1):23–42. January.
_____. 1973. *Science and Politics.* London: Macmillan.
Schmandt, Jurgen. 1982. "Policy Research in an International Setting." *Science* 217 (4564):987. September 10.
Thomas, Lewis. 1984. "Scientific Frontiers and National Frontiers: A Look Ahead." *Foreign Affairs* 62 (4):966–994. Spring.
Tong, David. 1978. "Diversified Energy Program Based on 'Much Higher Costs'." *Honolulu Advertiser.* November 1.
UNESCO. 1981. *Inventory of Regional Cooperative Programmes in Science and Technology: Asia and the Pacific,* 2nd issue. Jakarta: UNESCO Regional Office for Science and Technology for Southeast Asia.
U.S. Department of State. 1974. *International Scientific Cooperation—A Summary of Tangible Benefits.* Publication 8760, General Foreign Policy Series 285.
Walsh, John. 1982. "'Lack of Reciprocity' Prompts IIASA Cutoff." *Science* 216 (4541):35. April 2.
_____. 1983. "A 'Euro-Brookings' Enters the Lists." *Science* 219 (4581):152. January 14.
White, Gilbert, and Julius London. 1984. "Nuclear Winter Scenario." *Science* 224 (4645):110. April 13.

About the Contributors

Fereidun Fesharaki is leader of the Energy Program of the Resource Systems Institute, East-West Center, Honolulu, Hawaii, and coordinator of the institute's OPEC Downstream project. He is the author, co-author, or editor of more than ten books and monographs on petroleum and other issues in the field of energy, including *OPEC, the Gulf, and the World Petroleum Market* (Westview, 1983).

Edward D. Goldberg is professor of chemistry at the Scripps Institution of Oceanography, University of California, San Diego. He is the author of *The Health of the Oceans* (1976) and *Black Carbon in the Environment* (1985). He has been awarded the Guggenheim and NATO fellowships and is a visiting professor at Harvard University, University of Chicago, and University of Michigan.

Jesse L. Greenstein is Lee A. DuBridge Professor Emeritus of Astrophysics at the California Institute of Technology. His specialist scientific fields included studies of the compositions of the stars, and the origin of these compositions in nuclear process in stellar interiors. He led the National Academy of Sciences study of the future federal support of astronomy in the last decade.

John P. Holdren is professor of energy and resources at the University of California, Berkeley; faculty consultant in magnetic fusion energy at the Lawrence Livermore National Laboratory, and senior investigator at the Rocky Mountain Biological Laboratory in Gothic, Colorado. He is the national chairman of the Federation of American Scientists, a Fellow of the American Academy of Arts and Sciences, and a MacArthur Foundation Prize Fellow.

Sir Fred Hoyle was elected to the Royal Society of London in 1957, made an honorable member of the American Academy of Arts and

Sciences in 1964, and invited to be a foreign associate of the National Academy of Sciences in 1969. His numerous honors include the Gold Medal of the Royal Astronomical Society, the Burce Medal of the Astronomical Society of the Pacific, and the Royal Medal of the Royal Society. He was knighted in 1972. Among his publications are *The Relation of Physics and Cosmology* (1973), *Astronomy and Cosmology* (1975), and *Energy or Extinction* (1977).

John Hurley is director of the National Research Council's Board on Science and Technology for International Development (BOSTID). He is a member of the executive board of the Committee on Science and Technology in Developing Countries of the International Council of Scientific Unions (ICSU) and is involved in a range of other activities related to science and development. Before joining the staff of the NRC in 1970, Mr. Hurley was a Peace Corps staff officer in Malaysia, Fiji, and Washington, D.C. and, as one of the earliest Peace Corps volunteers, was a science teacher in Malaysia.

Bruce Murray is professor of planetary science at Caltech. From 1976 to 1982 he was director of the NASA/Caltech Jet Propulsion Laboratory. He co-authored *Earthlike Planets* (1981) with Michael Malin (his former Ph.D. student) and Ronald Greenley.

Clair C. Patterson is a Geochemist in the Division of Geological and Planetary Sciences at the California Institute of Technology, having been a member of the faculty there for thirty-four years. By choice, Professor Patterson has not been active in social affairs in science and has published works in refereed scientific journals.

Victor Rabinowitch, executive director of the Office of International Affairs of the National Research Council, has devoted more than 25 years to efforts related to science, technology, and international development; international science cooperation; and arms control, disarmament, and world peace. His interests have been reflected in numerous publications, including the editing of *Views on Science, Technology, and Development,* service on the board of directors of the *Bulletin of the Atomic Scientists,* and participation in many Pugwash Conferences on Science and World Affairs.

Robert H. Randolph was assistant director of the East-West Resource Systems Institute from 1980 to 1984, was previously a member of a U.S.-Soviet research team at the International Institute for Applied Systems Analysis, and is currently assistant director of the National Council for

Soviet and East-European Research. His publications have dealt with the history and organization of science, including international scientific cooperation, technological forecasting, and technology assessment, with emphasis on the USSR and the Pacific Basin.

Roger Revelle is professor of science and public policy at the University of California, San Diego. He was formerly director of the Center for Population Studies and Richard Saltonstall Professor of Population Policy at Harvard University. From 1950 to 1964 he was director of the Scripps Institution of Oceanography of the University of California. Revelle College at the University of California, San Diego, is named for him. Recently he was chairman of the Geophysics Film Committee of the National Academy of Sciences.

Glenn T. Seaborg is currently university professor of Chemistry, professor in the Graduate School of Education, Associate Director of the Lawrence Berkeley Laboratory and chairman of the Lawrence Hall of Science at the University of California, Berkeley. In 1961 Dr. Seaborg was appointed chairman of the Atomic Energy Commission by President Kennedy. He served in that position until 1971, having been reappointed by both presidents Johnson and Nixon. Winner of the 1951 Nobel Peace Prize in Chemistry (with E. M. McMillan), Dr. Seaborg is one of the discoverers of plutonium.

Richard P. Sheldon is a consulting geologist for the United Nations Development Programme and other international assistance programs attempting to discover and develop phosphate rock resources in the Third World. He retired in 1982 from the U.S. Geological Survey, where he served as Chief Geologist from 1977 to 1982. He was a research associate and leader of the Raw Materials project at the Resource Systems Institute of the East-West Center from 1977 to 1980.

Kirk R. Smith is a research associate in the Resource Systems Institute of the East-West Center, Honolulu, Hawaii, which he joined at its inception in 1977. His research and publishing deals principally with the relationship of resource utilization with environmental quality and economic development. In 1984 Dr. Smith was elected one of "America's 100 Brightest Scientists Under 40," a distinction granted only once previously, in 1954, to 20 scientists including Harrison Brown.

Rector Soedjatmoko is rector of the United Nations University, a post that he has occupied since 1980. A former ambassador of Indonesia to the United States, he was also a member of the Palme Commission, the

Independent Commission on International Humanitarian Issues, and the Club of Rome. In 1978 he received the Ramon Magsaysay Award for international understanding.

Victor L. Urquidi is a research professor at El Colegio de Mexico, Mexico City (he was President of El Colegio from 1966 to 1985). His past affiliations include the following: member of the UN Advisory Committee for the Application of Science and Technology to Development (ACAST), 1970–1977; president of the International Economic Association, 1980–1983; member of the Council of the United Nations University, 1973–1976 and 1981–1986; current member of the Board of the International Institute for Educational Planning; member of the Club of Rome; member of the Mexican Academy of Scientific Research. He is also the author of books, articles, and other contributions on *inter alia*, Latin American development, population, and science and technology policy.

Alvin M. Weinberg is Distinguished Fellow of the Institute for Energy Analysis, which he was instrumental in establishing. From 1955 to 1973, he was director of Oak Ridge National Laboratory, where he had worked since 1945. The originator of the pressurized water reactor, Mr. Weinberg has played an active role in the development of nuclear energy. Mr. Weinberg is a member of the U.S. National Academy of Sciences and of the National Academy of Engineering.

Gilbert F. White is Gustavson Distinguished Professor Emeritus of Geography and former director of the Institute of Behavioral Science at the University of Colorado, Boulder. He has served as president of the Scientific Committee on Problems of the Environment and as an adviser to the United Nations Environment Programme. He is co-editor of the UNEP report, *The World Environment, 1972–1982*.